STEAM, POLITICS AND PATRONAGE

STEAM, POLITICS AND PATRONAGE

The Transformation
of the Royal Navy

1815–54

BASIL GREENHILL
and
ANN GIFFARD

CONWAY
MARITIME PRESS

For

JGG

Great-Great-Grandson of HWG

© 1994 Basil Greenhill & Ann Giffard

First published in Great Britain 1994 by
Conway Maritime Press, an imprint of Brassey's (UK) Ltd
101 Fleet Street
London EC4Y 1DE

British Library Cataloging in Publication Data
Greenhill, Basil
Steam, Politics and Patronage: The Transformation
of the Royal Navy 1815–54
I. Title II. Giffard, Ann
359.00941
ISBN 0 85177 612 4

Designed by John Leath, MSTD
Typeset by The Word Shop, Bury, Lancs
Printed and bound in Great Britain by
The Bath Press, Bath

Contents

List of Plates

(between pages 96 and 97)

Sources for illustrations are credited in the full captions.

Introduction

There is a deep strand in our culture derived ultimately from the biblical conception of the sea as chaos which sees things maritime, and those who have followed the sea, as alien, other, incomprehensible and divided from ordinary human life. There are understandable reasons for this. Until relatively recently the seafarer was cut off from land society both by the long periods of isolation imposed by life in sailing vessels and by the all absorbing technology of his profession, which even developed a strong terminology of its own which the landsman did not understand.

In this book we have sought to treat the navy in the period of transition between the Napoleonic and the Russian wars not in isolation, as if it existed apart from society as a whole, but as one manifestation of that society, with all its dynamic creativeness, and readiness to initiate and to undertake what seem to us now to have been incredible risks and which also had its hardships, its discomforts and dangers, its violence and brutality. The navy, like society as a whole, was heavily politicised, and at this period, when patronage has been thought by some historians to have been on the wane, the navy, like the rest of society, was in fact still run largely on patronage, although there were already clear signs of the changes which were soon to come.

In suggesting, as we have done in this book, that the navy, far from opposing the development of steam propulsion, took the lead in various ways, it is important to bear in mind the realities of changing situations over the years between the wars when technical developments in the generation of steam power, its application to industry and transport ashore and to the propulsion of ships at sea, were as great and as rapid as developments in electronics have been in the late twentieth century. The Admiralty, the ever present and all important political and financial considerations permitting, were essentially pragmatic and on the whole realistic in their approach. Faced, as they usually were, with financial stringency and with successive alarms, real or imaginary, as to the intention of the traditional enemy, France, and as to developments in the only potential superpower other than Britain, the growing collection of states then known as Tsarist Russia, the Admiralty advanced with steam as fast as technical development allowed.

The birth of the steamship in the first half of the nineteenth century is a far from simple subject. Naval, political, industrial, financial, and merchant shipping developments are inextricably mingled and must not be treated in isolation from one another. On the other hand, the navy was not inhibited by the sole function of a merchant vessel, the requirement to make money, net profit on invested capital. The navy, with the long voyages of pioneer naval steamers in the 1820s and the successful operation of the Mediterranean packet service after 1830, tended to make the running, subject to its own restraints, in the development of steamship operation. This is particularly true for the development of screw propulsion. Its origins were purely entrepreneurial, but the navy had more use for it than the merchant shipping industry, developed it more rapidly, and gobbled up its entrepreneurial originators in the process. Here is a classic case of the interplay of the private and public sectors.

In the present work, we have tried to outline the current state of knowledge on this very important subject and to develop ideas first put forward by the late Rear Admiral P W Brock and Basil Greenhill in a little book called *Steam and Sail in Britain and North America* in 1973. In that book we challenged, and perhaps were the first to do so, the then widely held view that the Admiralty were obstructive to the introduction of steam power into the navy in the crucial period between the Napoleonic and Russian wars.

The view that the navy was excessively slow to develop and adopt steam propulsion was expressed on pages 194–96 of Volume VI of Sir William Laird Clowes's massive work *The Royal Navy – A History*, published in 1901. Laird Clowes's opinions were, perhaps, inspired by the correspondence of some early engineers whose ideas were ahead of the practicalities of their times. Since then the subject has not been seriously examined until very recently. Successive books on various aspects of naval history have repeated Laird Clowes's views, usually, like Clowes himself, devoting no more than a page or two to the subject, sometimes with a somewhat careless approach to detail. The navy itself has been most responsible for perpetuating this critical view of the wisdom of its former senior officers. Thus three distinguished Professors of History at the Royal Naval College at Greenwich, Sir Geoffrey Callender (who was also Director of the National Maritime Museum), Michael Lewis and Christopher Lloyd, were all successively responsible for repeating this interpretation of history without the rigorous examination it merited. Some recent writers, copying these classic sources, have continued to propagate this version of events, without original research. The result has been successive generations of senior naval officers who consider their forbears, who lived in an age of innovation, to have been hostile to developments demonstrably likely to benefit the service. This was not the case. We hope that this book will convince its readers that the evidence does merit further examination and other interpretations. Published work, notably that of Dr Andrew Lambert of King's College London and D K Brown, formerly Chief Constructor of the Admiralty Experimental Works, has in recent years strongly endorsed the view so briefly put forward in 1973.

The effects of the development of steam propulsion at sea have been incalculable and there is scarcely an aspect of late twentieth century life which has not been influenced by it, directly or indirectly. We have sought in particular to show that the history of this development cannot be treated as a continuity. There are dislocations which change the whole nature of the game – the paddle vessel had defects in both naval and civilian application which meant that as long as paddles alone were the sole means of propulsion the use of steam at sea was going to be strictly limited. The screw changed the whole scene for the navy and, initially to a lesser extent, for the merchant shipping industry. We have also sought to show the uses to which naval paddle vessels, with all their limitations, were successively and successfully put as technical developments increased their potential value to the fleets. For much the greater part of the period we cover, a naval steamer was, by definition, a paddle-propelled vessel, and it is therefore with paddlers, or 'flappers' as they were known to some contemporary naval officers, that this book principally deals. We have also sought to show that the attitude of many naval officers to the development of the steamer was more favourable than has been thought in the past. For a very thorough study of the sailing navy of this period see Dr Andrew Lambert's *The Last Sailing Battle Fleet*, published by Conway Maritime Press in 1991.

This book also deals, to a degree, with the little studied subject of steam-and-sail. There was a whole era, starting from the earliest years of the steamship and lasting well towards the end of the 1800s (and the navy may be criticised more for hanging on to the obsolete mystique of sail-assist to the end of the nineteenth century than for slowness in adopting power for propulsion at the beginning of that century), when in different ways and in varying degrees vessels were propelled by using power and sail together.

Indeed, this era lasted for much longer. Until roughly the middle of the twentieth century the motor schooner was a common and profitable vehicle of sea transport. Steam-and-sail was the power unit of almost all powered vessels of the period from 1815 to the 1880s. If the reader wishes to study the matter further – and it is of great, if highly technical, interest – we commend Chapter 8 of *The Advent of Steam* (Conway Maritime Press, 1993) in which one of the present authors, with Captain Peter Allington, examines the subject in some depth.

In all the matters mentioned above, the linking of the navy with society as a whole, the navy's attitude towards the introduction of steam propulsion, the history of the development of the steamship, and the use of steam-and-sail as a source of power, the views we have expressed and the conclusions we have reached are in some aspects novel. This was a period of transformation, in the Navy, as in society as a whole.

This is not a technical book. The technicalities of the early steamship have been dealt with recently in D K Brown's *Before the Ironclad* (London 1990) and have been dealt with thoroughly in chapters by Denis Griffiths, Ewan Corlett and others in *The Advent of Steam*. We have throughout this book when speaking of the power of steam vessels used simply the term horse power. The actual horse powers quoted are the nominal horse powers of the vessels concerned. In the early nineteenth century it was not easy to measure the actual power of a steam engine and as a result a nominal horse power was defined which was based on the geometry of the engine. This nominal horse power was quite accurate in the earliest days of steam at sea but rapidly departed more and more from real power. It is therefore a measure of comparison of the relative horse powers of steamships as they developed, and it is in this sense that we have used it. For an admirable explanation of the technicalities of horse power measurement and rating see Appendix 1 of D K Brown's *Before the Ironclad*.

In illustrating the significance of the political background for the individual naval officer, the workings of the patronage system, and the details of the employment of the steamers of the period after 1840 when they were becoming essential units of the fleets, if strictly limited in use, the Giffard papers have been invaluable. No part of this book is in any sense biographical, but Captain Henry Wells Giffard's career illustrates so clearly so many aspects of our subject as completely to justify the use of this material.

No book of this nature, involving many years of research and preparation, can be written without incurring considerable debts to many people. First and foremost our debt is to Dr Andrew Lambert, Lecturer in War Studies at King's College London. Many years ago, Ann Giffard found herself sitting at the same table in a library with a post-graduate student who was calling for very similar research material. Conversation revealed a meeting of minds on such subjects as the neglected but decisive significance on the outcome of the so-called Crimean War of the naval campaigns in the Baltic and the attitude of the Admiralty to steam propulsion in the early part of the nineteenth century. A working relationship has developed which has been of great mutual benefit to all three, with constant interchange of ideas and information. As far as the authors are concerned, never was a working relationship more stimulating and fruitful. It was, of course, 'Canada' Brock who pointed the way to this study, and it was Captain Karl Kåhre, President of the Cape Horners of Åland, who drew our attention to the importance of the technology of sail-and-steam. Barry Pinson QC helped us to understand the workings of the Magistracy of early nineteenth century England. General Edward Fursdon was the greatest help in interpreting attitudes to the varying challenges of service life. The Reverend Dr Ewen Corlett, Captain Søren Thirslund, formerly of the Danish Greenland Company, Captain W J Lewis Parker, United States Coastguard retired, and the late Captain Karl Karlsson of Wårdö in Åland all helped greatly in the interpretation of technical matters, as has Captain Peter Allington of Cotehele Quay on matters of seamanship, shiphandling and terminology. Professor John Vincent of the University of Bristol has helped us to understand the significance of the political dimension, and we also thank Sir Sydney Giffard, Captain H W Giffard's only great-grandson, the late Miss Maud E Giffard, Dr Robert Prescott of the Scottish Institute of Maritime Studies at the University of St Andrews, Lt Commander James Richard, Mr I D Gilroy, the late Edgar Erikson and his wife Solveig (who led us to study the Baltic dimension of the Crimean War from which all else follows), Mr Aatos Erkko of Helsinki for encouraging interest in the history of steam, and Dr Simon Chaplin for his diagnosis of the symptoms of tertiary malaria. We also thank Anne Barrie for her help, especially in the translation of Russian French, and Dr Alan Jamieson, Mrs Anthony Barnes and Mr Denis Griffiths for their assistance with research. We thank Robin Craig and John Munday for their constructive comments, as also Dr Michael Duffy, a colleague at Exeter University, for his helpful work on the final typescript. We thank the staffs of the Public Record Office, the Guildhall Library in London, the British Library, the Hampshire County Record Office, the Devon County Record Office, the Scottish Record Office, and the Musée de la Marine in Paris for their courtesy and helpfulness. Finally, our neighbour Mrs Peter Fearn has performed secretarial functions with speed, accuracy, and unfailing reliability. Where would we have been without her?

This book was Ann Giffard's idea. All these people have helped and we are most grateful. Besides controversial opinions there are bound to be errors in a work on this scale. The fault is ours and we hope they will be forgiven.

Basil Greenhill, Ann Giffard, September 1993

1

Tiger, Tiger, Burning Bright

At 5.30 in the morning of 12 May 1854 (30 April on the old Russian calendar) *Tiger*, Captain H W Giffard, a steam driven, paddle propelled vessel of the Royal Navy, grounded in thick fog 'about 3 miles south of Odessa . . . The wreck lies North 60° East (true) 800 yards from Svedny Fontan Church, about 600 feet from the beach and about 1000 feet distant from the abrupt edge of a table land 130 feet above sea level'.[1]

The British government had declared war on Russia on 27 March 1854, although the British, the French and the Russians had all been acting as if they were at war since January, and the Turks had been fighting the Russians since October 1853. This was to be the conflict which later generations (but not the war's contemporaries, who called it 'The War with Russia') were to misname the 'Crimean War'. So in the situation of war the Russian response to the grounding of *Tiger* was immediate. In the words of General Baron Osten-Sacken, the Governor of Odessa,[2]

I hasten to lay before Your Highness [Prince Paskevic, Governor of Poland, who has been described by a recent British historian[3] as the Tsar's 'military mentor'] the flag or jack of the British steam frigate *Tiger* of 400 h.p.

It ran aground, was set on fire, and blown up as it was impossible to get it afloat and bring it into the harbour because two other steamers prevented the attempt. The following are the details:

This morning, May 12, the frigate, which came in the direction from Sebastopol, got ashore near Kartazzi, about six versts from Odessa. The

1 The wording is taken from a memorial plaque 'erected at the joint cost of the Board of Admiralty and the British Community 1906'. A photograph of this plaque was found amongst the papers of the late Miss M E Giffard, of Lockeridge, Wiltshire. The plaque itself, presumably erected somewhere in Odessa, could not be found in 1985. Authority is given to the position of the casualty by the fact that the engraved wording claims that the plaque itself was made from metal recovered from *Tiger*.

2 As reported in the *Russian Invalide*, quoted in *The Illustrated London News*, 1854, p 521.

3 A D Lambert, *The Crimean War, British Grand Strategy Against Russia, 1853–56*, Manchester 1990, p 13.

position field pieces (18 and 12 pounders) of No. 2 Battery, 16 Brigade, under Lt. Abakoumoff, arrived from the Lustdorf colony before the other two steamers could assist the *Tiger*; and, supported by two companies of the Dneiper reserve infantry regiment opened their fire with such precision that, after the vessel had received several shots, and its Captain had lost his foot, she was forced to surrender. The enemy's shot flew harmlessly over the battery (evidently from the vessel lying on her beam), the colours were hauled down, and the Lieutenant, who had taken command, presented himself before me, and declared his crew prisoners of war. By my orders he sent his crew and boats ashore and laid down his and their arms. They and their wounded, five in number, were sent to quarantine. Meanwhile 8 pieces of the light position battery No. 2 (12 pounders) and the Horse Battery No. 11 arrived from Odessa with a battalion of the Sonzdal Reserve Regiment and the Reserve battalion of the Ukraine Light Infantry with two squadrons of Archduke Ferdinand's Lancers reached the shore. The enemy's wounded were not yet removed before two of the enemy's steamers were observed through the fog. As no means were at hand to float the surrendered vessel and get her into port and as more enemy vessels might also arrive at any moment, I ordered the stranded ship to be set on fire with shot. The two steamers of the enemy came within gun range and opened fire upon our battery. Colonel Granovitch maintained such a well directed fire during 2 hours with 12 pieces that the enemy's ships were compelled to retire out of range much damaged. Two men and three horses of the reserve battery were killed. Colonel Flensky and Lieutenant Smirnoff of the Second Light Infantry and the Tenth Brigade received contusions. We have made prisoners Captain Giffard, 24 officers and warrant officers and 201 seamen and marines. The *Tiger* was armed with 16 Paixhans (exploding shell guns). At half past seven she was completely burned.

Tiger had been cruising in company with two other vessels, Her Majesty's steamers *Niger* (14 guns, Commander L G Heath) and *Vesuvius* (6 guns, Commander R A Powell). The orders to Captain Giffard from his commander in chief, Vice Admiral James Dundas, were perfectly clear.[4]

You are to take the *Niger* and *Vesuvius* under your command and proceed to Odessa, and having scoured that Bay and the neighbouring coast and captured or destroyed all Russian vessels you may fall in with, return to this rendezvous by Sunday evening next.

---

4 PRO ADM 1/5627 Dundas to Giffard, 11 May 1854.

Niger had herself recently been aground while pursuing potential prizes –
small merchant ships carrying cargo for the enemy – and such an event was
not taken too seriously in the British Black Sea fleet at the time. Although it
appears that the keel of *Niger* was badly damaged, so that she was ordered
to take an early opportunity to go to Malta to be docked, writing of the
incident in a letter home Commander Heath was quite light-hearted.[5] He
said

> Sir Edmund Lyons gave me all possible consolation and told me how
> often he had gone on shore himself, and that in his opinion no small craft
> Captain could be worth much who didn't get on shore occasionally; he
> also quoted a famous letter of Lord Nelson's on the same subject . . .
> The Admiral laughs at my misfortune and I am to go to Odessa with
> *Tiger* and *Vesuvius* to look around and then to Constantinople [in fact he
> was sent to Malta] to be docked.

But the grounding of *Tiger* was an altogether more serious affair.
Commander Heath wrote home[6]

> May 13th – One does not realise what war really is until one has either
> suffered oneself or seen its effects on one's friend. *Tiger*, *Niger* and
> *Vesuvius* left the Fleet as I told you in my last letter, to look into Odessa
> and see if anything could be picked up in the way of prizes. We left about
> noon on the 11th and went on full speed. Captain Giffard, being senior
> officer, made us some signals as to what course he should steer during the
> night, and told us in case of parting company to rendezvous at Odessa.
> About six in the evening he was five or six miles ahead of me (for the
> *Niger* does not seem to go the faster for having the keel roughened and
> knocked about by the rocks), and we were obliged to stop half an hour to
> put something to rights in the machinery, so that when we were ready to
> proceed he must have been about 10 miles ahead; and besides that a
> regular Black Sea fog had come in, so one could not see the ship's length.
> I therefore gave up all idea of keeping company and steered my own
> course for Odessa arriving there in the morning . . . We heard the firing
> of guns occasionally in the direction of the shore, but knowing there was
> a large garrison at Odessa we concluded it was their exercise day. The
> guns were not continuous for an engagement and it was natural to
> suppose that if either of our companions were on shore the last thing they
> would do would be to fire guns, as their anxiety would be to avoid
> drawing attention to their state . . . when the fog rose . . . I discovered

5 Admiral Sir L G Heath, *Letters from the Black Sea*, London 1897, p 23.
6 Heath, *op cit* p 25.

the *Tiger* on shore, five miles to the southward . . . and went on as hard as I could to her assistance. *Vesuvius* came up from the southward just before me. We saw the poor *Tiger* within 30 yards of the beach, over which rose cliffs 120 feet high, crowned by no end of Russian field pieces and troops, the former shelling the *Tiger*. We opened our fire as soon as we had got within range, but it was clear the *Tiger* was in the enemy's hands, for she had no colours up; she made no answer to my signal "How can I assist you?" and no return to the Russian guns, nor could we see anyone on board . . . Powell, the Commander of the *Vesuvius* came on board and said he thought he had seen the *Tiger*'s crew marching up the hillside, so as nothing more was to be done . . . we steamed out of range and ceased firing. Smoke began to rise from the *Tiger* and she was very soon in a blaze fore and aft; whether her own crew or the Russian shells had done it we do not know. In any case it was the best thing that could have happened, for with a garrison at Odessa of 30,000 men and the ship 30 yards from the beach it would have been absurd to attempt and impossible to succeed in getting her off . . . In the meantime the fire was doing its work, the masts fell in succession, and the whole of the upper works were in flames.

The poor *Tigers* seem to have done their best to get off, their boats were out and they had laid out a stern anchor and thrown their guns overboard; but it is difficult to account for their being all made prisoners, unless it was that they were so hard at work that they didn't observe the rising of the fog in time to get away. Doubtless the first thing they saw was an overwhelming force almost over their heads; still I should have thought they would have taken to their boats and risked the chance of being shot in preference to the certainty of a prison.

The thick fog again came on at 8, and I left to return to the Admiral. We had three men slightly wounded by shrapnel, but none of any consequence; several balls struck the ship's side, but only those coming through the ports could do much harm at that distance. Poor Mrs. Giffard is at Malta with her children.

And so HM Steam Vessel *Tiger* burned down to her waterline as she lay grounded in a sea which is tideless but constantly varying as to depth. Her dismantling was put in the hands of a local scrap merchant, one Luigi Mocha, who proceeded to plunder *Tiger* even while she was still burning. Other, unofficial, plunderers, according to *Tiger*'s surgeon, Greek seamen who seized the boats in which *Tiger*'s men came ashore, were also very quickly at work and some personal effects left on board were lost forever.

Thus her destruction appeared to the Russians, who brought it about, and to the British spectators, who were powerless to prevent it. How did the events appear to the men on board? Because of the inevitable court martial which had to follow the loss of a naval vessel, they were careful what they said and wrote at the time, but after his repatriation an anonymous junior officer of *Tiger* published[7] a very vividly written account of the grounding and the subsequent events.

Relative to the loss of the ship, it will be at present only in our power to say, that the *Tiger* left the fleet during a dense fog off Sebastopol, and steamed in company with the steamships *Niger* and *Vesuvius*; that at about six of the following morning, and during the continuance of this dense fog, the *Tiger*, not being in sight of her companions, took the ground and became firmly fixed under what, when the fog abated, appeared to be a high cliff. A faint hope had been entertained at first, that our position might have been to the northward of the town of Odessa, at the head of the bay, in a part which would have rendered the approach of artillery a work of time, but now the height of the cliff clearly showed that the ship's position was south of the town, and probably not far off it, and very convenient for the arrival of the enemy's field battery. Guns of distress were fired, and signals with muskets were made to endeavour to procure assistance from our companions, supposed to be not far off, but all was a dense fog to seaward. Efforts were made to release the ship by throwing overboard guns, coals, &c., and by laying out an anchor, but all was fruitless, she was firmly fixed, and could not be moved. The enemy's battery was then seen taking up a position on the top of the cliff, right ahead of the *Tiger*, and the attack commenced; at first, the enemy fired high and cut the rigging and spars, but they soon got the range for the hull, and fired into that, and from some cause (probably their using carcases) they eventually set fire to the ship. The distance from the Russian battery was probably not more than 200 yards, and seeing this, it appears they reduced their charges of powder, and threw spherical case shot or shrapnell shell. The *Tiger* returned the fire from forwards on the upper deck as best she could, for the main-deck guns, not then thrown overboard, were useless, as they could not be brought to bear against the battery in its elevated position; then, again, the smoke hung about the guns' muzzle through the fog, and the effect of our shot could not be seen as to elevation. At length an enemy's shell burst just at our gun's mouth, and struck down Captain Giffard, John Giffard, midshipman; John Tranor, the captain of the gun; William Tanner, and the powder-boy, Thomas Hood, all of whom were severely wounded; others at the gun were struck, but not materially hurt. The wounded were immediately carried below, and shortly after this, on the Captain being prepared to undergo the operation of having his leg amputated, the fire-bell rang. The *Tiger* was burning forwards, near the

---

7 In Colburn's *United Services Magazine*, November 1854, pp 337–351, and December 1854, pp 552–565.

powder-magazine, and the enemy's shells were bursting so rapidly on the upper deck, it was almost certain destruction to any one that appeared. The Captain then ordered the ship to be surrendered, as he considered it would be useless sacrifice of life to continue the resistance. So a boat was sent on shore to say that we had surrendered as prisoners of war. The third lieutenant went in this boat, but returned to fetch the first lieutenant, who spoke French, and when he landed, he was detained and soon afterwards marched off, and orders were sent for all to come on shore immediately, as they were going to destroy the ship forthwith. The majority of officers and men went on shore in the paddle-box boats, and were also marched off, but it was necessary that all the amputations should be performed, and the wounds dressed, before the wounded could be removed. Messages hurrying us on shore, and threats of firing again into the ship, kept arriving, and under these trying circumstances one leg was taken from Captain Giffard, two from the young midshipman, one from the captain of the gun, and their wounds and the wounds of others dressed. The scene on the ship is impossible to describe, and it is difficult now to say at what time events happened, but it must have been about noon before these duties were finished, and those now left on the ship were two gigs' crews and about seven or eight officers.

During the amputations we received permission to bring on shore our clothes; but it is no easy matter without assistance, and in times when everybody has his own interest uppermost, to transport many of one's personal effects from the cabin to the shore. A few of the most necessary articles were put up in such packages as readily offered themselves, and the wounded having been passed through the main-deck ports, the Captain into his own gig, and the others into the second gig, we started for the shore. At this time the *Vesuvius* broke through the fog, and when we left the *Tiger* our friends were, apparently, as near us as our foes; but stern duty obliged us to turn our boats' heads towards the latter. It has been asked why we did not escape in the boats, but the idea of deserting the ship, I think, never entered the head of the Captain: nor did he think matters would become so serious. He seemed, I fancy, to think we could at any time drive the battery from the cliff; but its elevation gave the enemy too great an advantage for this. In the paddle-box boats had been deposited shot, ballast, an anchor, &c., and it is highly probable that, in running the gauntlet with our wounded, had we cleared the boats and tried to escape to our friends, a serious loss must have been sustained. Could the *Niger* or *Vesuvius* have found us out, and taken the fire away, or partly away, from us, perhaps we should not have been forced on shore as prisoners; but that the ship was doomed I think was certain, so soon as they brought their guns into full play, and more especially if they did, as I fancy, make use of carcases. It may be necessary to observe, that by carcases I mean iron shot with three apertures filled with a highly inflammable substance, which of course ignites when the carcase is discharged from the gun, setting fire to the substance struck. We scarcely touched the shore before the Russians resumed their fire, to destroy the ship, and the *Tiger* was on fire forwards; the magazine was flooded with water, and she was so riddled in the hull that the people on the troop deck could see daylight through the ship's bows before we left.

We partly ascended the cliff, at first immediately under the battery, and had to lie down whilst they fired over our heads. We were then again sent to the beach, where there was a motley group of soldiers and apparently Greek sailors from some of the merchant-ships at Odessa. These latter were armed as best they could be, and took as much interest in the capture as our enemies the Russians, and doubtless a warm interest in our personal effects; for in putting down the boxes to carry about the wounded, almost all our things were plundered, and we were hurried away up another part of the cliff, only bringing up the Captain, having insufficient men to carry the others, but being assured of their safety, and the impossibility of our returning to the beach for them. The *Vesuvius* had commenced firing, the *Niger* was hurrying from the harbour of Odessa to assist in the rescue, if practicable. The Russians were apprehensive of the vicinity of the allied fleets, and thus, before we could remove our own wounded companions from the scene, we were more in danger from the guns of our friends than from those of our foes. We were soon made acquainted that we were in quarantine, and every one kept us at bay as if we had the plague. Our swords being deposited on the ground near the General Osten Sacken, we met an official, who addressed us in English, and assured us of good treatment, but, at the same time, the necessity of getting the Captain out of the way of the shells then bursting over our heads. In vain we asked to have our other wounded companions brought up the cliff; we were assured that they would be taken care of, and thus we hurried away, and never saw young Giffard or the man Tranor again alive. In all probability young Giffard did not survive long; the man Tranor, it is said, lost blood from the tourniquet slipping, and the people not righting it. The boy Hood lived in the hospital a day or so, but he had been struck in the liver. Tanner, although severely wounded, finally recovered to be exchanged.

On the top of the cliff we found ourselves in a garden, or pleasure grounds, the country seat of Senor Catazzo, a gentleman of English descent; and it contrasted strangely with our previous position. We had passed a tedious and severe winter at Constantinople, before we made our entrance into a sea of fogs. After a monotonous blockade of Sebastopol, and the attack of Odessa, from 6 A.M. to 6 P.M., a few days before, we (after undergoing a scene which it is impossible to describe) leave our house (the gun-room) a pool of human blood, where the maimed limbs of our companions had been lying about us as those of animals in a slaughter-house, and emerge to become prisoners; then, suddenly, a scene of English gardening presented itself, under a May sun, with a different temperature to the sea level or the inside of a ship, and, assuaging for a time our passions, it brought to our minds recollections of peace and home. But this reverie was but momentary. The shells were whizzing over our heads, and pieces falling not far off; we see a horse and the rider knocked over, and we turn to take a last look, and see our friends, at sea, carrying on their murderous duty; and near and around we see stern, helmeted, foreign soldiers; and the battery which had brought destruction on our devoted ship (now smouldering a wreck), and the object of another fray, in which we can take no part; and, on a bier, our wounded Captain: so we hurry away, led by our interpreter, who assures us of safety and good treatment.

The first lieutenant and second in command of *Tiger*, Alfred Royer, on his return to Britain published an account of his experiences in which he wrote of the loss of the vessel.[8]

During one of the dense fogs so prevalent in the Black Sea at that season of the year, we had lost sight of our consorts; and although our course had been shaped with care to avoid danger, strong currents had carried the ship considerably to the westward of our reckoning. No land was visible; indeed we did not expect to see any for we supposed we were much nearer to the Tendra Spit than to the mainland . . . Happily the weather was calm so that the shock of the vessel, in striking upon, or rather between two rocks (as was afterwards discovered by Russian divers) was so slight, that it was scarcely felt, and we imagined she had grounded on a sandbank which we knew lay to the east of our course.

It was about half past five o'clock when we ran aground, shortly after, the fog seemed to grow thinner under the influence of the sun's rays, and revealed, to our astonishment, high land on our left. We then understood the critical position into which we had fallen.

As the fog cleared . . . we could discover the well-known figure of a Cossack on horseback, with long lance in hand, no doubt meditating on the expediency of galloping off to announce the news to his superiors, of the grounding of a steamer on the coast. To increase, if possible, the interest of the scene, we could discern two ladies, with pink parasols, promenading in their garden, which revealed the edge of the cliffs and these ladies, with many others who joined them later, were witnesses of all that occurred during the day . . . as the bright colours of their parasols were but dimly seen, they were once mistaken for fresh troops and ran great risk of being shot by our riflemen . . .

8 Alfred Royer, *The English Prisoners in Russia. A personal narrative of the First Lieutenant of H.M.S. Tiger, together with an account of his journey in Russia and his interview with the Emperor Nicholas and principal persons of the Empire*, London 1854.

It was necessary to give notice of our situation to the consort vessels and to warn them of the danger they were approaching, as they were doubtless steering the same course. We therefore made the fog signal by firing guns in quick succession, to inform them of our position; and it is possible that the first intimation of what had taken place reached the ears of the Governor of Odessa with the sound of our own guns . . . We felt convinced that we should soon be attacked by overwhelming numbers of artillery and musketry.

The attack was begun by the latter, the number of which we could not ascertain, as the Russians fired from under a bank, on that part of the cliff nearest to the ships: the balls came chiefly through the rigging, so that at the onset no-one was killed.

During the firing the boats were lowered and an anchor laid out in order to draw the ship off after she had been lightened. Every exertion was made and many things thrown overboard; but she was too firmly fixed on her rocky bed to be dislodged. There were one hundred and fifty men at work on the capstan; and this compact mass would have formed an excellent target for the musketry, but fortunately it was not visible from the shore, so that the fog was, to a certain extent, of use to us.

The cable being hove as taut as was prudent, without having moved the vessel, it was deemed expedient to prepare for resistance to the artillery, which we expected would soon open upon us.

The head of the vessel was the part nearest the shore; we stood pointing, as it were, with our jibboom to the cliff, the shore bearing away to our left, it was therefore requisite to form a kind of rampart in the front part of the vessel: this was done by hanging the hammocks of the men containing their beds and blankets, to a stout rope, from the rigging to the forestay on each side, thus intercepting the line of fire from the cliff above. The hammocks afforded protection from the fire of the musketry, while our men were free to fire from below them . . .

About half past nine the guns of the enemy opened fire. They consisted of eight twenty-four pounders, which had just arrived from Odessa; they were placed in a position nearly ahead of us on the cliff, so that their shot could rake the ship fore and aft, our guns at the same time being useless, as they could not be trained sufficiently forward to bear on the shore. It was therefore deemed expedient to send the men below, to cast the guns, now become useless implements of war, into the sea, in order to lighten the ship, and enable her to respond to the force supplied by the cable and capstan on the anchor laid out to the southward. The men were also thus kept out of unnecessary danger below the upper deck, while they effected the object we had in view – that of lightening the vessel – by throwing sixteen guns overboard. Still, to our great disappointment, the vessel did not move.

In the meanwhile we had contrived to bring one of the guns on deck, to bear upon the cliff, from under the hammocks, in response to the artillery opened upon us from above; but it may be easily imagined how useless was the firing upwards in such a situation.

A highly competent account of the disaster is to be found in the log of *Tiger*'s surgeon, Henry J Domville.[9] He wrote

From this time up to the 11th May we were with the squadron off Sebastopol cruising in cold, damp and foggy weather. On this day we started in company with the *Vesuvius* and *Niger* and steered in the direction of Odessa passing in the afternoon into one of the dense fogs whose darkness we had already experienced and which seem to prevail at this season in the Black Sea. On the morning of the 12th about 6 a.m. I was awoke by a shock and a grinding sensation conveying the impression that we had come in contact with another vessel, but we were soon alive to the reality and peril of our position as the ship had struck the ground not much more than her own length from the beach, and as the fog gradually cleared off we found ourselves lying under a cliff that rose above our mast heads at a distance of about 250 yards.

Every possible means were employed to get the ship off, by passing overboard guns, shot, anchors and other heavy materials, one anchor was laid out to seaward and the cable brought to the capstan at which as many men as could find room employed their utmost strength, aided at the same time by the reversed action of the paddle wheels moved by the full steam power . . . I quietly proceeded to prepare for the reception of wounded men and get all things ready as for general action and it was not long before my anticipations were effectually realised as about 9 o'clock a sharp fire of musketry was opened upon us from the cliff and the rattle of the small arms was soon intermingled with the louder report of the more destructive heavy ordnance every one of which was attended by a simultaneous crash on board as shot or shell came tearing through the spars and rigging or plunging through the decks. The first few shots were directed towards the masts but on obtaining a better range a discharge of shells upon our almost defenceless decks was kept up so vigorously that the ship was shortly on fire in two places and the Captain and four others brought below, dangerously wounded, from the forecastle, where an endeavour was being made to repel this attack with a solitary gun, the others having been thrown overboard or in positions unavailable for the defence of the ship.

As the Captain was being carried below he gave the order to discontinue firing and the men to retire to the shelter of the main deck and also that the Russian flag should be hoisted in token of surrender and

9 PRO ADM 101/123/5 132735.

that one of the Lieutenants should go on shore to inform the officer in command of the troops. Any further resistance would only have entailed a greater effusion of blood without any possible advantage occurring. Having delivered these orders he requested to know the nature and extent of his wounds and on hearing that he must lose one leg he only suggested the use of chloroform.

Why were paddle steamers still being built in the late 1840s, several years after Brunel, with the success of his great iron steamship *The Great Britain*, had convincingly demonstrated to the wide world that the screw propeller, not the paddle, was the answer to the problem of applying steam power at sea? Why also, several years after, had the Admiralty become convinced that the future of steam in the navy rested in its use as auxiliary propulsion in battleships and frigates using the screw, and had thus begun the long, slow, sometimes painful, abandonment of the vastly complex old sailing tradition and the way of life which went with it? How far had the Royal Navy progressed in the transition towards steam propulsion and how had that progress affected and changed the navy? How were steam vessels used in this period of transition, and for what functions were they suited at their various stages of development? In this period, when all steam vessels, however powerful their engines, had masts and sails, when were the sails used, and how were power and sail worked together? How far was the navy representative of its parent British society in an age of social change? How did naval officers acquire expertise in steam and what was the road to command of a steam frigate? What was a paddle steamer, with all her disadvantages, doing in the Black Sea at a time of war with the great power of Russia? How did this vessel come to be aground, fatally, within easy artillery range just outside the Russian base of Odessa?

2

Steam Before the Frigates

The answers to the questions asked at the end of the preceding chapter are not simple. They involve, first and foremost, the politics of the Tory and Whig parties which ruled Britain through the period covered by this study, and the complex interplay of the individuals, politicians, naval officers mostly with clear and well known political connections and industrialists intent on manipulating them, who were the decision takers. The answers also involve the development of engineering and of industry on shore, the development of the technology of the marine steam engine, of ship design and building, of armament, of communications. Deeply involved also is the state of society on shore, of which the navy was one of many manifestations, a society emerging from a rural state, with many traces of feudalism still remaining in the countryside, and with towns still run by merchant oligarchs. It was a society in which patronage played a very important role at every level. This society was also beginning the long, slow process of ceasing to accept the general brutality which in the past had always been regarded as normal. People's ideas about people were changing.

In the years between 1815 and 1854, which we must consider in attempting to answer these questions, the Royal Navy underwent the greatest transition in its history. At the beginning of this period it comprised sailing vessels of all types and sizes, the legacy of the great fleet which had been Britain's principal contribution to the defeat of Napoleon. In 1854 the fleet included numerous steam driven, paddle propelled sloops and frigates while the main fighting force comprised frigates and ships of the line equipped with auxiliary steam engines driving screws. By the end of the War with Russia in 1856, steam driven armoured floating batteries and numerous screw propelled steam gunboats had been added to the naval force. Together, the steam driven vessels made the British fleet by far the most powerful weapon which had ever existed at sea. These developments had a world-wide effect on the strategy and tactics of sea power. Here were the beginnings of a modern navy.

★ ★ ★

In considering the early history of the steam vessel, that is of the paddle steamer, the only type of steam vessel there was until the early 1840s, the distinction between the fully powered steamship and the vessel in which a steam engine was installed to provide power auxiliary to that derived from her sails must always be borne in mind. Most of the early working paddle steamers between 1815 and 1830, both merchant ships and vessels built at the government's expense and used for official or naval purposes, were fully powered steamships. Their sails, and almost all of them had sails, were used to support their engines in the way that is now called sail-assist. This was for several very good reasons. The hull form most efficient for the purposes for which the early paddle steamers were used was not efficient for sailing, and the presence of the paddles further inhibited sailing ability. Morever, investment in the early merchant paddle steamers was a high risk enterprise. Their market advantages over sailing vessels on the short sea routes with passengers and light cargo on which they could be employed profitably were speed and regularity of service. Hence, at an early date engines became powerful enough to provide marketable speed. Sails are of little use in fast, heavily powered vessels except for periodic sail-assist, especially for lightly laden paddle steamers with the wind on the beam and one paddle out of the water, when the use of sail on the masts on the fore part of the vessel may be essential to prevent her griping up into the wind, as an insurance against breakdown and for marketing purposes – because masts and sails were almost by definition what a ship had. A ship without masts and sails was not acceptable in the passenger market. It was seen as far too risky a vessel in which to take passage. For these purposes, on coastal and short sea routes a limited sailplan – known to contemporary seamen as a jury rig – sufficed. For a detailed study of the complicated problem of sails and how they were used in early steam vessels see chapter 8 of *The Advent of Steam* a volume of *Conway's History of the Ship*.

This book therefore deals with a distinct era in the history of the ship. It was the era of steam and sail. In modern terms it was an era of sail-assist for fully powered vessels and steam-assist for traditionally rigged sailing vessels. Steam and sail together provided the propulsive power. It was also an era of vessels operating on the margins between these extremes. In the ways in which power and sail were used, these vessels might be thought of as the warship and merchant ship equivalent of the late twentieth century motor sailing yacht in all her numerous variations.

Until the early marine steam engines achieved a reasonable degree of reliability and economy, which they did in the 1830s, both naval and merchant paddle steamers were used mainly for relatively short passages around the coasts of Britain and across to the continent, although the pioneering naval paddlers *Lightning* of 1822 and *African* of 1823 made much longer voyages at the beginning of their careers. Thus naval and merchant requirements for steamers were not dissimilar, although merchant shipping requirements tended to put the emphasis on speed and naval requirements on towing ability. There were, of course, many tugs amongst the early commercial steamers. Once marine steam engines developed to the point at which relatively long regular sea passages (as opposed to one-off delivery passages of new ships to distant owners) could be contemplated in the mid 1830s, naval and merchant shipping requirements began to diverge. The merchant shipping industry developed the paddle steamer as a fast, fully-powered vessel with auxiliary sails for use in emergency and to provide power as sail-assist for the engines. The deck log of the first passage from Bristol towards New York of *Great Western* in 1838 (see page 54) shows continuous use of sail when the course was four points or more from the wind. The course, however, was that of a fully-powered steamship and was not varied to maximise the use of sail power. *Great Western* appears to have followed the great circle course across the North Atlantic. The engineer's log contains numerous references to the sails set, to sail handling and to the different power settings used with different sail combinations and in varying weather conditions. The use of sail and steam was continuously and closely coordinated. Thus on 15 April 1838, the engineer's log reads

> 4 A.M. larboard outer plummer block brasses hot; cooled down with water. 6 A.M. let one fire out in each boiler, viz., worked with eight furnaces; put expansion on 9th grade; average revolution during the time thirteen per minute; sails doing much good; average consumption of coal during the time, say five and a half hours, 19¼ cwt. per hour . . . Meridian, put expansion on 7th grade; kindled one more fire, viz., nine at work; . . .

These vessels were used on those deep sea routes on which they could be made to pay dividends, that is with passengers and light cargo, on the transatlantic service and the service to the Mediterranean. But the high fuel consumption of their still relatively inefficient propulsion units meant that a government subsidy for carrying mail was almost a necessity for successful operations. The vessels in this category included the Great Western Steamship Company's *Great Western* of 1838, the first successful trans-atlantic liner which operated without a mail subsidy, and a paddle steamer which was never really improved on, *British Queen* of the British and American Steamship Company of the following year, the early Cunard vessels of the 1840s on the Atlantic service, and the early vessels of the Peninsular Steam Navigation Company on routes to the Mediterranean in the mid 1830s.

For these vessels highly sophisticated sail-assist rigs were required. Merchant steamships were a high risk investment. Crew costs had to be reduced as far as possible. It was unsafe to reduce the numbers of engineers and firemen but the number of seamen could be reduced if labour saving simplified rigs were developed. Moreover, reduction in the amount of rigging aloft meant reduction in windage. Pioneer merchant steamship builders and owners showed quite remarkable skill and adaptability in breaking away from the enormously strong influence of traditional sailing ship technology. They developed the schooner rig from the small two-master to a mighty six-master. Work aloft was almost eliminated. Gaffs were made standing, the sails brailing to the masts. Topmasts could be housed from the deck, gaff topsails were set flying and not stowed aloft. These rigs were made possible by the liberal use of iron wire in place of natural fibre. It looks at the present state of research as if the four masted schooner was 'invented' by the team responsible for designing the rig of *Great Western*. Certainly, the pioneer iron screw driven Atlantic liner *The Great Britain* was the world's first six masted schooner.

The navy's requirements for paddle steamers capable of long voyages were quite different and highly complex. The navy had world-wide responsibilities and effective naval ships had to be capable of extensive voyages. The development was therefore towards vessels with traditional sailing rigs, since they could never carry enough fuel, given the consumption of contemporary engines, to steam for long distances. A naval vessel also had to carry the large crew necessary to fight the ship, her guns and ammunition, and the supplies necessary to feed her men, the whole amounting to a heavy cargo. At the same time, her guns had to be so disposed that she was as efficient a fighting machine as possible. These requirements were really incompatible as far as the paddle steamer was concerned, and the naval paddler was in practice limited to certain special, but very valuable, functions. What those functions were and how they developed with the vessels is one of the chief purposes of this book to explain. The problem of steam propulsion for the navy was, in the end, met by the abandonment of the paddle in favour of screw propulsion, that is propulsion by what is now loosely called a propeller. This is the driving mechanism of almost all ships in the late twentieth century. The navy used the screw in fully rigged warships, capable of world cruising under sail fitted with auxiliary steam engines, which gave them manoeuvrability in restricted waters and in action, and safety in bad weather, to a degree never before known. These steam screw battleships and frigates of the 1850s, which could fire full broadsides in the manner of sailing vessels, something the paddlers could never do, were the most formidable fighting machines which had ever existed at sea.

The early history of the steamship, therefore, is not a continuity. It is in two very distinct parts represented by paddle propulsion and screw propulsion. Between 1815 and the late 1840s the paddle steamer, to a degree limited both by her inherent defects and by the technology of the period, reached a plateau of development for both naval and merchant purposes. The development of propulsion by screw during the 1840s introduced new elements of flexibility of use and efficiency for both naval and merchant shipping purposes, but more especially for naval, which enabled the steamship in due course to come of age. Covering as it does the period from 1815 to the War with Russia in 1854, this book inevitably deals principally with some aspects of the first part of the history of the naval steam vessel, the paddler, or 'flapper'.

The early history of steam propelled vessels is associated with river transport. Considering the circumstances, this is entirely to be expected. There was a long period of adapting crude and unreliable machinery developed for use on land to the driving of rotating paddles. These paddles had to be designed and developed as an entirely new application of power for transport on water, and this was done long before the steam engine was adapted to the regular propulsion of land vehicles. But the potential advantages of the application of power to river transport – increased speed, regularity, carrying capacity, and the ability to move upstream – were sufficient to encourage rapid development in an age which considered the inland waterway, rather than the road, as the natural highway for the movement of goods in bulk. On inland waterways the disadvantages of the early steam propulsion units could be overcome. Regular refuelling on the banks of rivers or canals solved the problem of the vast consumption of fuel of early engines. Unreliability was less important when a broken down vessel could easily tie up to the bank and wait assistance.[1]

So the paddle steamer began her commercial career on the Clyde and the Hudson, the Seine, the Elbe, the Neva, the Thames, the St Lawrence, the Rhine, the Swedish lakes, the Ganges, the Brahmaputra and, with the beginnings of the opening up of the west, in the United States the advantages of the river steamer were so great that already by 1819 some one hundred steam vessels had been constructed there, as opposed to forty-three in the whole of the British Empire.[2] Between 1829 and 1840 no less than 729 elaborate passenger steamboats were built in the United States for service on the western rivers. As an American historian has put it, the steamboat changed 'the relations of the West which may almost be said to have changed its destiny'.[3]

A steamboat service to Gravesend from London was established in 1815 with *Margery*, Clyde-built, which was towed through the Forth and Clyde Canal (her paddle wheels had to be removed as she was too beamy for the locks) and sailed down the east coast to London. She remained in service on the Thames for only one season and was then sold to French owners. On her delivery passage in March 1816, she steamed from Newhaven to Havre in 17 hours, and was the first steamer ever to cross the channel.[4]

1 In the period 1815–1820 the early steamers on the Thames 'had often to be laid up for repairs to their machinery, sometimes for three weeks together'. Fraser MacDonald, *Our Ocean Railways*, London 1893, p33.

2 Smith, *A Short History of Naval and Marine Engineering*, Cambridge 1937, p 16.

3 Morrison, *History of American Steam Navigation*, New York 1958, p 191.

4 Spratt, *The Birth of the Steamboat*, London 1958, pp 92–95.

The first long coastal passage to be made under steam in British waters (and, moreover, one on which two passengers were carried, one of them a woman) was that of *Thames*, built on the Clyde as *Duke of Argyle* in 1814. She had a side lever engine of 14 horse power operating at 2 pounds per square inch of steam pressure. In 1815 she was sold to London owners and, too beamy to be got through the Forth and Clyde Canal, she was steamed to the Thames via Dublin, Wexford, Romsey Island (making the first steam crossing of the Irish Sea in twelve hours), and then through Jack Sound off the Pembrokeshire coast and to Milford Haven. Here her master, George Dodd, amused himself by steaming round the Irish Mail packet under sail. *Thames* next put into St Ives, round Land's End, and put into Plymouth where a demonstration of steaming ability in the harbour created a great sensation. At Portsmouth, *Thames* was visited by Admiral Sir Edward Thornborough, Rear Admirals Sir Hyde Parker and Sir James Gordon, and twenty-two captains. Thornborough later wrote to Dodd 'Captain Hope, of the *Endymion* [frigate, 40 guns], wishes he had asked you to give him a tow; I really think you would have moved him at a good rate; for my part, I am quite astonished at the swiftness of your vessel'. Thus *Thames* narrowly missed a further place in history as the first steamer ever to tow a British warship. *Thames*'s passage to London was of some 758 nautical miles completed in 122 hours, steaming at a mean speed of 6.2 knots. The vessel subsequently served between London and Margate and later London and Gravesend with success. She was clearly very fortunate both in her hull design and her machinery.[5] Captain Dodd was subsequently involved with *Thames* and other vessels in passenger service on the river, but he did not prosper and died in poverty in 1827.

Thereafter, the development of the paddle steamer for commercial use on short runs with passengers and light cargo was steady, if not rapid, but it was marked by fairly frequent commercial failures and disasters of various kinds. By 1827 there were 225 steamships registered as of British ports under the Merchant Shipping Acts, many of them tugs but including *United Kingdom* of 1000 tons, a Leith to London packet of 200 horse power built in 1826, which was perhaps the largest steamer built to that date. In the same year, 1827, the first regular service beyond home trade limits was established with the Dublin–Bordeaux sailings of the Dublin and London Steam Marine Company.[6] The short sea routes and inland waterways were soon saturated and ten years later there were still only 624 steamships registered.

5 Dodd, *An Historical and Explanatory Dissertation on Steam Engines and Steam Packets*, London 1818, and *The Dictionary of National Biography*.

6 *Oral communications from Mr Robin Craig, formerly of University College London, and Dr Freda Harcourt, Queen Mary College London.*

The development of steam power for naval use was not lagging behind the application of steam in the private sector. There had been steam pumping engines at Portsmouth since 1799 and the famous machinery for making ships' blocks which was designed by Sir Marc Brunel, father of Isambard Kingdom Brunel, was driven by a steam engine. As early as 1814, before the paddle steamer had evolved to a point at which it could have serious applications for the navy, Simon Goodrich was appointed Mechanist to the Navy Board and remained its adviser on engineering matters for many years.

The progress of the Admiralty's adoption of steam power afloat can be followed in some detail in the papers.[7] An early experiment was made in 1816 when a steam vessel, *Congo*, was built in Deptford Dockyard for an expedition to explore that river. Not surprisingly at this very early date, when a steam service on the Thames had only just been established, she was a failure; the accounts are conflicting, but it appears that her machinery was too heavy for her hull as designed. By 1815 the correspondence in the Goodrich Papers in the Science Museum reveals that a bucket dredger with a steam engine to work the machinery – and, it was suggested, to drive paddles through bevels – was under construction at Portsmouth for use at Sheerness and Chatham. This dredger followed on the successful work of the Cornish engineer Richard Trevithick, whose steam dredger of 1806 had been used to excavate the entrance to the East India Dock on the Thames.[8] The new dredger may in turn have played a significant role making possible the continued use of those dockyards, which were silting up.

At this time it is apparent from the correspondence that the Navy Board were being bombarded with suggestions for steam vessels. Among their advocates were cranks and men without substance, but advocates of a different kind were the famous civil engineer John Rennie, then employed on the design of the Plymouth breakwater amongst other projects and to whose advice the Admiralty attached much importance, and Sir Marc Brunel. Some if not most of these proposals were submitted to Simon Goodrich for approval, and his comments are to be found in his papers. Also to be found are his comments after inspection of new commercial steam vessels with which the Navy Board were keeping in close touch, thus

20th May 1817. Went on board the *Britannia* steam packet just arrived at this port to ply between here and Ride [Ryde] 15 horse steam Engine vessel 50 tons Paddle wheel of Iron Arms 8′ diam. paddle of plate iron 3′6″ long 1′6″ deep set upon the arms not quite in the direction of the radius but a little inclining towards the tangent on the ascending side of the Circle. The Boiler a Waggon Boiler of pl. iron with 2 fires

7 *PRO ADM 92/1 – 3 Steam Dept. 106/Navy Board Correspondence.*
8 *Spratt, op cit*, pp 89–90.

underneath with ash pits into the bottom of the vessel but which was lined with Bench work and covered over. Steam Engine stood on one side of the Boiler with Beam under the Cylinder and the half of the beam on the Cylinder side split in two with rising connecting rods on each side to cross Brass on the tops of the air pumps and Piston Rods. The length of stroke by recollection 3 ft. a crankshaft with an Iron wheel about 2'6″ diam. driving a transverse Flywheel and paddle wheel shaft by another iron wheel of about the same diam. to drive the eccentric for working the sliding valves of the Engine.

Both the Boiler and Engine completely under the deck and the whole outside surface of the Boiler was uncovered and made the place below excessively hot. The bottom of the boiler placed upon the Bench work.

From time to time towing trials of various kinds were carried out, often at Rennie's instigation, but the steamers during this period were not powerful enough to tow large naval vessels. It is apparent that the naval authorities were well aware both of the potential value of steam propulsion at this stage in its development and of the limitations imposed by inadequate power, excessive fuel consumption, unreliable engines, lack of knowledge in designing steam vessels, and the stresses imposed on flexible wooden hulls by heavy reciprocating machinery. By 1819 better results were being achieved. On 6 August 1819, C Robb, Commissioner at Deptford Dockyard, wrote a letter which exactly sums up the probable utility of a steam vessel to the navy at the stage of development such vessels, and their machinery, had then reached.[9]

Robb to Navy Board 6/8/1819
I beg to observe a steam vessel of sixty Horse Power would be a great utility and saving to the Government, and therefore humbly propose to your Honourable Board that one may be built to serve this Port, Woolwich, Sheerness and Chatham, of old timber that may be used from ships taken to pieces. She would be of great saving in towing men of war out of the Ports when ready for sea, as they are sometimes detained two, three and four weeks waiting for a wind. In transporting ships from one Port to another without any delay, as there would be no occasion of rigging them or putting an additional quantity of ballast on board. And also in transporting stores from one yard to another; and in the last case there would not be any occasion for burning coals (unless the stores should be immediately wanted) as she could be navigated by light sails. A vessel of this kind would do more business than two or three Lighters, and in my opinion, not be more in the expense of building than one of the Large Lighters as she would require no finery. In time of War the

9 PRO ADM 106/3443.

advantages of such a vessel would be incalculable in the despatch of storeships to join convoy, and in the prompt execution of yard orders.

But the Commissioner's ideas were, in fact, overtaken. On 29 November 1820, the Navy Board made a most significant submission to the Board of Admiralty.[10]

Navy Board to Admiralty:
Sir,
In reference to the directions of the Lords Commissioners of the Admiralty of 23rd May last for building a steam vessel on the plan proposed by Mr. Rennie for the purpose of towing men of war out of Harbour in the Thames, Medway, etc. we desire you will be pleased to acquaint their Lordships that we have prepared a draft for building a vessel accordingly, but at the same time to submit to them as two steam vessels are building by the Post Office on a plan which promises some improvement, whether it may not be advisable to defer proceeding with the vessel until they are launched.

It is apparent that the Admiralty now considered that the time had come to design and build a steamer specifically for naval use as a towing, general purpose and experimental vessel. But it is equally apparent that because they were short of funds, as a result of the great reductions in the naval forces after the end of the Napoleonic Wars (as they were to be more than once in the history of the development of steam propulsion), they were only too happy for the private sector (or in this case another government department) to make the running and bear the development costs. The expense of building and running the packets, the mail carriers to Ireland and the Continent, was carried by the Post Office, but some of the vessels were built (on recovery of cost from the Post Office) in Royal Dockyards on the Thames.[11]

The two steam vessels referred to in the foregoing letter were built at Rotherhithe on the Thames and engined by Messrs Boulton and Watt. They began a service from Holyhead to Dublin in May 1821. By the end of that year both vessels had made over 140 crossings of the Irish Sea, with an average passage time of seven and a half hours.[12] They had been built in response to new competition for passengers (which the Post Office sailing packets carried as well as the mail) provided by two new commercial steamers built for the Holyhead–Dublin route in 1819 and 1820 respectively.

10 PRO ADM 106/2280.
11 Adm to Navy Board, 8 January 1822, and reply of the same date. Post Office to Admiralty 22 April 1842. PRO ADM 12/210.
12 Bagwell, 'The Post Office Steam Packets, 1821–36', in Craig, ed, *Maritime History*, Vol 1, Newton Abbot 1971, pp 4–28.

The better construction of the new Post Office vessels proved crucial. The older steamers were unable to compete with the new Post Office steam packets. From now on, steam packet routes blossomed and many new services were to be opened up in the next five years.[13] Competition was intense, and in these years of the early 1820s the paddle steamer made great strides forward both technically and commercially.

However, as tended to be increasingly the case throughout the century, the requirements of the navy and of the merchant shipping industry began to differ. Goodrich was in London in July 1821, inspecting the new Post Office packet ships. He approved their design, but even at this early stage he asked how a 'towing engine' should be different from one 'calculated for speed only'. What the navy wanted at this stage, when there was no possibility of operating steamers on anything but short passages around the coasts, was an efficient and reliable towing machine capable of long working passages. The emphasis in the merchant shipping industry was on a vessel so fast and reliable on short runs that, despite the fear of the unknown and the well justified fear of boiler explosions, she attracted sufficient numbers of passengers to pay her way despite the considerable investment cost she represented and the high cost of operating her.

The new naval vessel was eventually laid down at Deptford in November 1821 and launched in May 1822. She was named *Comet* and was designed and built at Deptford under the supervision of the master shipwright of Woolwich Dockyard, Oliver Lang. She was 115 feet long and was equipped with side-lever engines operating at a steam pressure of four pounds per square inch and developing 80 horse power. She was given a two masted schooner rig. Some stokers were recruited from the steam dredger. Thus we have the appointment of one Robert Watson to be a stoker[14]

> he having been accustomed to that business on board the Steam Engine for raising mud.

Comet was not listed as one of His Majesty's Ships until 1831 but Brown[15] and others have been in error in describing her as a 'harbour tug'. Her duties were more varied and her range of operation much greater. For instance, on 4 April 1823 it is noted[16] that the 'dredging machine' was ready to go to Portsmouth to dredge the harbour bar, that the dredger was capable of raising 70 tons of shingle per hour, and that *Comet* was to tow her from Woolwich to the Solent. On 2 March 1824, the yard officers at Woolwich informed the Navy Board that *Comet* was to tow *Maidstone* to Northfleet

13 Body, *British Paddle Steamers*, Newton Abbot 1971, pp 55–57.
14 PRO ADM 106/1796 Woolwich, Commissioner to Navy Board 15 July 1822.
15 Brown, *Before the Ironclad*, London 1990, p 47.
16 PRO ADM 106/1797 Woolwich, Yard Officers to Navy Board 4 April 1823.

and the following day to take the packet *Kingfisher* to sea, 'Reach or the Nore'.

If the duties of *Comet* were varied they were nothing to those of her immediate successor in the service, *Lightning*, a naval vessel of great historic importance. She was also built under Oliver Lang's supervision at Deptford, and measured 126 feet overall and 111 feet 10 inches between perpendiculars with a beam of 24 feet 8 inches. She was fitted with two side-lever engines of 50 horse power each by Maudslay, Sons and Field at a cost of £5350, and she was rigged with two masts carrying gaff sails brailing to the weather, and later with a single square-topsail on the foremast. But she was a fully powered steamer and the use she made of her small sail plan was probably limited. She was launched on 19 September 1823 and her birth seems to have followed on an Admiralty decision to order steam vessels to be based at Portsmouth and Plymouth of size for two engines of 50 horse power.[17]

Lightning began her working life on towage duties and on 21 September 1824 Goodrich reported that Joshua Field, of the engineering firm Maudslay, Sons and Field, had reported that she could make 11 miles per hour at 26 revolutions towing a frigate going free, that is with the wind abaft the beam. The wind strength was not noted. On 19 May 1824 Goodrich noted

> Go out with *Lightning*, steam vessel, and tow in the *Nieman*, 28 guns. The engines perform remarkably well.

On 4 June 1824, within nine months of her launch, the Navy Board reported to the Admiralty[18] that they were preparing to send the steam vessel *Lightning* to Algiers under Mr Gage, master attendant at Portsmouth, with the transport *Admiral Berkeley*, to carry her coals. Four days later she was reported as leaving for Spithead in the evening. She would be ready to sail from there once the transport had arrived. A squadron under command of Vice Admiral Sir Harry Neale was being assembled with the purpose of bombarding Algiers, whose ruler had violated the British Consulate and seized two consular servants, this after numerous acts of piracy on the high seas. The passage to Algiers, the longest yet made by a naval steamer, and probably longer than any made by a fully powered merchant steamer to that date, was evidently made in order that there should be a steam vessel available to tow ships into positions of advantage to threaten Algiers. *Lightning* appears to have remained in North African waters for about a month but, after some preliminary actions in which one Lieutenant George Evans, later to command *Lightning*, took an active part, the ruler of Algiers gave way to the threats and came to terms. There was no bombardment and

17 PRO ADM 106/2283 and 2284.
18 PRO ADM 106/2287.

Lightning was not in action. She sailed for home on 27 July, calling at Gibraltar and Lisbon. She coaled at Lisbon for two days and arrived at Plymouth nineteen days out from Algiers.[19]

Lightning was subsequently employed on towing and other duties all around the southern coasts of Britain. She was also the subject of a number of experiments in such matters as water-changing apparatus, steam valves and the desalination of boilers. Thus, on 30 August 1825, the Commissioner at Portsmouth wrote to Goodrich[20]

The Navy Board say the Service to which these vessels may be applied on the occasion of a future armament render it essential that every point connected with their equipment should be placed in time of peace on the most advantageous footing, the Navy Board are very anxious to settle the question as to the preference which should be given to Copper or Iron Boilers, and as Copper Boilers cannot be used for a long voyage unless some mode of getting rid of the salt be established you are to avail yourself of the opportunity of the removal of the *Dreadnought* from this port to Milford of making such experiment in the *Lightning*, which is to accompany her, and in which you are to proceed, as may serve to determine the efficiency of the apparatus in Question and make correct observations on the State of the Brine during the course of the voyage and back, reporting on your return to this yard the State of the Boilers.

The Commissioner went on to say that the Navy Board considered this matter very important 'bearing on the Improvement of the said vessels, with special reference to long voyages at Sea'.

Less than a year later *Lightning* was at the great Russian naval base of Kronstadt, 18 miles out into the Gulf of Finland from the then Russian capital, St Petersburg. She had gone there as escort for *Talavera*, 74 guns, and other vessels which took the British representatives, including the Duke of Wellington, to the funeral of Tsar Alexander I. In the Goodrich Papers can be found a letter from *Lightning*'s acting engineer, John Chapender, to Goodrich,[21] reporting on the passage home. *Lightning* left Kronstadt on 1 July having been in the Gulf of Finland since early June 1826, and escorted *Gloucester*, 74 guns, to Copenhagen, partly towing her, taking ten days in what were apparently contrary winds. On passage from Copenhagen to Sheerness *Lightning* sheltered from a gale in a Norwegian port and then made a three day passage to Sheerness 'which made our running better than 200 miles in four and twenty hours'. As soon as she returned to Britain *Lightning* was employed in towing a 74 gun ship from Sheerness to

19 Laird Clowes, *The Royal Navy*, London 1901, pp 235–237. Kennedy, *The History of Steam Navigation*, Liverpool 1903, p 40.
20 The Goodrich Papers, Science Museum.
21 Quoted in Smith, *op cit*, pp 20–22.

Chatham, then on a towage job from Woolwich to the Nore. On 2 August 1826, she was due to take a barge containing the personal effects of an ambassador to rendezvous in the Downs or at Portsmouth with HMS *Ganges*, in which the ambassador was to take passage.

Thus *Lightning*, a highly successful vessel, was the first of the naval steam vessels to be employed on regular deep sea passages, passages more ambitious than merchant paddle steamers were making regularly at this period. An attempt by the General Steam Navigation Company to establish a service to St Petersburg a year later was a failure. The next steam vessel to be built, *African*, was described in a letter from the yard officers at Woolwich to the Navy Board in the following terms.[22]

> Yard Officers to Navy Board 14/12/1825.
> We beg to acquaint you that His Majesty's Steam Vessel *African*, went down the River yesterday as far as Longreach. Mr. Maudslay and Son, the Master Attendant Mr. Peake, Assistant Master shipwright, the Foreman of the New Works and Mr. Peake junior attended, and we beg leave to state that in our opinion no machinery could act better, nor any steam vessel give more satisfaction, as far as we were able to judge, and beg to propose her going down to Greenhythe on Friday next to bring up the *North Star* to this port.

Robin Craig[23] has drawn our attention to reports in *Lloyd's List* of the sailing from Gravesend for Sierra Leone of a vessel named *African* under the command of one Austin on 3 January 1826. She sailed again from Ramsgate, 'London for Sierra Leone', on 12 January having been 'assisted in here, with loss of rudder, having been on shore', and arrived at Falmouth, after lying five weeks in Portsmouth, no doubt under repair, on 18 February. She sailed again from Falmouth on 2 March. Robin Craig assures us that there was at this time no vessel named *African* registered under the Merchant Shipping Acts. It would therefore appear that this was the naval vessel. Newbury shows that she successfully completed her passage, and thus she was indeed a pioneer among ocean-going vessels using steam-and-sail. Such a voyage is a very long way from the employment as a harbour tug which has so often been ascribed to naval steamers of this period.

African was followed in the next four years by a number of paddle steamers. By 1828 there was a small fleet of such vessels available for towing, despatch carrying, and general duties. This included *Alban* of 1824, *Echo* and *Confiance* of 1827, and *Meteor* and *Columbia*. A good idea of

22 PRO ADM 106/1799 Woolwich.

23 In an oral communication of 21 March 1892. The *Lloyd's List* reports appeared on 6, 10, 13 January, 17, 21 February and 7 March 1826. See also Newbury, *British Policy towards West Africa: Select Documents 1780–1874*, Oxford 1965, p 142.

their general employment can be gained from a Plymouth yard report on the work of *Meteor* in April 1826.[24] On 1 April she towed *Windsor Castle* down the harbour; on the 8th she towed *Genoa* and *Reynard* from the Hamoaze to the Sound. From the 15th to the 17th she towed what is described as a 'lump' from Plymouth to Milford, 'for laying and repairing moorings for the quarantine service'. On the 19th and 20th she made passage back to Plymouth and on 23 April she left Plymouth for Sheerness.

These little vessels were naval steamers and as such played a very useful and increasingly important role. They were not ships of war. The steam vessel was not at this time capable of being developed into an effective fighting ship and, as the Admiralty was well aware, there was no need at this stage to hasten her steady evolution, in which they were playing an effective part.

It is perhaps necessary to point out at this stage that the communication attributed[25] to Lord Melville, First Lord of the Admiralty, 1812–27 and 1828–30, in which he is alleged to have written to the Colonial Office in 1827 to state that the Admiralty 'felt it their bounden duty to discourage to the utmost of their ability the employment of steam vessels', appears to be a fabrication.[26] Indeed, in view of the fact that most of the developments described so far can be attributed to Melville's administration of the navy under a Tory government, it seems a most unlikely statement for him to have made, at least in the form in which it has been frequently quoted. He was the head of an efficient administration which included the Navy Board, the subordinate body with a long and complex history which was charged with the civil administration of the navy. This administration achieved the postwar reconstruction of the fleet, which became the most powerful of the age of the wooden warship, as Andrew Lambert has shown in *The Last Sailing Battlefleet* (London, 1991). Lambert has also suggested (in the opening chapter of *Steam, Steel and Shellfire* (London, 1992) that if there was any opposition to steam propulsion it came from the Navy Board, which tended to be more conservative than the Board of Admiralty. The Navy Board was abolished for political reasons in circumstances described later in this chapter.

Lightning carried a crew of twenty or so: the commanding officer, two mates, a steward, a cook, nine seamen 'to serve as stokers and coal trimmers', two boys first class, two engineers and two boys in the engine room department. It is probable that until 1828 the commanding officers of these early paddlers were civilians, or half-pay masters and mates re-employed in a civilian capacity. The vessels, although by now often described as 'HM Steam Vessel', did not appear among the listed naval

24 PRO ADM 87/2, 29 July 1826.

25 By Sir John Briggs, *Naval Administration, 1827–1892*, London 1893, p9, and numerous later naval historians repeating him, down to the present day.

26 See Brock and Greenhill, *Steam and Sail*, Newton Abbot 1973, p 11.

ships. But on 4 December 1827 a significant communication was sent by the Navy Board to the Admiralty.[27]

> In obediance to the command of the Lord High Admiral [the Duke of Clarence, soon to become King William IV] signified by your letter of this date, we beg to propose the following as the proper establishment for steam vessels. One Lieutenant, one mate, two engineers, twelve men (including stokers).

On the same day the Duke signed the commissions of Lieutenant George Evans RN for the command of *Lightning*, and those of Lieutenants Bullock and Hay to command *Echo* and *Meteor* respectively. These officers thus became the first commissioned officers of the Royal Navy to be appointed to the command of steam vessels. In January 1828, *Lightning*, *Echo*, and *Meteor* duly appeared as HM Ships in the quarterly navy list, thus making official the birth of steam as an element in the Royal Navy's power. *Lightning* was to go on to have a very long and distinguished career. Immediately after commissioning she became the yacht of the Lord High Admiral, and indeed, this is possibly why the commissioning took place. A note of 25 March 1828 shows the cost of her conversion as £75 2s and three farthings. Later in her life she featured in the magazine *Punch*, then a national institution. In connection with the crossing to Ostend of a Royal Personage, the magazine printed the following doggerel.[28]

> Though Canute could not check the wave
> When rapidly the tide was heightening,
> Victoria her orders gave
> And at her bidding stopped the *Lightning*.

She went on to do important survey work in the Irish Sea under the command of a famous and controversial officer, Edward Belcher, in the mid-1830s. During the War with Russia, the so-called Crimean War, she was under the command in 1854 of a full post captain, B J Sulivan, arguably then one of the two most able officers in the navy, and the hydrographic work done by *Lightning* made possible the destruction of the great naval base being built by the Russians at Bomarsund in the Åland islands.[29] In 1855 she was again in the Baltic and took an active part in blockade duties. She then returned to more mundane duties, acting as a tender to *Duke of Wellington*, and in the 1860s returned to survey work. In 1868 she made a short voyage in the course of which work of seminal importance in the

27 PRO ADM 106/2292.
28 Quoted in Smith, *op cit*, p 20.
29 See Greenhill and Giffard, *The British Assault on Finland*, London 1988, especially Chapter 13, and Lambert, *The Crimean War*, especially Chapters 12 and 13.

history of oceanography was completed.[30] In 1870–72 she was back on survey on the west coast of England, after which this historic vessel, now 50 years old and still equipped with her original side-lever engines, was broken up at Devonport.

In September 1828, *African* was preparing for a voyage to Ancona on the Adriatic coast of northern Italy carrying a 'messenger from the Colonial Office'. Lieutenant Grigg had been appointed in command and he received personal instructions from the Comptroller of the Navy, Admiral Sir Thomas Byam Martin, as follows.[31]

September 28, 1828.

Dear Sir,

I am most anxious that you should use every possible exertion in getting the *African* ready for service, and you must take every opportunity to go about in our steam vessels to pick up a knowledge of the movements, etc., of such vessels, and it will be a great point to get a Mate who has been in such a vessel. . . .

Your lower masts ought to be as snug and low as possible, with a lofty fore topmast, so that you may have the least resistance when going head to wind, and the greatest spread of canvas when going free.

I wish you to consult with Mr. Stone and make every possible arrangement for stowing the largest quantity of Coals, informing me how much the vessel will be able to take – if a quantity can be stowed equal to 12 days consumption, which I doubt, it would then be unnecessary to incur the expense of keeping a supply for you at Ancona.

Mr. Grigg, *African*, Steam Vessel, Deptford.

Already in 1828 the Admiralty was contemplating the establishment of its own engine maintenance unit. Byam Martin not unnaturally turned to one of their two chief engine builders, Maudslay, Sons and Field, for advice. The correspondence went on[32]

Navy Office
Oct. 21, 1828.

Sir Byam Martin is very much obliged to Messrs. Maudslay and Field for their readiness to afford him any information as to the necessary buildings etc. to enable the Navy Board to repair their own Steam

30 Ritchie, *The Admiralty Chart*, London 1967, pp 322, 341.
31 Byam Martin MSS, BL Add 41, 397, 146.
32 Byam Martin MSS, *op cit*, 154.

Engines and perhaps to make their own boilers, it is even possible that such an arrangement may be the commencement of a plan for manufacturing in the Dock Yard the whole of the machinery, which Sir B. Martin thinks it candid to state, because he should quite understand and admit the reasonableness of Messrs. Maudslay & Field declining to assist in promoting an object which, in the end, might prove prejudicial to their interests, – if, however, after the communication there is no objection to Mr. Field's going to Portsmouth, Sir Byam Martin will be glad to meet him in Portsmouth Dock Yard on Friday morning at ten o'clock.

Mr Maudslay replied

> Lambeth,
> Oct. 21, 1828.

Mr. Maudslay presents his compliments to Sir Byam Martin and begs to inform him that it is the wish of both Mr. Field and himself to meet the views of the Hon'able Board as much as possible. Mr. Field will certainly be at Portsmouth on Friday as proposed, and he begs to join Mr. Maudslay in acknowledging Sir Byam Martin's candid method of treating the subject under discussion.

It was, in fact, to be 1835 before the maintenance unit, the 'Steam Factory', was set up at Woolwich, and many years more before the navy built its own engines.

The paddle propelled steamship having become a recognised part of the navy, the construction of small vessels for the sort of general duties which have already been described was continued, and by 1831 there were a dozen or so in service. After 1830, when steam was introduced into the Mediterranean packet service, some of these, including *Meteor, Echo, Confiance, African* and *Carron*, were employed in carrying mails. This was an exacting service requiring regular sailings and many days of continuous steaming. It was operated not by the Post Office but by the Navy, which thus inaugurated the first regular long distance service to be operated under steam. A contemporary summed up what was involved.[33]

> The most extensive line of steam navigation, of which we have yet had any lengthened experience, is that of the Admiralty packets, which for several years have maintained a regular communication between this

33 Lardner, *Steam Communication with India*, Calcutta 1837, p 20. Lardner, notorious as a controversialist on the subject of steam propulsion at sea, is here dealing with contemporaneously well known facts.

country and the Ionian Isles, Egypt, and occasionally Syria. The stages of this line have been – first, from Falmouth to Gibralter, 1,010 miles; secondly, from Gibralter to Malta, 970 miles; thirdly, Malta to Alexandria, 860 miles. So far as Alexandria, then, here is a voyage of 2,800 miles performed with certainty and regularity for a long continuance.

These vessels (which took a month to make the round voyage to Corfu, though the sailing vessels which preceded them had often taken three) were employed (the Admiralty being reimbursed by the Treasury) alongside some vessels bought from civilian owners for the purpose. These included the steamers *George IV* and *Duke of York*, purchased from Jollife and Banks for £12,500, including furniture and fittings, to carry mail and passengers to Corfu. The lieutenants appointed in command were required to pay by instalments for their furniture 'considering the great profits to officers commanding such vessels' – an interesting sidelight on the advantages of being appointed to command of a steamer.[34]

Engines were becoming more reliable and fuel consumption more reasonable. Merchant paddle steamers were increasing in numbers on short sea routes, but it was not until 1833 that the first steam assisted crossing of the Northern Atlantic was made by a vessel designed as a fully powered steamer, and that in an east to west direction, the hard way. This was the *Cape Breton*, 104 feet long, built at Blackwall for three London shareholders in the same year and equipped with two 35 horse power engines on her delivery passage for use in connection with the coal mining operations at Sydney, Nova Scotia. She arrived in Sydney on 3 August 1833.[35]

The establishment of a regular transatlantic service was still five years off. Given the limitations of the paddle steamer at this stage it is not surprising that no other ocean route had yet been developed, or indeed was to be until after 1840, although under the influence of Samuel Seaward (see page 48) two full rigged ships in the India trade in the late 1830s, *Earl of Hardwicke*, 1600 tons, and *Vernon*, were fitted with diminutive paddles driven by engines of such low power that they can have done no more than render the

34 PRO ADM 12 1829–1830 and 106/2295 186 of 18 May 1830.
35 See *The Mariner's Mirror*, Vol 50, p 145 and Vol 52 p 328, and Hyde, *Cunard and the North Atlantic 1840–1873*, London 1975, p 3. The claim that the Canadian-built *Royal William* crossed the Atlantic using steam alone and without recourse to 'sail-assist' in 1833 and was the first vessel to do so which was made in a number of late nineteenth century histories of the steamship and has since been repeated in numerous books was conclusively refuted by James Walker in *The First Trans-Atlantic Steamer*, London, second edition, 1898. Walker demonstrates that she made an orthodox passage using both steam and sail and sail alone for a number of days. *Royal William* sailed on her passage to England thirteen days after *Cape Breton* had already arrived in Canada. The first vessel to cross the Atlantic steaming continuously was *Great Western* in 1838. Even she was dependent on sail-assist not only as an additional source of power but to make it possible to maintain course with a strong wind on the beam.

vessels more manoeuvrable in the restricted waters of the Hooglie.[36]

The establishment of a regular commercial service to the Iberian peninsula was to begin only with the formation of the Peninsular Steam Navigation Company in 1835, five years after the navy began to maintain a mail service under steam, and this company was not financially successful until it obtained the subsidy of a government mail contract in 1837, thus enabling the navy to use its steamers elsewhere – although a further twenty-six steam vessels, originally built for the Post Office, were transferred to Admiralty jurisdiction in 1837 in a process of rationalisation. Indeed, it was not to be until the 1840s that merchant steam vessels, frequently aided financially by mail contracts, all with sail-assist in one form or another, blossomed forth on a limited number of middle range, deep sea routes.

The difficulties are made clear in the 29th Half Yearly Report of the General Steam Navigation Company of London, published in 1839.[37]

> For several years after the general introduction and application of steam navigation, large and indeed extravagent expectations were formed of the profit to be acquired. The cost of the management of steamships was judged from the results of the first five years, from the returns obtained while the ships were in perfect condition and before reparations to any serious extent had been required . . . The expenses required in order to maintain steamships in a proper state of efficiency and repair have been found to reach so large an annual amount that, of the numerous steam companies which have been formed, scarcely one has been found, upon review of their operations for ten years, able to maintain for the average of that period, a dividend of five per cent; consistently of a proper sum to the maintenance of their capital, while, in many instances, the operations have terminated in the sacrifice of almost the whole of the property embarked. Steam boats have been found to require in a very great degree the exertion of the most indefatigable activity and rigid economy in every particular of their employment and conduct in order to obtain from them any returns . . .

A paper by Gordon Jackson[38] paints a very vivid, entertaining and fully documented picture of the financial, managerial and operational difficulties

36 Greenhill and Giffard, *Women Under Sail*, London 1971, p 63. Body, *op cit*, p 75. MacGregor, *Merchant Sailing Ships 1815–1850*, London 1984, pp 174–175. The principal document is Seaward, 'Memoir on the Practicability of Shortening the Duration of Voyages By the Adoption of Auxiliary Steam Power To Sailing Vessels', *Transactions of the Institute of Civil Engineers*, Vol 3, London 1842, pp 385, 400.

37 Quoted in Palmer, 'Experience, Experiment and Economics: Factors in the Construction of Early Steamships' in Matthews and Panting, eds, *Ships and Shipbuilding in the North Atlantic Region*, St Johns, Newfoundland 1978, p 236.

38 Jackson, 'Operational Problems of the Transfer to Steam: Dundee, Perth & London Shipping Company, c1820–1845' in Smout, ed, *Scotland and the Sea*, Edinburgh 1992.

met by a steamship company in the 1830s. Jackson observes that 'Although transport historians usually view steamers as a cost effective move into modern efficiency, the early ones were costly experiments tending to ruin each other in a desperate search for superior freights'.

In 1835 Peter Ewart, who had formerly worked for Rennie and for James Watt, was appointed Chief Engineer and Inspector of Machinery to the Navy. The construction of the maintenance unit for steamers, the Steam Factory, was eventually begun at Woolwich in 1836, and by 1840 it was complete, with John Dinnen, who had been an engineer in *Lightning*, as one of its senior staff. But the difficulties in the way of the construction of large paddle propelled war vessels for long range service were considerable. As is explained in Chapter 7, the long term solution was to be provided by the screw propeller. By the early 1830s numerous schemes had been put forward for the propulsion of ships by means other than paddle wheels, including at least one, by Robert Wilson, as early as 1820 which was so much on the right lines as to provide the eventual solution.[39] This was the placing of the screw propeller between the sternpost and the rudder of a vessel, the lines of which at the stern had been designed for the purpose.[40].

In practice in the early 1830s, therefore, there was no practical alternative to paddles, and propulsion by paddle was unsatisfactory. Murray summed up some of the reasons very well in 1851.[41]

Variable Immersion the Grand Objection to the Paddle Wheel.
We have already hinted that the grand objection to the paddle wheel is the unequal 'dip' or immersion of the boards, consequent on the varying draught of water, as the coals and stores continue to be consumed on the voyage. A vessel, for instance, with a displacement of 12 tons per inch of the load line, burning perhaps 460 tons of coals during a long run, will swim 3 ft 6 ins lighter, from the consumption of the fuel alone, at the end than at the beginning, so that it is only in the middle of her voyage that the wheels can have the dip best calculated for them . . . When the wheels are too deeply immersed, then they may sometimes be 'reefed' by disconnecting the boards, and securing them nearer the centre.

Another major difficulty with the paddle steamer is obvious. In anything like a rough sea, as the vessel rolled, one paddle or the other was out of the water for some of the time and the system was working at half or less than half efficiency. The vessel had to roll very little to begin to bring about this

39 Wilson, *The Screw Propeller*, Glasgow 1860, p 17. Although Wilson did not benefit from his original thinking on the placing of the screw, he later prospered as a partner in Nasmyth's engineering works.

40 Lambert, *The Royal Navy and the Introduction of the Screw Propeller: 1837–47* in Fisher, ed, *Innovation in Shipping and Trade*, Exeter 1989, and Brown, *op cit*, Chapters 9 and 10.

41 Murray, *Rudimentary Treatise on Marine Engines*, London 1852, pp 109–110.

situation because the advantageous dip at which the paddle worked most efficiently varied with the speed of the vessel, the depth to which she was loaded and the diameter of the wheel.

But the problem of variable immersion does not end here. When a paddle steamer was in the second half of a relatively long passsage and her coal consumption had reduced her draught by perhaps three or four feet, with the wind on the beam her angle of heel led to an increased turning effect by the leeward and more deeply immersed paddle. The vessel therefore had a constant tendency to turn up into the wind. Bearing in mind the inherent difficulty of steering a paddler (see page 47) various devices had to be adopted to counteract this tendency to carry excessive weather helm. The log of the first passage of *Great Western* towards New York shows that when the vessel was carrying weather helm from this cause the anchor chains were shifted over to windward and the predominance of canvas set was forward of amidships – a proper use of sail-assist to counteract a fully powered paddle steamer's tendency to turn up into the wind in certain conditions.

In addition to these obvious difficulties the paddle steamer suffered from an inherent weakness which imposed limitations on the cargo and fuel carrying capacity of the merchant paddle steamer, and the fuel, armament and stores capacity of warships. The difficulty was summed up by Campbell McMurray, Director of the Royal Navy Museum at Portsmouth.[42]

. . . in the first place steps have to be taken at the design stage to ensure that the wave profile abreast of the paddle should be reasonably flat, or at least, not likely to form a hollow immediately in front of the floats. Should the latter take place the thrust of the float takes place in something less than the full, free, flow of water, leading to excessive slip in the action of the float and consequent loss of efficiency. The second point is related: it is vital to ensure that the bow diverging waves trail aft *outside* of the paddles, since when they come inside, serious vibration is encountered in the running gear, bringing attendant damage. The solution to these and associated problems is often related to the fineness of the entrance and run, combined with their length viz a viz the total immersed length of the vessel. The outcome is usually to provide such ships i.e. fast, passenger-carrying paddle steamers – with much lower block coefficients than would be thought acceptable for general deep sea work.

The expression 'low block coefficients' simply means that the vessels had to be long, lean and narrow. Such a shape strictly limited the carrying

---

42 McMurray, *Old Order, New Thing*, London 1972, pp 22–23. McMurray's book is a lucid exposition of the paddle steamer which should be read by everyone concerned with this phase of naval and merchant shipping history.

capacity, and therefore the commercial viability, of a merchant vessel. She could not carry bulk cargoes, which were the great majority of cargoes, coal, grain, ores and so forth, but was limited to passenger carrying and the transport of light, high value, high freight materials. This perhaps did not matter so much for vessels employed on short runs in relatively sheltered waters where fuel costs were of less concern than speed. But such vessels, ideal for river and lake use, beyond a certain speed become unstable and are unable to cope with the stresses imposed by the big seas of the oceans. As far as the navy was concerned the fuel, ammunition and stores a naval vessel could carry, and therefore her range, were limited, and also the weight of armament which could be fitted and the disposition of that armament fore and aft in the vessel's length. The naval vessel had, in effect, to be a bulk carrier. The presence of the great side paddles meant that, instead of being able to mount a broadside of guns – and the broadside still dominated naval tactics in the 1820s and '30s because of the nature of the guns available and the difficulty of transmitting orders – her armament was limited to the fore and after parts of the vessel. At this stage in the 1830s, before the introduction of the pivot gun in 1841, to carry her heavy guns – various guns, but in the 1830s perhaps two long howitzers (84 pounders) and a number of 32 pounders – in her ends meant that the naval steamer had to have, not the sharp hull at the ends which made for efficient working of the paddles, but full bodied, round ends, like the old sailing warships. Sharp ends simply did not have the buoyancy to support the heavy guns.

It follows that the naval steamer at her best could only be a design compromise of limited functions. This was the more so since her paddles were highly vulnerable, although possibly less vulnerable than was usually supposed at the time. Lying parallel to the enemy and slugging it out with broadsides of solid shot or primitive shell fired horizontally was out of the question. Slugging it out in broadsides was, quite rightly, in those days when commanding officers had very little control over their fleets because of the poor communications, what naval tactics were still all about, shell firing guns or no shell firing guns.

Common to the merchant ship and the naval steamer were other and even more fundamental problems. One emerged from the nature of the paddle itself. The ideal diameter had to be established and the ideal length of the paddle boards. The paddle was inefficient, partly because the only time when the board acted perpendicularly to the water was when it was vertically below the centre of the wheel. Various solutions were tried and a feathering system was adapted for merchant vessels operating on short services where there was not much variation in depth of immersion during a passage because not much in the way of fuel, water and stores was consumed. But the installation of a feathering system meant that the boards could not be sent out to the perimeter of the paddle as a vessel floated higher and higher as she consumed her various weights on a long passage, in the manner described by Murray in the quotation on page 43. The effect of the feathering systems, which were complex in operation, is well summed up by McMurray.[43]

> The reaction thus engendered is to keep the floats approximately normal to the effective surface during their passage through the water, so that the whole of the thrust will be in a sternward direction.

The feathering system can be seen in operation in the port paddle wheel of the steamer *Reliant*, preserved intact on public view at the National Maritime Museum at Greenwich.

The feathering system was not widely adopted in the navy for the reason given above: naval vessels had to be capable of long passages at maximum efficiency, and the reefing system of the boards was preferred. The complex feathering system was also considered vulnerable in action and difficult to maintain. Nevertheless, they were tried. A report[44] from Byam Martin to the Admiralty of 26 April 1830 gives an account of trials with such wheels in *Confiance* of 100 horse power, which beat *Columbia*, 120 horse power, Post Office packet, hitherto the faster vessel. Oliver Lang believed the feathering paddle was worth an extra knot on speed, but they were less confident of its ability to survive long periods of working and suggested that, as a trial, *Confiance* should be sent out with the next Mediterranean mail.

Charles Jordan, a shipbuilder and surveyor of great experience, wrote of the feathering paddle float[45]

> the steamer . . . had been fitted with feathering paddle wheels, and while proceeding down the river at full speed one of the floats of the starboard paddle wheel suddenly broke adrift and crashed through the top of the paddle box, where the author was standing, and it was only by his leaping on to the bridge deck between the paddle boxes that he escaped injury. This description of paddle wheel, although admirably designed with a view to rendering the wheel more effective, was very liable to accident.

Yet another problem arose from the poor handling characteristics of paddle steamers at low speeds. The rudder of a paddler had no slipstream from the screw to render it immediately effective when the vessel got underweigh or was coming alongside, and in consequence had low manoeuvrability except in the case of vessels in which the paddles could be

43 McMurray, *op cit*, p 25, Appendix B.
44 Byam Martin Papers, *op cit*, 398.
45 Charles H Jordan, *Some Historical Records and Reminiscences Relating to the British Navy and Mercantile Shipping, Lloyd's Register*, London 1925, p 18.

operated separately. Jackson (see page 42) refers specifically to the managerial and financial consequences for an early steamship company of the fact that 'In close encounters steamers were difficult to stop and impossible to steer'.

Another, wider, problem emerged from the fact that the ships and the engines were built by different firms and by men steeped in entirely different traditions. Shipbuilding was still in a very unscientific state and a great deal of contemporary engineering was still essentially empirical. Merchant shipbuilders were not disposed towards programmes of experimental development and here the navy was more advanced in its approach. As Buchanan and Doughty put it[46]

> in the experimental period up to the mid 1830s . . . every steam installation, no matter how small, was significant in affecting later development.

But it was a long time before the hull and the engines were conceived as a whole, the one intimately interlinked with the other.

A third problem was even more fundamental. For both merchant ships and naval the whole technique of engineering had to develop, not only in the obvious major ways but in small but fundamental ways without which no general progress could be made. Thus the availability, cost and quality of various metals was fundamental; early machine tools had to be invented; without lubricants, oils and greases no machinery could operate and new lubricants had to be perfected which could withstand high temperatures. In due course such apparently but misleadingly insignificant matters as screw threads had to be standardised.

But there was a greater problem than all these. Although in the 1830s and '40s steam engine technology was advancing very rapidly indeed, nevertheless all steam engines suffered from a fundamental defect which imposed strict limits on their use as a means of propulsion at sea. These early marine engines were single cylinder reciprocating engines like a small modern petrol engine, with cylinders and pistons and a crankshaft to convert the reciprocating action of the piston into rotary motion to turn the paddles. Although things were steadily improving, the way the steam was worked meant that up to 90 per cent of its potential power was wasted. This in turn meant that the vessel had to carry many times as much coal as she would have done if her engine had worked at, say, 60 per cent efficiency. Every ton of coal carried meant that a ton of cargo could not be carried, so it would at once be obvious that the merchant paddle steamship had very strict limitations. In 1841, Samuel Seaward FRS read his paper to the Institute of

46 Buchanan and Doughty, 'The Choice of Steam Engine Manufacturers by the British Admiralty 1822–1852', *The Mariner's Mirror*, Vol 64, pp 327–347.

Civil Engineers which put the problem nicely in contemporary terms[47] – it is to be remembered that Seaward was still thinking in terms only of paddle propelled vessels, the first real experiments with the screw in the Screw Propeller Company's *Archimedes* were only then being carried out.

> Notwithstanding the numerous improvements which have been made in the form and dimensions of the hulls of steam vessels, and the perfection to which the machinery has been brought, still the weight of the latter, together with the space required for the fuel, has rendered it hitherto impractical to extend the duration of the steam voyage beyond the period of 20 days, without the necessity of taking in a fresh supply of coal. It must therefore be concluded that until some great reduction can be made in the weight of the engines and the amount of fuel required to keep them in motion, the use of steam as the sole moving power must be limited to voyages of three weeks' duration, a period of time wholly inadequate for the performance of an Indian or South American voyage.

Similarly, the range of operation of a warship under steam was strictly limited, while under sail her performance was often gravely impaired because the paddle boxes and paddles imposed limitations on the spacing of the masts, so that she was a poor sailer and often could not keep station with sailing vessels on naval manoeuvres. The spacing of the masts of the paddle frigates of the 1830s and '40s, as the illustrations to this book show, looks very odd to eyes accustomed to the conventional mast spacing of the sailing vessel. Moreover, even though various devices were developed by engineering firms for the ready disconnecting or declutching of the paddle wheels when the vessels were under sail, the freely rotating paddle wheels still imposed a drag on the vessels under canvas. It was not until a light, small, economical engine became available that the steam merchant vessel, even screw driven, could compete with the small wooden sailing ship in world trade and this was not to happen until the middle of the 1860s. Thus *Lloyd's Register* for 1853 shows merchant steamers representing only two per cent of all vessels listed.

In November 1830, the Tory government, which had been in power since the early years of the century with very little break, fell and Lord Melville was replaced as First Lord of the Admiralty by Sir James Graham. The shift in political requirements was marked. The policy of the Tory administration had, with the recent traumatic memory of the French Revolutionary and Napoleonic Wars, been to prepare for another major conflict and hold the navy in a state of economical reserve in readiness for it. They pressed forward with the steam paddle vessel as fast as was necessary, and as the new technology allowed, and used her more ambitiously than did the

---

47 Samuel Seaward, *op cit.*

merchant shipping industry – for the good reason that the Admiralty did not have to face shareholders who had put capital into high risk ventures. The Whig administration of the ten years after 1830, while still concentrating on the possibility of war with France, saw a small active fleet as an agent of power, a fleet in being to enforce British policy by its very existence.

The Tory government in its last period had commissioned the building of a further group of steamers including *Dee*, larger than any of her predecessors, which has been seen as the first real steam warship. She was the first steamer capable of carrying a significant armament, and her design appears to have been influenced by contemporary merchant shipping practices. Armed initially with two long 32 pounders and later with four 32 pounders, her construction marks the real beginning of steam vessels as part of the navy's fighting force. Even so, she was seen initially as potentially a dual purpose vessel, as the documentation shows.[48]

> Order a 701 ton st. v. at Woolwich to replace *Dee*. Of a peculiar form having receptacles for the paddle wheels built in the body, this principle has long been in practice at Liverpool and has been found to answer the purpose particularly well, as it allows of greater space on deck, protection to the wheels, and prevents deep rolling and pitching. We beg to remark (at the same time) that it is not intended in the first instance that the vessel shall have ports, but have spaces framed for them as shewn by the ticked lines in the Draught, which can be opened at little expense if required, and her internal accommodation will be so arranged that she may serve either as a ship of war, or for the conveyance of troops.

The device of giving the vessel a narrow waist in which the paddles were housed became universal in naval paddlers built after *Dee*, and is illustrated in the draughts of *Tiger* and other vessels reproduced in this book. As this document shows, *Dee* was not laid down as a sailing vessel, as some authorities have maintained,[49] but she was built in the place of a sailing vessel which was to be called *Dee*.

In France, General Paixhan, an eminent artillery officer, who had solved the old problem of the horizontal firing of explosive shells, had since the early 1820s been advocating the building of a fleet of fast paddle steamers armed with exploding shell guns. Such a fleet, not dependent for its manning on the great pool of experienced seamen which Britain had and France did not, would, he argued, render the British fleet ineffective and enable France to overcome the might of the British navy which had played so large a part in France's defeat.[50]

48 PRO 106/2292 (73–4, Navy Board to Admiralty, 4 April 1827).
49 For instance, see Brown, *op cit*, p 51.
50 There is a useful summary of General Paixhan's ideas in Robertson, *The Evolution of Naval Armament*, London 1921, pp 165–175.

General Paixhan's proposals were the subject of much contemporary controversy and they were, in fact, impractical because, just as Britain had a complete superiority in seamen, so also she had complete superiority in industrial power, and French industry was incapable at the time of producing the marine steam engine that Paixhan's fleet of fast paddlers would require.

Nevertheless, in 1830, at a bombardment of Algiers which was actually carried out and led to French annexation of the territory, seven lightly armed French paddle steamers, equipped with machinery built in Britain, were meant to be part of the attacking force, although only two of them reached Algiers. Within two months of the new Whig administration taking office, the following Admiralty Order was promulgated.[51]

> 10 January, 1831.
> Steam vessels. Four to be built immediately one each by the Master Shipwrights at Portsmouth, Plymouth and Woolwich, and one by the Navy Board – to be of 220 Horse Power each and to carry a 10 inch gun of 80 hundredweight.
> A second class of steam vessels to be prepared to 500 tons and two engines of 70 Horse Power each. One tug steam vessel will be attached to each of the Ports, viz, Portsmouth, Plymouth and Sheerness.

This was followed by an exchange between Graham and Byam Martin[52] as follows.

> Sir James Graham to Sir T. Byam Martin 22.1.31. extract
> Steam, also, must change the character of the next war with France, and if we have not a superior force of armed steamboats in the Channel our own shores will be unprotected – and our homeward bound trade will be exposed to constant and inevitable danger. It is impossible that these important considerations can have escaped your attention – but I am anxious to hear from you, how many steam boats properly armed you could bring forward for Channel Service.

> Sir T. Byam Martin to Sir James Graham 27.1.31.
> Of steam vessels (an expensive description of force) we have eleven, as shewn with their respective condition in the accompanying list. Most of these vessels were intended to be kept in ordinary constantly ready for service but it was thought expedient by the Admlty that a portion of them should be commissioned some years ago, and the consequence is that several of them are now requiring repairs to their machinery etc.
> The *Dee*, a steam vessel of large class now building, will be ready in

51 Byam Martin, *op cit*, 368/259.
52 Byam Martin, *op cit*, 399/16.

May – & preparations were making for another previous to your recent directions for constructing three at different Ports.

The mode and extent of arming these vessels is that prescribed by Admiralty Order dated 16 Nov. 1830.

It is satisfactory to know that this country has a greater command of Steam Vessels (and many of large size) than perhaps all other nations together. In the event of a war, a sufficient number might no doubt be hired and armed for the protection of the Trade in the Channel, with such means within reach, it was perhaps, prudent and economical not to incur great expense in forming an extensive Establishment of such vessels, while the Machinery and its' application are subject to continual experiments with the view to improvement.

The final paragraph of this exchange sums up very well the fluidity of the technical situation and one aspect, to which we have referred before in this chapter, of the Admiralty's attitude to the private sector.

The following month the urgency was emphasised. Byam Martin wrote the following communications.[53]

To Commissioner Ross   18.2.1931.
My Dear Sir,

It is a sad thing at such a moment as the present to give the Master Shipwrights of the large yards the task of preparing a plan of a steam vessel, but there is so pressing an anxiety on the part of the Admiralty to hasten forward vessels of that description that it is necessary you should give Mr. Roberts a *written* direction to hasten it as much as proper *attention* to the subject will permit, and tell him I fully expect enquiry from the Admty. on an early day to ask what progress has been made.

To Oliver Lang   21.2.31.
You must push forward with the *Dee*.

And then in June to Graham,

To Sir James Graham   16.6.31.

I am far from underestimating the growing importance of steam as applicable to War, and can well imagine its capability of improvement & extended power, so as to exceed even the ascendancy which has been predicted, but, if in the meantime our naval rivals continue to build ships of the largest class it surely is not fitting that this great naval country should abate its preparation on the vague ground of anticipated improvement in steam.

53 Byam Martin, *op cit*, 35 and 65.

I submit that even the certainty of prospective loss to any amount of money ought not to put us off our guard, but on the contrary, whatever may be the means of warfare persisted in or adopted to by other nations, the safety of this empire depending as it does upon our superiority at sea, requires that we should take the lead so as to be capable of meeting the united force of the World of whatever description that force may be. So, in the progress and improvement of steam as applicable to Naval purposes, this country must secure a superiority over others, and if we have hitherto confined the building to a few vessels of this class while steam, as regards the Navy, was in its infancy, and daily gaining in its power, it has lately been decided that the time is arrived for making an addition to the force of this description, and we may feel confident that the means of this country, and the skill of our manufacturers, cannot fail to give us a superiority over others in steam as we have had heretofore in vessels of a description more congenial to the habits of our practical seamen.

steamers building:

Dee & Medea	at Woolwich
Phoenix	Chatham
Salamander	Sheerness
Rhadamanthus	Plymouth

Add 41,368

Sir James Graham's motives may have been other than to guard against a hypothetical and unreal threat from French steamers. His intent was the abolition of the Navy Board and the removal of Byam Martin, who had strong Tory connections and connections with King William IV, with whom he had served. Allegations of neglect of the development of steam were one device to seek to discredit both Comptroller and Board. The post of Comptroller was abolished in 1832, and the Navy Board was also abolished in a general reorganisation of naval administration.

The new vessels were still lightly armed, but the uses to which they were put, although towing was still an important function of the steamer, were wider. Thus the beautiful *Rhadamanthus*, placed under the command of Commander George Evans, who as a lieutenant had been the first naval officer to command *Lightning*, was involved in blockade and peace-keeping duties on both sides of the Atlantic. She was the first steam powered vessel of the Royal Navy to cross the Atlantic. Her exploits in the West Indies are described in the next chapter. These four vessels, *Salamander, Phoenix, Medea* and *Rhadamanthus*, of over 800 tons each, equipped with engines of 220 to 260 horse power and armed with purpose built, 84 hundredweight 10 inch shell guns, the largest guns in the fleet, proved most reliable and they were followed by others of the same kind. The navy now had a core of experienced steam vessel officers who were rapidly gaining operating experience of steamers in all conditions. Stoking was becoming recognised as a specialist function – the absence of experienced stokers for the navy in the 1820s had been something of a handicap. Repair and maintenance facilities were building up, together with spares, at the dockyards. Maintenance was an expensive process, particularly because (rightly at this early stage) there had been no attempt at standardisation of engines. Boilers needed constant attention and frequent renewal.

Naval and merchant shipping moved forward together, using the same engine builders, the same shipbuilders, and to some extent the same designers. Of the eight or nine available engine builders of the period, the Admiralty favoured Maudslay, Sons and Field and Messrs Boulton and Watt. Of the twenty-seven steam vessels on the Navy List in 1837,[54] six had been engined by the latter (mostly with engines of lower power), and ten by the former company which, after 1832, tended to be commissioned to build the navy's more powerful engines. As we have already seen, the Admiralty also turned to Maudslay's for advice and co-operation in a wider field in the kind of relationship which exists between the Ministry of Defence and some contractors in the late twentieth century. The year 1837 was to be very important for the history of the paddle steamship. In that year two notably large steam vessels were being built at Pembroke, *Gorgon* and *Cyclops*. These, the first naval steam vessels of over 1000 tons, have been described as 'the first steam frigates'. This title is not really justified because a frigate by definition had her principal battery on the main deck with a weather deck over and was ship rigged. *Gorgon*, apparently rigged as a schooner and later as a brig, carried her six 32 pounders on the weather deck. But certainly with engines of 320 horse power and a heavier armament than any vessel which had gone before, they can be regarded, despite their limitations, as the first steamships with some real fighting capacity. Here again, the navy and the merchant shipping industry went hand in hand. In the same year, 1837, the first true fully powered, deep sea merchant steamship, *Great Western*, was building in Bristol to designs by Isambard Kingdom Brunel, son of Sir Marc Brunel who had played a role in the introduction of steam power into the navy. *Great Western* was both larger and more powerful – 212 feet on deck as opposed to the 178 feet of *Gorgon* and 190 feet of *Cyclops* and, with 450 horse power, nearly half as powerful again as the naval vessels. But those responsible for her construction acknowledged their debt to Oliver Lang, to whom is sometimes attributed the design of *Lightning* and many other early naval steamers, and to Sir William

54 Smith, *op cit*, p 52. Quoting Otway, *Elementary Treatise on Steam*, London 1834, and later editions.

Symonds, the Surveyor of the Navy.[55] In turn the navy was to benefit from the operational experience gained with *Great Western*. Her master, James Hosken, was a lieutenant on half pay who had had a very varied career, in the navy, in command of Post Office packets, and in merchant ships. Re-employed in the War with Russia in 1854, he was posted and eventually became a vice admiral, his interest being strong enough to ensure this despite his putting *The Great Britain* ashore through gross navigational error in 1846. In an autobiographical sketch[56] he wrote

> During this time (from 1837) I was frequently thanked by the Admiralty for information on steam progress . . .

Great Western had a cam control which gave nine points for shutting off steam during the piston stroke. The power which could be applied without varying the engine speed was therefore highly flexible and could be, and, her first log shows, constantly was, varied to match the power developed by her highly sophisticated four masted schooner sail-assist rig. The sails were, equally constantly, set and furled to gain maximum advantage from the wind. Operated in this way, with continuous attention to power applied from both steam and wind, she demonstrated for the first time in history that a fully powered paddle steamer could operate profitably on the North Atlantic without subsidy, albeit with extensive annual maintenance. She was an epoch making vessel, never really improved on, and she had great influence on the development of the steam warship, French and American as well as British.

Gorgon and *Cyclops* differed from *Great Western* in a very important respect. All the steam vessels previously discussed were powered by side-lever engines. Those of *Great Western*, as of so many naval vessels, were built by Maudslay, Sons and Field of London, who at that time had built more large engines[57] than any other firm and therefore were the natural candidates to build the engines, the most powerful marine engines constructed to that date, for the new ship.

Murray described the side-lever engine in simple terms.[58]

---

55 Griffiths, *Brunel's Great Western*,Wellingborough 1985, pp 14, 56. This scholarly and thorough study of this historic vessel is strongly recommended. Among other things it indicates some of the difficulties met with in operating even this splendid and successful vessel.

56 *Autobiographical Sketch of the Public Career of Admiral James Hosken*, Penzance 1889, p 17. See also Hosken, *The Logs of the First Voyage, made with the unceasing aid of steam between England and America, by The Great Western, of Bristol*, Bristol 1838.

57 In 1838 they had built fourteen marine power units of 300 horse power or more, the first being the 400 indicated horse power engines of *Dee*, in 1827. See *Henry Maudslay, Sons & Field Ltd.*, Maudslay Society, 1949.

58 Murray, *op cit*, pp 2, 4.

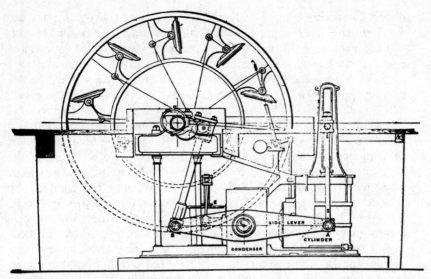

A side-lever engine. The drawing also shows, diagramatically, the working of the paddle float feathering mechanism. (From Gordon, *The Marine Steam Engine*, 1845)

In all marine engines the required object is to give a rotary motion to a horizontal shaft – either the paddle shaft in the case of paddle-wheel steamers, or the screw shaft in the case of vessels propelled by the screw. The earliest form of engine used for this purpose was the side lever, or beam engine, in which the reciprocating motion of the piston rod is transferred through upright side rods and the horizontal side levers to the connecting rod, which then gives the shaft its continuous rotary motion by means of the crank. . . .

Side Lever Engine – Its Advantages. – It is said that the side-lever engine was the first employed in a steam boat. This construction, with the arrangement of which the reader is doubtless familiar, has several advantages which enabled it for a long while to resist innovation. Perhaps its chief merit consists in this, that the weights of the moving parts are so balanced, the one against the other, that the piston when not acted on by steam is nearly in *equilibrio*, and ready to start in either direction with the smallest application of force. The great length of the connecting rod also admits of the motion of the piston being transmitted to the crank in the most equable and effective manner, and the moving parts of the engine are supposed to do their work with less friction and wear than are to be met with in any other kind of engine. It can hardly be wondered at, therefore, that the side lever engine was long a favourite, and indeed that it still continues to be so in certain cases and under certain conditions.

Disadvantages Of The Side Lever Engine. – There are two very important conditions, however, in the economy of a sea-going steamer which the side lever engine does not fulfill – namely, lightness of weight, and compactness of form. As these properties were found to be most essential in the machinery of a war steamer, it soon became apparent that some other arrangement of parts must be adopted which would admit of the same power being stowed in less compass, and a portion of the weight of the machinery saved for additional coals, or stores, or armaments.

Adoption Of The Direct-Acting Engine. – Hence the adoption and general use of direct-acting engines in the Royal Navy, by which means (in conjunction with the adoption of tubular boilers) the length of the engine room was diminished by about one-third, and the total weight of machinery by two-fifths. It may be observed here, that the weight usually allowed to side lever engines, flue boilers with water, and paddle wheels, is one ton per horse power; whilst direct-acting engines, with tubular boilers and water, paddle wheels, etc., scarcely exceed twelve hundred-weight per horse power. The distinguishing feature of all direct-acting engines consists in the connecting rod being led at once from the head of the piston rod to the crank without the intervention of side levers: And as it happens (unfortunately, we think) that this kind of engine is capable of almost endless variety, each manufacturing engineer has introduced his own child into the steam navy, where scarcely two pairs of direct-acting engines are to be found alike.

McMurray has written and illustrated the best modern description of the working of a side-lever engine.[59] In it he quotes an unnamed contemporary text book.

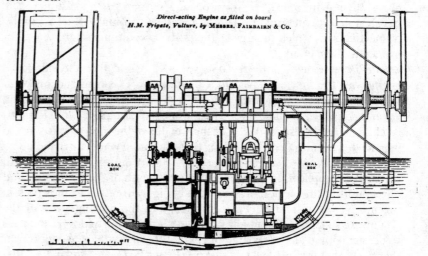

Direct-acting Engine as fitted on board
H.M. Frigate, Vulture, by Messrs. Fairbairn & Co.

Direct acting engines. (From Murray, *Marine Engines,* 1852)

59 McMurray, *op cit*, pp 26–35.

this class of engine is capable of working when in such a bad state of repair that the same condition in any other form of engine would prove dangerous; moreover, it seems to require far less care and attention than are usually found necessary with marine machinery.

They could be run by relatively unskilled engineers. To quote McMurray himself

these were engines that 'ran on the peak o' your cap' a reference to the clearance given the bearings. But no disadvantage that . . .

Besides engines in several museums, a pair of side-lever engines survives, perhaps the only ones in the world today still in the vessel for which they were built.[60] These are in the steam tug *Reliant*, preserved in the main display hall of the National Maritime Museum at Greenwich. Although built at the beginning of the twentieth century, these engines differ little from the side-levers of all the early naval and merchant paddle vessels, and, presented in the environment of the vessel, they are an example of the techniques of early marine engineering of the greatest value and of international importance.

Gorgon and *Cyclops* were equipped, not with the tried and trusted side-levers, but with the first direct acting engines of the type described in the quotation from Murray above to be installed in naval vessels. They were built by Messrs Seaward and Capel and claimed to be 60 tons lighter and also smaller than side-lever engines of the same power would have had to be. Direct acting engines can be seen in various forms in a number of paddle steamers in Europe in the 1990s.

The origins of the decision to install direct acting engines in these vessels are now obscure. It appears that they were originally to have side-levers of lower power, but in the end these engines were installed in other vessels and an order placed with Seaward and Capel for engines each consisting of a vertical cylinder mounted underneath the paddle wheel crank shaft and connected to it by a short connecting rod. So great was this departure from normal marine practice at this time that this type of engine became generally known as the *Gorgon* Engine. In the next five years the Admiralty was to order the building of thirty-eight more engines, more or less half and half side-lever and direct acting of various kinds.[61] The monopoly of two or three builders was broken, although Seawards built no fewer than sixteen of

60 A pair of side-levers also exists in the intact hull of the steamer *Eric Nordevall*, of 1837, at the bottom of Lake Vättern near Vadstena in Sweden. This vessel is being fully recorded by divers and may possibly be raised and conserved in due course. See Cederlund, *Rapport över den Marinarkeologiska und ersökningen av Hjulångfartyget E. Nordevall 1985–1988*, Stockholm 1989.
61 Buchanan and Doughty, *op cit*.

these engines, and the Admiralty became the subject of a campaign of criticism, probably instigated by Seaward's rivals, notably the Scots firm Robert Napier, for concentrating orders with them. It was alleged in Parliament and elsewhere that Seaward's engines were unreliable and very expensive to maintain, but Buchanan and Doughty's examination of the facts and figures suggests that they gave rise to no more difficulties than should be expected from a revolutionary new design, and that in a few years the difficulties were overcome. Nevertheless, the fact that the Admiralty concentrated its orders for engines with Thameside engineering firms and continued to do so for many years is not without political interest.

By 1840, only two years after *Great Western* had initiated the world's first regular deep sea steamship service and only twelve years after the first steamers had appeared in the Navy List, that list showed nearly fifty steamers and thirty-two vessels employed on the mail packet service. With the building of *Gorgon* and *Cyclops*, which were really big steam sloops, the paddle-propelled steam warship matured into an essential part of the fleets. From them were to be derived a generation of big steam sloops, eight of which, *Cyclops, Hecate, Hydra* and *Gorgon*, all with six guns, and *Medea, Phoenix, Stromboli* and *Vesuvius*, all with four guns, took part in operations off the coast of Syria in 1840.

3

The Navy and Society

So much for the ships, but what of the officers who were in charge of them, and the men who sailed them? Especially, what of the senior officers, the commanders and post captains and the admirals, brought up from early youth in the mastery of the immensely complex technology of the wooden sailing vessel, with wooden masts and spars, natural fibre rigging and hemp canvas sails? They served in a navy in which their careers were subject to family and political interests from a very early stage. Although the situation gradually changed as the Admiralty began to gain more and more control of the detail of day-to-day administration during the period covered by this book, the majority of these officers, who had joined the navy in the years of the French wars or soon after, had been recruited, not by the Admiralty, but by individual captains.[1]

The potential officer joined a ship as a Boy First Class, or Volunteer, at the age of twelve, thirteen or fourteen. The start of his career depended on parental connections with the captain of the ship, who might be persuaded (sometimes in return for fifty pounds or so a year in allowance) to take their son. The captain might in so doing be looking after the interests of members of his own extended family. The Admiralty had control neither of the numbers of young men who were recruited, nor of their quality. The right to enter 'young gentlemen' was a jealously guarded perquisite of captains (and, at various periods, of commanders in command of ships). After 1815 young gentlemen could not be admitted without Admiralty approval, but this was so freely given it had at first little effect in controlling entry.[2]

This system of recruitment may seem strange, even irrational, to the late twentieth century mind, but it is always unwise to attempt to judge the past with the mind of the present. This was a society before the age of bureaucracy. Given the nature and history of that society it is difficult to see in what other ways officers could have been recruited. Although in the late

1 For a study of the evolution of Admiralty bureaucratic control of the recruitment and promotion of naval officers in the nineteenth century see Dandeker, 'Patronage and Bureaucratic Control – The case of the naval officer in English Society, 1780–1850' in *British Journal of Sociology*, Vol 29, No 3, September 1978, pp 300–320.
2 Lewis, *A Social History of the Navy, 1793–1815*, London 1960, p 159.

eighteenth century there had been no great barrier against the commissioning of men whose social status was not that described as a gentleman, and
some nine per cent or more of officers were former seamen,[3] in the much
smaller navy of the 1820s and '30s well connected officers necessarily tended
to obtain the limited appointments available to the exclusion of 'officers of
lower social status who had gained advancement during wartime, when the
service was large and merit considerations more at a premium'.[4] Nearly half
the officers at this period came from the peerage, the baronetage, the
landed gentry, and almost all the rest from professional families (which
meant, for the majority, from families involved with the fighting services,
the law or the church).[5] This was still a society in which the power of the
landed gentry and the landowning titled classes was paramount. Their
power had in fact recently been increased as land came into demand for
industrial development and its value was accordingly enhanced. The power
and prestige of the landowner was in fact enormous.[6] They were still the
real government of the countryside, and in some places were to remain so
well into the twentieth century. Their power over tenants could be absolute.
Within living memory at the time of writing, a farmer in the parish in which
this book was written was deprived of his tenancy after he had shot one of
his landlord's pheasants.

As magistrates with extensive administrative functions, they dispensed
justice after a fashion; as landowners in their various capacities they dealt
with the building of roads and bridges, hospitals and almshouses, with
education and law and order. They upheld the church which in turn upheld
them. They did much of the work of the County Councils before the
establishment of the latter in 1888. As a standard work on the subject
explains,[7]

> We must also remember that the justices sitting both in and out of
> quarter sessions had taken over a great many of the administrative
> functions of the older legal courts and also had had many more such
> functions imposed on them by statute, with the result that in the
> seventeenth and eighteenth centuries they were the chief organs of local
> government . . . in the eighteenth century probably a fair proportion of
> the country gentry were on the commission of the peace . . . The period

3 Rodger, *The Wooden World: An Anatomy of the Georgian Navy*, London 1986, p
266.

4 Dandeker, *op cit*, p 311.

5 Lewis, *The Navy in Transition*, London 1968, p 22.

6 See, for instance, W L Burn, *The Age of Equipoise*, London 1964, especially pp
305–312, and J V Beckett, *The Aristocracy of England, 1660–1914*, Oxford 1986,
especially pp 451–460, for his examination of the effects, or rather the absence of them, of
the Reform Act of 1832.

7 Radcliffe and Cross, *The English Legal System*, 3rd ed, London 1954, pp 191, 194
and 205. This source contains an admirable account of the magistracy and its functions.

from 1650 to 1820 is the great era of the justices of the peace. In it they were the real governors of the English countryside.

In the towns the position was less satisfactory. In the words of Radcliffe and Cross[8]

The inefficiency of the constables and the corruption of the local magistracy combined to make the enforcement of the criminal law in London and other large cities extremely unsatisfactory in this period, and eventually produced a demand for the modern system of qualified and salaried police magistrates.

The professional classes, living to some extent off the droppings from the tables of the landowners and often connected with them as younger sons or nephews, or as the descendants of younger sons, identified their interests with the landowners and they, too, were becoming more powerful. As the century wore on, although the Admiralty gradually extended its power over recruitment and training until it was absolute, the social basis of recruitment became steadily even narrower. By the outbreak of the War with Russia in the middle of the century the Admiralty Board was nominating 70 per cent or more of new entrants, and they were the relations of men of rank and fortune, supported by (if not related to) senior politicians of the party currently forming the government.[9] In the first half of the century the service was extremely politicised and it was still in the hands of a relatively small group of families. In this, as in many other ways, it reflected the society from which it emerged and which financed it, a society in which the political character of the powerful office of Lord Lieutenant of a county was still unconcealed, and magistrates were appointed by the Lord Chancellor on the recommendation of local Members of Parliament.[10]

There was, however, a second way into a naval officer's career which, by the second decade of the nineteenth century, when the future senior officers of the paddle frigates and sloops were entering on their careers, was becoming more important, although it still provided only a minority of future officers. This was through the Naval Academy at Portsmouth, an official foundation of the early eighteenth century which took boys at thirteen or so and gave them a basic, but quite wide, education including arithmetic, English, French, drawing and dancing, before they first went to sea. Opposed by some senior officers, partly because it threatened their privileges of nomination of potential future officers and partly because

8 Radcliffe and Cross, *op cit*, p 204.

9 Rodger, 'Officers, Gentlemen and Their Education, 1793–1860', paper given at the Anglo-French Naval History Conference, Portsmouth, March 1988, published in *Les Empires en guerre et paix* 1793–1860, Vincennes 1990, pp 139–154.

10 Lee, 'Parliament and the Appointment of Magistrates', *Parliamentary Affairs*, Vol 13, 1959–60, No 1, pp 85–94.

many of them (and this tendency is not unknown in the navy down to the present day) despised intellectual pursuits, nevertheless it gradually prospered and in 1806, during a brief period of Whig government, was enlarged, reorganised, dubbed The Royal Naval College, and put under the command of an efficient and experienced officer (of Whig family) about whom we shall have a good deal more to say later. There were further changes in 1816, and gradually through the second, third and fourth decades of the century the college gained in status until the minority of entrants which it was producing became something of a respected élite among junior officers. By 1831–32 exactly one-third of midshipmen promoted to lieutenant were college products. These young men were Admiralty approved entrants whose parents could afford the fees of the college, which were comparable with those of a contemporary public school. So the process of further narrowing the social basis of the navy was developed.[11]

But, however they had entered the service, once on board a ship the further education young gentlemen received still depended in the 1820s through to the 1850s on the organisation provided by the captain, rather than on any formal training requirements. As Dandeker states[12]

> The skills of a 'Naval officer' were essentially a collective body of *seamanship skills*, with a limited amount of theoretical knowledge . . . The dominant emphasis was on 'customised practices' rather than on formalised theoretical knowledge.

Even in the steam frigates they lived in squalid conditions far down on one of the lower decks and on poor food. In the words of one of them who joined the paddle frigate *Magicienne* as a volunteer in 1853[13]

> . . . at the early age of 12½ years, I joined HMS *Magicienne* in Plymouth Sound, and took my place in the midshipman's berth, as it was then called in a frigate. My uncle, the Captain, had sent his gig for me, so I went on board in style. Apropos of sailing with relations I do not think it advisable. It is not over pleasant to hear a near relation growled at, as all captains of men of war are occasionally. There is always a chance of your relative either showing favouritism to you, or going to the other extreme, and being more strict than with other young officers. I was very soon made acquainted with the customs of a midshipman's berth, not a very good school for a youngster of 12 years of age, and the drinking and

11 Rodger, *Education*.
12 Dandeker, *op cit*, p 305.
13 Daniel, *Some Reminiscences of a Midshipman in the Fifties*, 1906, place of publication not given, printed pamphlet, copy in the possession of Mr R S Craig, formerly of University College London, pp 3, 8 and 9.

swearing habits in those days were something too dreadful to write about . . .

. . . Our midshipman's berth was almost below the waterline of the ship, so that we always burnt an oil lamp, and the only means of warming the berth in very cold weather, such as we experienced in the Baltic, was by means of a red hot shot placed under the table. The berth was on the lower deck, and only about the size of a large stateroom in one of the present Atlantic liners, with seats or lockers all around the table, which was in the centre, and, as we had some dozen officers in the berth, including mates, midshipmen, naval cadets, a second master, master's assistant and a clerk's assistant, as they were respectively called in those days, it was rather close quarters . . . Our hammocks were all strung on the same deck as and outside the midshipmen's berth, and our sea chests, which held all our kit, washing materials, etc. near them.

Another young volunteer of the same vintage wrote[14]

We certainly were shockingly fed in those days. Growing youths much imbued with sea air, used to fare very badly; but when it is considered how little was paid in the shape of mess money it is no wonder. On joining you found £10 as an entrance fee; and the mess subscription was one shilling a day, with your rations thrown in. The rations were the same as those allowed to the ship's company: a pound of very bad salt junk (beef) or of pork as salt as Mrs. Lot, excreable tea, sugar and biscuit that was generally full of weevils, or well overrun with rat, or (in hot climates) a choice retreat for the detestable cockroach.

Montagu was franker in his private letters home.[15]

> *HMS Princess Royal*,
> Spithead,
> February 1854.

My dear Father,

. . . I have got the command of the captain's cutter which is very jolly as I shall always fetch all the ladies off . . . I was very miserable the first day, for it was such a change to what I am accustomed at home to come in to all the swearing and bad language they use. I made up my mind from the beginning not to make use of these expressions. You will be sorry to hear that none of them read their bibles, not even on Sunday. I always get up before them and then go and read my bible in the gun room before they are dressed . . .

14 Rear Admiral the Hon Victor Montagu, *A Middy's Recollections, 1853–60*, London 1898, p 12.
15 NMM San/T/101 (MS 60/008).

Spithead,
5th March, 1854.

My dear Brother,

. . . I get up at half past six and go into the gun room when I am
dressed and do my daily devotions and have breakfast at eight. Before
breakfast they call us on deck to see the topgallant yards go up. After
breakfast we go to the Weapon Instruction which is at nine o'clock. We
then work until one o'clock and then have a light luncheon and do what
we have to do until half past and then we dine and do what we like for the
rest of the day and at half past seven we have to stand by our hammocks
which means we have to see the men get their hammocks down and we
have tea and turn in when we like but it never is later than half past nine
because we are always so tired.

Wednesday,
8th March, 1854.

My dearest Father,

. . . I am getting a little acquainted with the rigging now I have been
aloft about eight times. I went up to the mizzen top. I never was so
astonished in my life as when I got up there, the height looks nothing on
deck . . .

There is such a fine fleet at Spithead it is quite worth coming to see.
There are eight line of battleships. We are the senior ship, bearing the
flag of Sir Charles Napier.

Montagu was a godson of the Queen and he wrote to his father on 8 March
1854, after she had reviewed the fleet.

My dearest Father,

Did you hear of my speaking to Her Majesty!? She said she had not the
pleasure of seeing me since I was quite a little boy. I made two graceful
bows with a step back at each bow and mumbled something; then the
captain said in a whisper, 'get in the boat again'. I then jumped down like
a little squirrel. We have all to keep watch now. The pilot is going ashore
with the letters so I must say goodbye . . .

The contrast in his life between the very rough conditions in the gun room
and presentation to the Queen illustrates one of the social phenomena of
the first half of the nineteenth century. There is no doubt that a competent
and experienced lieutenant was as completely soaked in the technology of
that vastly complex product of carpenter and blacksmith, the wooden sailing
ship, as the most professional seaman, yet often he emerged as a
sophisticated man of the world and of broad cultural background, albeit
some naval officers of the mid-nineteenth century would seem today to be

pretty rough customers. Some, out of touch with higher command for months on end, fell victims to the subtle corruption of petty power.

In a good vessel volunteers were trained quickly and thoroughly. Thus, young Daniel, recently promoted a midshipman, after only two years in the steam frigate *Magicienne* was capable of correctly handling a relatively complex situation.[16]

> Although the *Magicienne* was a paddlewheel steam frigate, she was a square-rigged vessel (barque rigged), and we were frequently under sail only, the paddlewheels being disconnected and fires banked, more especially when blockading ports in the Baltic, in order to save our coal so that I had every opportunity of learning how to handle a ship under sail. I remember on one occasion, when midshipman of the watch, Captain Vansittart came on deck and told the officer of the watch (one of the Lieutenants) to go below to dinner, and had me on the bridge, and ordered me to take charge and to turn all hands up and shorten sail, and it must have been rather amusing to see a youngster, barely 15 years of age, carrying on, and giving the necessary orders in executing this manoeuvre.

Take as a further example the case of Lieutenant Astley Cooper Key. Son of a surgeon to Prince Albert, he entered the navy in 1835 at the age of thirteen. By 1843 he was a junior lieutenant in HM Steam Vessel *Gorgon*, which in May 1844 was blown ashore at Montevideo in Uruguay. Her crew laboured to refloat her for five and a half months, at last succeeding on 29 October. Cooper Key's account of this feat[17] shows the most intimate practical knowledge of all aspects of seamanship involved in a remarkable operation. He moralises, in the manner of the period, apropos his captain (Charles Hotham) on the procedure for acquiring such skills.[18]

> No man can have confidence in his own powers, unless the early period of his service has been devoted to the studies suited to his profession, and these studies should be pursued with a zeal to acquire an entire mastery of the subjects, for the subjects' sake themselves, making them wholly his own . . . the young officer should energetically seek to improve every opportunity of gaining practical experience.

The fact is that the skills necessary to handle and maintain a wooden square rigged sailing ship were so complex as to require total absorption from a very early age. It has recently been suggested[19] that the seaman of

16 Daniel, *op cit*, pp 19–20.
17 Cooper Key, *A Narrative of the Recovery of HMS Gorgon*, London 1847.
18 Cooper Key, *op cit*, p 111.
19 Eric W Sager, *Seafaring Labour, The Merchant Marine of Atlantic Canada, 1820–1914*, McGill–Queens University Press, Montreal 1989.

the pre-industrial, the long sailing ship age, at sea, was simply another form of skilled craftsman, a 'working man who got wet'. This he was, but the isolation in which the seaman, and usually the merchant ship's officer, lived for very long periods, surrounded by his own kind, cut off from the cultures and normal social life ashore, marked him, often for life, as a different person from even the most specialised of workers ashore. Those of us who, like the authors of this book, have known closely many among the last survivors of the world of the sailing ship, in Britain, in Scandinavia, in the United States, can testify that many, perhaps most, of these men never fully adjusted to normal social life ashore, but always felt sharply cut off from those with whom they had little shared experience. Coleridge's Ancient Mariner was a social phenomenon who died only with the last of the men of the sailing ships – and this took place as late as the early 1980s.

How much greater was this isolation in the early nineteenth century when the level of craft and skill was expected to be such that it was normal practice to send down the upper masts and spars and the vastly complex gear of a square rigged vessel *at sea* in bad weather. This was necessary in order to reduce both windage and the shock stresses to the natural fibre rigging and the wooden structure of the vessel, which were transmitted from the violently moving weights aloft. It was also necessary in a paddle steamer steaming into a fresh to strong head wind in order to reduce the drag presented by the masts, spars and rigging. The log of the first passage of *Great Western* from Bristol towards New York contains a number of references to the housing of topmasts and to yards and gaffs sent down, operations conducted as a matter of course during a passage of only fourteen days or so. This frequent handling of the masts and spars must have made more work for the crew than was normal in a sailing vessel, though the efficient and relatively simple four masted schooner rig required less maintenance work than that of a barque or ship.

Moreover, an able seaman was expected to be able to play a skilled part in major rigging operations if a vessel was damaged or dismasted at sea.[20]

The standards of seamanship in a good class vessel were, to modern eyes, almost unbelievably high. Thus, on 15 April 1838, the deck log of *Great Western*[21] records

---

20 See, for instance, R H Dana, Jnr, *The Seaman's Manual*, London 1855, and G Biddlecombe, *The Art of Rigging*, London 1848. To read Dana in particular is to gain a very good idea of the kind of skill expected of a fully trained seaman or ship's officer in the mid nineteenth century. It is to be remembered that a warship, unlike a merchant vessel which carried the minimum number of men necessary to sail her, employed, especially in wartime, besides her prime seamen, a limited number of ratings whose duties, working guns and on deck, did not necessarily call for the skills of the able seaman.

21 J Hosken, *The Logs of the First Voyage, made with the unceasing aid of steam between England and America, by The Great Western of Bristol*, Bristol 1838. We are grateful to Denis Griffiths for bringing this important source to our attention.

OCCURRENCES AND REMARKS

Commences with strong winds and squally; all sail set to advantage. At 5, got the after gaff up, and set the sail; swayed the topmast up. At 6, passed a French chassmaree, apparently bound to the Banks of Newfoundland to fish. At 7, spoke the brig Henry Brougham, on the starboard tack, bound to London, and requested to be reported; set the squaresail and gaff topsails. At 8h. 40m. squally; carried away fore-topmast, two feet above the cap; the top-gallant-mast and yard and fore cross-trees were carried away by its fall; all hands employed clearing the wreck until 6, P.M.; carpenter getting other spars ready. At 2, P.M., finished the spare topmast, got it up, and rigged it; exchanged colours with an American ship, standing to eastward. At 4, fidded it, and set up the rigging, and got the topsail yards across. At 7h. 30m., in squaresail and gaff topsails, braced the yards up; watch employed securing the spars, &c. on deck. At midnight, strong winds and squally; engines performing well,

The job of clearing the wreckage, making new masts and spars and getting them aloft and re-rigging them was completed in eight or nine hours, during which the wind was Force 7 on the beam with the vessel steaming at ten knots. Such operations on vessels are now carried out in a shipyard using scaffolding, hard hats, and following all the requirements imposed by safety at work legislation, and probably take many days' work. Aboard *Great Western*, as aboard all her contemporaries, merchant and naval, the necessity to conduct them at sea in bad weather without slowing down the vessel was taken for granted, and not considered a matter for any special comment. The acquisition of the necessary skills left little opportunity for the acquisition of other knowledge, even had the seaman's social isolation permitted of it.

Nevertheless, many naval officers of the early nineteenth century do seem to have succeeded in bridging both worlds and to have acquired deep knowledge of the pre-industrial seaman's skills as well as a broad, often, by the standards of their successors today, a very broad, cultural background. They were sophisticated men of the world – albeit usually for ever (almost literally) tarred with indications of their profession in speech and habits. These men were able at least to some degree to bridge the void between the seaman's world and that of the landsman. The secret perhaps lay in the social background to which they frequently returned for sometimes long periods on half pay, and which provided a counter to obsessive and narrow technical professionalism and to the effects on personality of the harshness of life on board, which persisted until they reached a senior rank.

Moreover, in considering the hardships of life as a junior officer at sea, it must be remembered that even the most prosperous way of life between country house and London mansion in the first half of the nineteenth century was very rigorous when compared with life at the end of the twentieth. These conditions of living have been well rehearsed by historians, but it may well be useful very briefly to remind the reader of some of them. To list merely the obvious, there was almost no indoor sanitation except by commode or chamber pot, which had to be carried away and emptied after use. There was no efficient means of washing, either of clothes or person. In consequence, people and their environments had a powerful and unpleasant smell which sometimes amounted to what would now be considered an overwhelming stench. Thus Harriet, sister of Elizabeth, wife of Captain Thomas Fremantle, writes in her diary of 19 December 1804[22]

> *Stowe*. This is Lady Buckingham's birthday. In the evening we all danced with the tenants. Mr Winfield was my partner, I laughed a great deal to see the different mixture of people. We could hardly breath it was so hot and the smell was beyond anything.

Food was often coarse and dirty. Children, slowly gaining immunity, were subject to frequent bouts of food poisoning. Despite the roaring log fires most country houses were draughty, damp and extremely cold. The washing water brought to the bedrooms by servants was often lukewarm by the time it arrived. There was no waterproof clothing to provide effective protection in a life that was lived quite largely out of doors. In the 1820s and '30s, there was in most districts no transport for either man or message faster than a good horse could maintain on a long journey. Travel by coach was almost unbelievably uncomfortable; travel by passenger carrying smack or schooner, say from Scotland to London, equally so and even more hazardous, if sometimes faster.

Children were often brought up in cold attic nurseries whilst undergoing a gamut of diseases, dysentry, whooping cough, scarlet fever, blood poisoning, diptheria, tuberculosis, cholera and appendicitis, which in some families carried many of them off and left the survivors familiar with death, but immune to a number of infections, before they reached maturity.[23] The children's fiction, like the children's upbringing of the time, prepared them for the hard lives and for the deaths that lay ahead of them. One of the authors of this book recollects books in her grandfather's house which may possibly have been part of the childhood reading of Captain Giffard of *Tiger*, in which powerful and dangerous moral links were made between

22 Fremantle, *The Wynne Diaries*, London 1953, p 373.

23 Sir James Kay Shuttleworth wrote 'Owing in a great degree to neglect and mismanagement half of the children born in 1831 died in 5 years'. *Four Periods of Public Education*, p 131, quoted in Pinchbeck and Hewitt, *Children in English Society*, p 349, vol 2, London 1973.

children's behaviour and the familiar, death, such as 'if you are not a good girl your sick little brother may die and then what would you feel?'

Raging toothache ended only in extraction without anaesthetic. In many families whipping with birch twigs or leather strap was the normal domestic punishment for boys and girls alike.[24] Children grew up aware of industrial accidents in which hundreds of men could be killed at one time, and of the losses of scores of vessels at sea in one gale, both to some extent the product of what W L Burn[25] called the 'almost juvenile casualness displayed towards dangerous substances and dangerous circumstances', the sort of casualness nowadays associated with the third world and with socialist societies. Children grew up perforce aware of, and accustomed to, the brutalities, so often rehearsed by historians, of a judicial system which matched the social conditions. They knew of public executions, and in the early years of the century had perhaps witnessed the whippings of both men and women on the village green, which were ordered by the magistrates after what would now seem to be somewhat rudimentary judicial proceedings. There is an old Dorset rhyme[26]

They hanged the men and flogged the women
That stole the sheep from the village common.

In these circumstances the floggings in the navy, which have attracted the attention of so many writers who have treated them as if they were unique to that service, were taken for granted.

The adult survivors of the process of growing up in these conditions tended to be people with a very high pain threshold and the ability not to identify too readily with the suffering of others, together with a highly efficient bodily defence system against disease. They were often people of great energy and endurance. These are very important factors which must always be taken into account when considering living conditions and social

24 See numerous accounts of nineteenth century childhood and, for instance, I and P Opie, *The Oxford Dictionary of Nursery Rhymes* , Oxford 1955, especially pp 37, 42, 46 and 101. For a modern popular study of the treatment of children at this and earlier periods, see Kevill-Davies, *Yesterday's Children – The Antiques and History of Childcare*, London 1991. The author has a telling observation: 'They beat small children violently because so many died, and they were afraid they'd go to hell if there was any sin left in them'. See also Walvin, *A Child's World,* London 1982, and Pinchbeck and Hewitt, *op cit*.
25 Burn, *op cit*, p 298.
26 This may well be founded on two actual cases. The legal situation in the late eighteenth and early nineteenth centuries was complex, but the men may have been convicted of larceny – having been found guilty by jury at an assize court of the theft of articles of the value of twelve pence or more, which was punishable by death, and the women of petty larceny or misdemeanour before a magistrate, that is the theft of articles of lesser value, which was not a capital offence. Even so, there may well be an element of political propaganda in the doggerel, since only a fifth to a ninth of the death sentences passed were actually carried out. See Radcliffe and Cross, *op cit*, Chapter XII, especially pp 194–203.

attitudes before the second quarter of the twentieth century. The survivors of youth under these conditions still had a limited expectation of life in a world in which there was very little effective medical treatment. A simple fracture could mean lameness for life, a compound fracture gangrene and death. Pneumonia could, and did, carry them off at any time, and they were in consequence always very concerned about 'chills'. Back trouble, mercifully less common among a smaller, less well fed, people than it is now, for any manual worker could mean slow starvation. Tropical diseases were often lethal. Malaria, 'marsh fever', common in southern Europe and among the men of the Mediterranean fleet, although in its most common form rarely fatal, could ruin a man's health and, through its debilitating and depressing effects impair judgement and professional performance.

For women, there were no sanitary towels, much less tampons. To be married, although the alternative might be loneliness, social patronage, perhaps poverty, was to take a conscious decision to hazard the perils of childbirth, the principal cause of death in females. Women who could afford it retreated from childbearing into being 'sofa-mothers',[27] or were forced to the sofa by conditions now relieved by hysterectomy or hormone treatment.[28] When a young couple at the altar swore mutual fidelity 'till death do us part', their average expectation of shared life was perhaps at most twenty years. A second, or even third, marriage – and family – following on the death of the first wife in childbirth was very common, and was motivated partly by the necessity of having someone to look after the household. The modern phenomenon of stresses in a marriage, in the middle age of the partners, too often simply had no opportunity to develop. Late twentieth century men and women transported in time to the early decades of the nineteenth, when the men of the paddle frigates were in their formative years, would find a world which would seem to them incredibly hard, dangerous, violent, dirty and brutally cruel. Indeed, in many ways they would find even the world of the early twentieth century almost equally alien. Certainly it requires an act of well informed imagination to form any accurate impression of the way these people looked at the world. But these are the men – and women – who played their parts in the events this book records.

This act of imagination can be helped by reading, for instance, Surtees's *Mr Sponge's Sporting Tour*, published in 1852. Here there is a brilliant account of country society, a saga of people of the period portrayed without romance and with reality. The men and women of the upper and middle classes and those who aspire to those classes are very hard people. The

27 A term used at a later period by Carola Oman in *An Oxford Childhood*, London 1976, pp 146 and 163.
28 Davidoff and Hall in *Family Fortunes*, 1987, p 337, give the case of Ann Martin Taylor who bore children from the age of twenty-five to forty-one, which meant that she was pregnant for more than half of those sixteen years.

country farmworkers and the servants are a deprived and to some extent brutalised lot. At sea the distinction was between the officers and those aspiring to be officers and the men. Gogol's *Dead Souls*, published ten years earlier, paints a similarly realistic picture of the even more brutal society in the Russia with which the navy was soon to come into conflict in the Baltic and Black seas.

It is against this background, very briefly rehearsed here, that the lives of young sea officers in the early nineteenth century must be considered. The navy was not detached from the rest of society. It was the product of that society. It had the same standards and in its ideas, methods and procedures, in the powers given to those in authority and the way they used them, it followed its parent body. Indeed, a fairly close parallel can be drawn between the powers and attitudes of the magistrate ashore and those of the post captain in the navy in the matter of dealing with the maintenance of law and order and the punishment of offences against it.

Montagu's descriptions, already quoted, are all the more valuable because they describe a period of transition from what he calls the 'remnants of barbarism' to the period after 1860 when conditions both on shore and at sea began rapidly to improve, and because he seems to have been in some ways quite a sensitive man. Nevertheless, he was a product of his age. On joining his first ship, the steam-screw line of battleship *Princess Royal*, 91 guns, in December 1853, at the age of twelve, he immediately underwent an experience which would now be considered traumatic, requiring many months of remedial counselling. To this twelve-year old it was merely distressing.[29].

> My first obeisance to the Quarter-Deck (I had been warned to be very particular about this) – must have lacked finish. My troubles were not over with that ceremony. I'd hardly finished saluting the Officer of the Watch when a blue-jacket fell from out of the main rigging on to the Quarter-Deck gun within a yard of me. He was killed instantly and the sight was very painful.

Montagu is a particularly good example of the dichotomy of the seaman officer who was also a cultured man of the world. He was the second son of the Earl of Sandwich, his mother a daughter of the Earl of Anglesey, who had commanded the cavalry at Waterloo and lost a leg. All he says of his childhood was that he was 'educated by a private tutor'. From the age of twelve years and six months his only further education was that provided by experience on board Her Majesty's ships. Nevertheless, at the age of fourteen he was able to carry out a delicate negotiation with the French commander in chief in the Crimea.[30]

29 Montagu, *Recollections*, p 10.
30 Montagu, *Recollections*, pp 51–52.

We soon had our army ashore on a sandy beach not many miles from Kertch itself. Next day, while we were on the line of march, my uncle, Lord Clarence, happened to be in close conversation with Sir Edmund Lyons, when the Commander-in-Chief, suddenly observing me near at hand, called me up, and said 'Here, youngster: can you talk French?' On my answering 'Yes', he said 'Go at once and find the French General-in-Command' (pointing me out the direction I should find him), 'and tell him that I wish the English Jack could be hoisted alongside the Tricolour as soon as that fort is captured. Mind you say so very civilly and in your best French'. Off I ran as fast as my legs would carry me across the plain. Singling out what appeared to me to be a body of French Staff Officers, I asked the first among them to point me out the General-in-Command. Luckily, that potentate was among the bunch of officers. I felt nervous and shy; but, mustering up courage I stood, cap in hand, delivering my orders. To my horror, he seemed to demur, and asked me a heap of questions before he at last consented and desired me to inform the Admiral that his wishes should be carried out. I had been told to bring back an answer; but for the life of me I could not find the Commander-in-Chief for a long time. However, when I did find him he seemed pleased. He said, 'I see the Union Jack is up alongside the French Flag. Well done, my boy! What's your name and who is your father? Tell your commander I am much pleased with you.' I did feel proud.

Later evidence in Montagu's book suggests that he had similar fluency in German.

The captain of *Princess Royal* was Lord Clarence Paget, eldest son of Montagu's grandfather by the latter's second marriage. The relationship ensured for young Montagu a small degree of special treatment on board, while the family connection ensured very special treatment when he went ashore in ports like Istanbul, where there was a strong British community. Thus, again like so many of his contemporaries, he lived in two worlds, carrying out the normal duties of a cadet, and in due course midshipman, on board, but wined and dined at the Embassy ashore as a junior member of an aristocratic family. Daniel provides a further example.[31]

During the spring of 1856, we were mostly at Plymouth, and Captain Vansittart took me one evening, after dining with him and other of my brother officers at Moorehead's Royal Hotel, Devonport (among his guests being Prince Ernest of Leiningen), to a large dance given by the Hon. Mrs Keith Stewart, at which were present all the elite of Plymouth and the neighbourhood. I remember being asked to dance with a Lady

Ernestine Mount Edgcumbe, then quite a little girl of 12 or 13, and although I was only 15 myself, I am afraid I considered her almost too juvenile for a partner, and should have preferred to dance with someone rather older[32] . . . The Prince was there, and I can recall to mind that many of my juvenile partners, with feminine curiosity, asked me to point him out to them, all of us being in uniform on the occasion.

After two years or so a recruit could qualify as a midshipman. After 1839 the candidate had to take an examination. Six or so sea-going years later, during which time he might serve some years as a mate, a non-commissioned half-way house to a lieutenant's commission which after 1861 became the commissioned rank of sub-lieutenant, he could sit (or perhaps stand was a better term since much of the examination was practical) his examination to qualify for a lieutenant's commission.[33] There was no standard of examination set by a central body. The rigour, or otherwise, of the test depended on the three captains who comprised the examining board. It is probable that the candidate's connections and political affiliations were sometimes a factor in his success or failure. When (and if) he was appointed to the office of lieutenant on board one of Her Majesty's ships depended again, as had his first appointment as a volunteer, on his 'interest'. This term was used to encapsulate his family and political connections, connections with people prominent in naval or social life, or in political life or in the life around the Royal Household, and this interest was a matter of almost obsessive concern to all officers below the rank of post captain if they were not absolutely confident of having very powerful connections. Interest, of course, depended in part on the politics of the current government. For most of the early years of the nineteenth century until 1830, the sons of Tory families prospered in the navy. After 1830, when the Whigs gained power, Whig families were the more fortunate.

Qualification as a lieutenant did not ensure the young officer employment in the navy. A legacy of the inflated navy of the Napoleonic era was the unemployed lieutenant. As late as 1842, almost 65 per cent of qualified lieutenants were on half pay ashore, or serving as masters or mates of merchant ships. Thus the masters of the pioneer transatlantic passenger steamers were unemployed lieutenants. Richard Roberts commanded *Sirius* and *British Queen*, and he was lost with *President*.[34] We have already

32 Lady Ernestine Mount Edgcumbe never married and passed her later years at Honicombe House on the edge of the Mount Edgcumbe's Cotehele Estate on the west bank of the Tamar, 14 miles north of Plymouth. In the 1970s, elderly ladies living in the neighbouring parish of St Dominic, where this book was written, told the authors of her custom, before the First World War, of ordering her coachman to put the whip across the shoulders of any girl at the roadside who failed to curtsey as her carriage passed by.

33 But after 1831 half the mates and midshipmen were supposed to be selected from among men who had already passed their examination for lieutenant. See Dandeker, *op cit*, p 317.

34 See Mould, *Captain Roberts of the Sirius*, Cork 1988.

referred to James Hosken who commanded *Great Western* and *The Great Britain*. These were the crack ships of the late 1830s and '40s. The masters and mates of most merchant vessels of this period began life as seamen with no interest beyond, at the best, good connections in their local seaport town, as so many naval officers had done in the preceding century. Moreover, until the Merchant Shipping Act of 1851, they were not subject to examination or any system of establishing their competence. In these circumstances it is not surprising that, with the basis of naval recruitment becoming steadily more restricted as the century advanced, the social gulf between naval officers and the masters and mates of merchant ships increased, although the opportunities of the latter to improve their financial position were sometimes greater than service in the navy could offer during the long nineteenth century state of relative peace.[35]

Many lieutenants who had been promoted during the years of wartime shortage and whose interest was weak were beyond further sea service after long years of unemployment. Thus, the chances of employment for a young man coming into the navy as a first class volunteer and with good interest were much better than the figures suggest. Nevertheless, as Professor Michael Lewis states,[36]

> every stage in the process of advancement . . . meant an individual contest with neighbours to 'catch the eye of the selectors'.

In the early 1850s the title, but not the rank, of lieutenant commander was coming into use to describe lieutenants appointed to the command of small vessels. But the next stage in the career of the lieutenant who managed to find further employment at sea was promotion to the rank of commander. This depended, again, upon interest and a suitable occasion to provide interest with an excuse to promote the officer. Sometimes, where the interest was strong, the excuse, as we shall see in the case of Captain Giffard of *Tiger*, could be a very thin one indeed. Usually it was some particular piece of professional competence – or what could be represented as professional competence – more rarely, as what could be represented as a display of gallantry or initiative in one of the numerous so-called minor wars, in China, in South America, in the Syrian Campaign, in actions against slavers, which took place between the end of the Napoleonic Wars and the War with Russia of 1854–56.

A commander was in command, that is captain in all but rank, of a vessel of the navy below a sixth rate. He commanded a brig or a schooner (all

---

35 For a good account of the life of an unemployed lieutenant who turned to merchant shipping at this time and prospered, see Septimus March, *Memorials of Charles March*, London 1867.

36 Lewis, *Transition*, p 50.

naval schooners were small two masted vessels) or he served as the second-in-command, or chief executive officer, of a larger vessel, such as a ship of the line, a large full rigged ship carrying sixty or more guns. Many officers did not achieve more than the rank of commander. Some, in numbers several hundred in the period covered by this book, perhaps men with moderate interest, achieved the rank after years on half pay as lieutenants and became half-pay commanders, usually with no possibility of further service. These officers were officially described as holding the rank of retired commander. Those whose interest was strong enough, and whose careers provided the occasion to promote them further, took one more vital step in the selection process and were made post captains, captain of a ship of war of substantial size. In the period with which we are concerned in this book, this step depended almost entirely upon interest. One man with the right family connections whose family politics were those of the government in power at the crucial time could be a post captain within nine years of first going to sea. Amother might take twenty years or more and might spend much of this time ashore. Many were never employed at sea again after promotion to post captain. In the 1840s it was said that nearly half the post captains in the navy had never served afloat in their rank.

The greatest of the post captain's privileges in the mid nineteenth century was automatic further promotion. Once a post captain there was absolutely nothing, short of death or dismissal, which could stop his relentless move up the list as his seniors in appointment died, right through to the rank of full admiral or admiral of the fleet. As men died, so those below then moved up the captain's list, then the rear admiral's list and so on. This process could not be stopped or by-passed. The most brilliant junior captain could not acquire higher rank until his turn came. Thus it was perfectly possible for a post captain to have served a year or two (perhaps no time at all) at sea in the rank, and never to have been employed again when thirty years later he was promoted vice admiral. On half pay, perhaps in civilian employment, or as a Member of Parliament or country landowner, he went up the naval tree. If the right political party was in power, if the officer was in other ways sufficiently well connected, if his career provided an adequate excuse, he acquired Companionship of the Bath and in due course, having achieved flag rank, perhaps a knighthood. Not until the 1860s was this system to be changed. Once again, the right to automatic advancement with the social prestige and money that went with it was accepted as an entirely natural right. It can be seen, therefore, that promotion to the rank of post captain was vital to the young officer. Once there his future was assured. If an officer was not posted he was branded as a man lacking the right connections.

In this respect, as in so many others, the navy merely reflected the practices of society as a whole. In all aspects, politics, the Civil Service, the armed forces, the law, the church, the East India Company, finance, industry and commerce, patronage was still the norm in nineteenth century Britain. It was the way society worked and it should not be assumed that it was corrupt. Indeed, how else could a pre-bureaucratic society operate? As J M Bourne states[37]

> patronage was a fact of life, as unremarkable as it was obvious, and for which a definition was neither wanted nor needed. Anyone who was ignorant of the existence, nature and importance of patronage would have been thought a fool and regarded as an object of pity.

To live in the first half of the nineteenth century was to live in a period of increasing stress. Great changes were taking place in society, in the distribution of wealth where new people were coming up, desperately afraid always of slipping down again. Very slowly, although historians dispute their true extent and nature, changes were taking place in the distribution of political and certainly of financial power, especially after the passing of the Reform Act of 1832. By the middle of the century, the advance of technology was affecting everybody's lives. Fundamental developments happened extremely quickly. The maximum speed of communication, which had been about eight miles an hour, as in the world of the Romans, changed between 1825 and 1845 to one in which fast travel on an expanding network of railways was something which people of even moderate income could enjoy, albeit in what would now be considered unbelievable discomfort. And the beginnings of instant communications by electric telegraph, the wires of which ran alongside the railways, were penetrating public consciousness. As we saw in Chapter 2, the adoption of steam propulsion by the navy was pressed forward to the limits that wisdom, practical possibilities and the nature of the administration allowed. Steam propulsion accelerated profound developments in the navy which affected the young men first. Gradually, the navy became bureaucratised. Control over entry, promotion and retirement became centralised as the century wore on. Impersonal rules to a degree replaced interest, facilitated by the specialisations which developed in officers' skills. But these rules themselves could ensure that the navy continued to provide a career as officers for only a very limited number of social groups.

Great changes were, of course, taking place ashore as well. The rising standard of living following on industrialisation, the development of a literate middle class, the spread of newspapers with a level of factual reporting which was to reach a climax during the War with Russia, the widespread reading of socially aware novels, of which Dickens, George Eliot, Charlotte Bronte and Mrs Gaskell are perhaps the most read today,

---

37 Bourne, *Patronage and Society in Nineteenth Century England*, London 1986, p 3. For a study of patronage in the Church see Dewey, *The Passing of Barchester*, London 1991.

the increase in travel, the lessons of the French Revolution, these and many other factors resulted in a gradual change in social attitudes. It was almost as if human beings in Britain had suddenly become aware of the brutality of past ages, and of their own times. These brutalities were no longer taken for granted and it sometimes seems as if, like Adam and Eve discovering their nakedness, society became self-aware. Thus industrial conditions, particularly in such matters, for instance, as the employment of children and of women underground (now at the end of the twentieth century again legal) and the number of hours in the day children were allowed to work were improved through legislative action. Duelling, with its inevitable tragedies, once a hallmark of a gentleman, ceased by the middle of the century.

In the particular matter of the punishment of offenders, from the end of the Napoleonic Wars campaigns were mounted, increasingly, for the amelioration of penalties both ashore and afloat.[38] Already in the 1830s some officers in the navy were beginning to command for long periods without recourse to punishment. Commander, later Admiral Evans, of HM Steam Vessels *Lightning* and *Rhadamanthus*, to whom reference in detail will be made in the next chapter, as early as April 1834 was commended by the commander in chief, West Indies Station, for having ordered no punishments of any kind for the last three months of the preceding year. Captain Bartholomew Sulivan, later to show himself as perhaps the most brilliant of all his naval contemporaries in the War with Russia of 1854–56, when in command of the beautiful brig *Philomel* in the mid 1840s, received Admiralty commendation for two years of blank returns for punishment – an achievement, according to his biographer, brought about largely by showing his crew that he had confidence in them. In the same commission he went for four years without a single desertion, an almost unheard of achievement in this period.[39] In the War with Russia there were already post captains who never ordered flogging. Lord Paget of Montagu's *Princess Royal* was one of them, as was Keppel of the screw steamship of the line *St Jean d'Acre*.[40] The research of Eugene Rasor[41] shows that in the twenty years preceding the War with Russia flogging had already been greatly reduced, and that ten years later its use as a punishment had virtually ceased. It had been abolished in the United States Navy as early as 1850. There is some evidence also that by the 1850s the actual administration of flogging had become less brutal than in previous generations, although we should consider it incredibly brutal today.[42]

38 Rasor, *Reform in the Royal Navy*, Hamden, Connecticut 1976, p 51.
39 Sulivan (ed), *Life and Letters of Admiral B. J. Sulivan*, London 1896, pp 68 and 111.
40 Greenhill and Giffard, *The British Assault*, pp 127 and 139.
41 Rasor, *op cit*, especially p 128.
42 See C Sloane-Stanley, *Reminiscences of a Midshipman's Life, 1850–59*, London 1893, p 283. Sloane-Stanley never saw streams of blood or severe lacerations caused by flogging.

In this, as in many other ways, the navy, conservative and with a reputation for brutality dating from the Napoleonic Wars which it took at least a century to eliminate,[43] was perhaps moved from without by public opinion rather than from within. As Rasor put it, 'outside pressure and sensitivity to the navy's public image were decisive factors'.[44] Another factor was the development of technology in gunnery and steam propulsion. Not only did this require more of the officers, a more sophisticated type of rating, less likely to commit breaches of discipline through sheer stupidity, began to appear in naval vessels. Byrn summed up the situation very well with the expression 'the discipline of publicity'.[45] By the 1830s conditions for the men of naval vessels, that is the seamen and those specialists not holding warrants or commissions, the 'ratings', were already beginning slowly to improve from what Montagu had thought of as the 'horrors of barbarism', although by late twentieth century standards they were still rigorous in the extreme. From the end of the Napoleonic Wars the navy was dependent on volunteers for seamen. The press gang was never used after 1815, although as Lambert has recently pointed out,[46] whatever public opinion might have been it would almost certainly have been used had the national emergency of war with France developed. But there was still no organised naval service for the lower deck, as the navy called – and still calls – the great majority of its members. There was simply a national pool of seamen, the majority in merchant ships, from which the navy sought to draw its recruits when a ship of war was commissioned. The captain and junior officers had to find the crews who were recruited for one commission only, that is usually for three years or so. Even if the ship was lucky and recruited prime professional seamen rather than a mixture of humanity, the crew were, in literal fact, a gang of craftsmen and sea-going labourers of differing degrees of skill recruited for the one job of taking the vessel around for the duration of the commission. The great majority of them had no sense of a naval service or of a career in the navy and there was certainly little to encourage them to think on such lines. Thus the first year of a ship's commission was spent in attempting to build the gang into an effective team for handling and fighting the ship. For the second year the ship was reasonably efficient. During the third year things ran down as the end of the contract approached, and at the conclusion of the commission the crew was dispersed. The whole process had to be gone through again next time the vessel was commissioned. Generally speaking, the navy was under no obligation to these men.

43 The origins of this reputation are now under academic challenge, and it is fact that in 1806 the powers of captains to impose some of the more draconian penalties were abolished. See Byrn, *Crime and Punishment in the Royal Navy*, Brookfield, Vermont, USA 1989, pp 1–30.

44 Rasor, *op cit*, p 56.

45 Byrn, *op cit*, p 233.

46 Lambert, *The Crimean War*, p 29.

If the lives of the officers and their families were, by modern standards, very hard, those of the men and their equivalents ashore were very much harder. The professional seaman, to survive at all, had to be totally inured to physical hardship but he had regular food, pay, and rudimentary medical attention from the ships' surgeons. On shore, many agricultural workers and factory employees and their families, growing up in earth-floored cottages or back-to-back urban terraces, without sanitation, with water drawn from a communal well or pump, with heating and food alike strictly limited by their cost, were never clean, rarely dry, rarely warm or adequately fed. And for them there was virtually no medical attention available.

As we have said, the men themselves tended to be isolated from the mainstream of society by the nature of their total occupation. As a result they were sometimes naive, and the great majority of them could be easily led provided they had confidence in those who led them. Cooper Key[47] gives an example which also reveals contemporary attitudes.

> . . . to a reasoning man, therefore, no actual advantage resulted from the mere change of position of the ship, nor could a more satisfactory influence be drawn than heretofore; but 'Jack' does not reason, he sees the effect, *that* is sufficient for him. The ship had moved once, and of course she can be got off . . . The men worked with a more hearty goodwill, if possible, than ever.

With the great developments, social, political and technical, in the first half of the nineteenth century, it was increasingly obvious that this system of manning the navy had to change. Engineers were not the only specialist ratings for whom this hit or miss system was completely inappropriate. Gunnery was advancing rapidly and the introduction of the exploding shell into the Royal Navy called for a new dimension of skill and resulted in the setting up of the gunnery school, HMS *Excellent*, at Portsmouth in 1830. Gradually, a pool of volunteers began to form up, men who tried to go from one naval ship to another. Some of them, graduates of the gunnery school, were engaged for five or seven years, renewable, with extra pay and good prospects for promotion in the non-commissioned ranks to warrant gunner. A very few of them were encouraged by a system introduced in the 1820s by which a man who could show a total of twenty-one years' service in the navy, not necessarily continuous, qualified for a small pension. But a pension was not much of an inducement in a society in which the expectation of life was such that few lived to enjoy it.

Conditions for ratings thus slowly improved. There was more room, the ships were bigger, in the 1830s and '40s the height between decks increased,

47 Cooper Key, *op cit*, p 62.

and the food, appalling as it still was, tended to improve also. On board the steamers, water was much more readily available than in the sailing ships of the old navy. The rum ration was halved in 1834 from half a pint to a quarter of a pint a day, with consequent improvement in behaviour and competence, as well as health. Consequently, there were fewer punishments for drunkenness. One might think that many of the seamen of the eighteenth and early nineteenth centuries could rarely have been sober. Many of them were worn out and unfit for further service from the age of forty. The ration was halved again in 1850, and by then tea and sugar could be taken instead of spirits, a move which was not universally popular and which led to some riotous behaviour.

But although some men tended to stay with the navy, being a naval rating was not yet a profession. The profession was seafaring and the majority of men stayed in merchant ships. Some moved from merchant shipping to the Royal Navy, backwards and forwards. Consequently, a newly commissioned ship of the 1830s might spend three months lying at anchor while her officers desperately tried to collect sufficient volunteers to man her. This kind of practice would never work with steamers, and the gradual introduction of steam with other factors at last brought about some change. In 1846 leave with pay between commissions was introduced, and it is apparent from the muster roll of *Tiger* that by 1849 a system of good conduct badges had been introduced, but an attempt to create a reserve of men who signed a contract to serve afloat in wartime was a failure. Not until 1853 was a really serious effort made to create a peacetime naval service for ratings with improved pension conditions and 'continuous service' for ten years or more.

In 1849 it had been estimated that to man the fleet ready for sea in wartime, some 46,000 extra ratings would be required. When the War with Russia broke out in 1854, the great majority of seamen were far away in merchant ships all over the world, enjoying better food, better pay under wartime conditions, and often better conditions than they expected in the navy, and they were simply not available to volunteer for the navy, even in the somewhat remote eventuality of their wishing to do so. Britain was not dominant in the world's sea-carrying trade for nothing.

4

Steam and the Naval Officer

As to the attitude of naval officers to steam, there is a good deal of evidence that by the early 1840s the understanding of steam was seen as the road to the future and an early post captaincy. We have already quoted a contemporary Admiralty communication which indicates the financial advantages to young officers of command in the steam packet service to the Mediterranean (Chapter 2, page 41). Young Victor Montagu's attitude as recorded in his biography and his letters is very interesting. *Princess Royal*, in which he began his career as a volunteer, had been authorised and laid down as a sailing vessel in 1841 but completed in 1853 as an auxiliary screw steamship of 400 horse power. Although she had been twelve years in the building she was, therefore, when Montagu joined her, a brand new vessel on her first commission. Montagu's introduction to the navy was thus in a screw steamship of the line, and he saw his first active service in the Baltic fleet of 1854, which comprised largely steamers (that is, paddlers) and screw propelled vessels. As a result he was of the first generation to think of such ships as the representative naval vessels, although it was only two years since this steam screw battlefleet had come effectively into existence and only six years since an end had been made to ordering the construction of new purely sailing vessels for the navy. Montagu was delighted to have the opportunity of returning from the Baltic in a vessel without a steam engine in order to have had a little experience of what he already regarded as 'the old navy'.[1] He wrote

> . . . in October, my uncle, knowing that there was little chance of my seeing any more active service (as I was not in very good health), took the opportunity of transferring me to his old friend Harry Eyre's ship, the *St. George*, a sailing three-decker of 120 guns.
>
> The sailing squadron had received orders to leave for England: so in October four beauties – the *Neptune* (120 guns), the *St. George* (120 guns), the *Monarch* (84), and the *Prince Regent* (90) – made for England; and a very interesting and instructive sail we had down the North

1 Montagu, *Recollections*, pp 32–33.

Sea . . . Everything was done quite in the old style; and thus I can fairly claim the distinction of having belonged to the old school – anyhow to the remains of it – as all the ships of this squadron were minus engines and boilers.

The *Monarch* was far and away the fastest ship, though in a breeze the *Prince Regent* held her pretty close. Off the island of Bornholm we were caught in a fresh gale; and, the *St. George* being a very crank old craft, it was deemed advisable to send her upper deck carronades down into the hold. As we were short of water and provisions, the extra weight of these guns below counteracted our want of ballast. A three-decker in a gale of wind was rather a curious being. Under close-reefed topsails you could not lay her near enough the wind to enable her to meet the seas comfortably. The effect of the wind on her huge sides was to drive her bodily and very fast to leeward: in fact, you simply drifted.

It was pleasant to watch these ships speeding gaily on their course for England. We carried on when the weather permitted. The *Monarch* was generally in the van, showing us a high turn of speed. After sunset, or soon after, we collected and sailed in two lines; and, as was customary, took in a reef or two off the topsails, to make all snug for the night. When daylight broke, every stitch was set again.[2]

Another contemporary observer of the sailing scene, a Russian, Ivan Goncharov, who made a voyage half round the world as captain's secretary in the Russian frigate *Pallada*, and who later was to become world famous as an author, notably for that classic comment on some aspects of Russian society, *Oblomov*, wrote[3]

as I have started to speak about sails, let me tell you incidentally how sailing impressed me. Many people take pleasure in it and see it as proof of man's dominion over the stormy element. I see it quite oppositely as a proof of his inability to master the sea. Look closely at the setting and trimming of the sails, the complexity of the apparatus – this network of rigging, ropes, cords, ropes' ends and twine in which each member has its special purpose and is an indispensable link in the general train. Consider

2 A further indication of the double world in which these young gentlemen lived on board HM ships is given by Captain (later Admiral Sir) Henry Keppel's reference to Montagu's illness:

on visiting Clarence Paget in the *Princess Royal* I found a cot hung up, with a chubby faced boy down with fever. It was Victor Montagu, the young son of Lord Sandwich, midshipman and nephew of his captain. We met afterwards in China and elsewhere.

Keppel, *A Sailor's Life under Four Sovereigns*, London 1899, vol 2, p 223. Keppel's letters to his brother-in-law, Harry Stephenson, (NMN/HTN/52a) show that the treatment of the young cadets under a captain's care could be most enlightened, with frequent runs ashore in foreign ports, experience in other ships in the squadron, plenty of sport and wide social opportunities.

3 Goncharov, *The Voyage of the Frigate Pallada*, London 1965, pp 27–28.

the number of hands setting the system in motion. And yet how imperfect is the result of all this ingenuity! The time of arrival of a sailing ship cannot be fixed, there is no contending with a head-wind nor any reversing should the ship run aground; it is as impossible to turn about at once as it is to stop dead instantly. In a calm the ship drowses, in a head wind she tacks, that is zigzags and cheats the wind, but only a third of the distance she sails is directly ahead . . . In each rope, in each hook, nail and plank, you read the history of those instruments of torture by which mankind has won the right to sail the seas with a fair wind . . . Perhaps it is beautiful to look at a ship broadside on with her white sails set, gliding over the boundless mirror-like surface of the waters as if she was a swan, but when you find yourself inside the impossible web of rigging, then you see in sailing, not the proof of ascendancy, but rather the abandonment of hope in a complete victory. A sailing ship is like an old cocotte who raddles and powders, puts on ten petticoats and laces herself into corsets in order to beguile her lover . . . In vain did they take me to see how beautifully the sails bellied out to leeward and how the frigate, heeling over on her side, clove the waves and scudded along at twelve knots. 'A steamer won't go like that', they said to me. 'But, on the other hand, a steamer goes all the time.'

The presence of engines on board Her Majesty's ships meant, as we have already indicated, the presence of engineers to drive and maintain them. That presence was one manifestation of the great and complex changes which were beginning to take place in the navy in the 1830s and '40s. As we have already suggested, these changes were brought about partly by pressures from the shore and partly by the advent into the service of the skilled professional, skilled, that is, in specialisations other than those of the handling and maintenance of the wooden sailing ship. Thus the status of the doctor, the schoolmaster, the paymaster, the gunner, was greatly improved during this period. It will become evident in later chapters that the surgeon of *Tiger*, Dr Domville, was a highly competent professional man educated to a higher standard than his companion officers and treated by the captain as a friend. These changes were reflected in the accommodation allocated to the various ranks. To quote Daniel[4]

The Doctor was named Clarke, and the Assistant Surgeon, Dr Dugald McEwan, later on for many years Surgeon on board the Royal Yacht. Their mess was called the gun room (not ward room) in those days in a frigate. The engineers, who, in those days, were rather a rough lot, and very different to the more refined and scientific engineer officers of the

4 Daniel, *Some Reminiscences*, p 9.

present day, had a mess of their own except the Chief Engineer, who messed with the gun room officers . . . The warrant officers also had their own separate mess on the lower deck.

Tiger's muster roll of March 1854 is divided, as far as naval officers are concerned, into three. The first list covers Commissioned Officers, Military Branch, who comprise the captain, the lieutenants, the mates (sub-lieutenants after 1861), the master, the second master and an acting second master. The master's function was navigation and under the captain he was entirely responsible for the navigation and pilotage of the ship. He was not under the orders of the lieutenant in the normal course. He has no modern naval equivalent and he could, and often did, move easily into the position of master of a merchant vessel. The second list includes the Commissioned Officers, Civil Branch. These comprise the paymaster and his two assistants, the surgeon and his assistant, the chief engineer and his four assistants, the chaplain, the naval instructor and two principal clerks. The third list is of the subordinate officers, the midshipmen, the naval cadets and the junior clerks. The hierarchical structure of the old navy was under a challenge posed by events. The effect on the seaman and the sea officer who had devoted his life to the technology of the wooden sailing ship has never been summed up better than in a few further lines by Goncharov.[5] He wrote

> Woe to the seaman of the old school whose whole mind, science and art, backed by his self-esteem and ambition, are centred in the rigging. The conclusion is foregone. Sails are for small ships and manufacturers of modest means, all other shipowners have taken to steam. Big sailing ships are not being built in a single naval dockyard; even old ones are being converted to steam. While we were in Portsmouth naval docks [in 1853] they half dismantled the completely finished ship and put a steam engine in.

The newcomers, especially the engineers, were interlopers who threatened the vested interests of the ship's establishment. The consequent alienation applied particularly to the engineer because he threatened the very fundamentals of the old way of life. Consciously, in the case of the more able and intelligent officers, unconsciously probably with many, the engineer was seen as a person who would in future perform the most important function on board the ship, that of making her go, from which process all her other functions followed. But these men who were usurping the first function of the sea officer and the seaman were not from the closed world of the wooden sailing ship and the even more closed world of the naval officer within it, but from the shore, and from the totally alien

5 Goncharov, *op cit*, p 28.

environment of the foundry and the workshop. They did not even come from the same geographical regions as the majority of ships' officers, who were from the south of England, but rather from the north or Scotland. They spoke with different accents, their social mores were completely different. They came from the new world of technology which was to have such profoundly liberalising effects on shore. Here was fertile ground for resentment and, of course, for snobbery. Again the Russian Goncharov, looking at British society and the British engineer from outside[6]

The mechanic or engineer does not fear being reproached for his ignorance of political economy; he has never read a single book about it. Do not start a conversation with him about the natural sciences, or about anything except engineering, for he will show himself pitiably limited, though sometimes his limitations may hide tremendous talent; he is always keenly intelligent, but his intelligence is devoted wholly to the mechanical. If you are a man with a liberal education a conversation with him in your hotel would be boring, but should you own a factory you would want to employ him or give him an order for his products.

The profession of engineering at this early stage in its history was almost as all absorbing as that of handling wooden sailing ships. The alienation which could develop between traditional naval officers and their engineers could have adverse effects. This led the Comptroller of the Navy, Admiral Sir Thomas Byam Martin, already, as early as 1830, to seek the opinions of distinguished engineers on the problem. This fact is of considerable interest as evidence of the concern which the Navy Board felt on this matter. In response to a request for his opinion on the efficiency and status of naval engineers, Joshua Field of Maudslay, Sons and Field, the engineers on the Thames, wrote on 16 December 1830, as follows[7]

Your engagement at the Admiralty this morning prevented me from entering so far as I could have wished into the subject on which you did me the honour to consult me.

With reference to some of the Steam Vessels in His Majesty's Service, the machinery could not be better managed. The *Lightning* and *Comet* are instances which confirm this remark, but in some of the commissioned vessels the case is far otherwise, and I think it can be accounted for chiefly from the want of a better understanding between the Officers and the Engineers, this arises very much from the education and previous habits of the only men qualified to manage these engines being quite at variance with the education and discipline of the Navy; having enjoyed in manufactories and workshops a loose kind of independence they do not

6 Goncharov, *op cit*, p 43.
7 The Goodrich Papers, 1618, Field to Byam Martin, 16 December 1830.

readily fall in with that respectful and submissive demeanour necessary in the discipline of a King's ship. On the other hand the officers do not make allowances for men so differently brought up from those men they have been accustomed to deal with, frequently treating them with harshness, and without understanding the subject, interfering with them in the exercise of their duty, which finally drives the best qualified men out of the Service, since such men can always find good employment in private vessels or workshops, this leads to the advancement of the second and third assistants, and even the stokers to the office of first Engineer, thus putting the most valuable machinery and the safety of the vessel into the hands of men who, but for such a train of circumstances, would never have been deemed worthy of such a trust. The only remedy which occurs to me is after selecting a well qualified man for first Engineer to make his position on board more respectable than it is at present, by giving him some rank in the ship and making him responsible for his department, having proper control over his assistants and stokers without interference of anyone on board excepting the general control of the Commander.

Every vessel should have two apprentices in the engine room who will in time be qualified for 1st Engineers and being brought up in the Service will fall into Naval discipline as a matter of course.

Some arrangements by which the objects of the foregoing remarks can be obtained and attention paid to the regulations drawn up in conjunction with Mr. Goodrich (for the preservation of boilers, etc.) would ensure the better working of His Majesty's Steam Vessels and avoid the frequent repairs to their boilers, etc.

With great submission, I have made these observations and have the honour to be,

Your obedient servant,
JOSHUA FIELD

In his *Elementary Treatise on Steam* of 1834, Commander Robert Otway advised officers of steam vessels as to what should be their attitude to the chief engineer. He said

further more, by showing this deference and mark of respect to that officer it serves as an example to the men on board who will more readily look up to him as their superior in every point of view.

Five years later, Commander R S Robinson was pursuing the same theme. Robinson had taken a great interest in steam and, after the publication of his book, he was appointed in command of *Phoenix*, paddle sloop, four guns, and then of *Hydra*, paddle sloop, six guns, in which he distinguished himself in the Syrian campaign and was posted. He was an aggressive and strong minded man. He became post captain of *Colossus*, 80 guns, in the Baltic in the War with Russia and in due course Comptroller of the Navy in 1861. He retired as a rear admiral. He wrote[8]

> We all know what a valuable class of men the boatswains of the Fleet have always proved, yet with the smartest and best boatswain that ever came afloat, an officer would not feel easy to know nothing about the rigging, and trust all to him.
>
> So with the very best of engineers, no person in command ought to be, or I should think could be, conscientiously satisfied, in ignorance of the names and nature of the power which is to move him.
>
> I hope to be excused for saying a few words to my brother officers on the subject of engineers:– they are a most valuable body of men, it is our duty and our interest in every way to befriend them; they possess knowledge which we do not, their lives have been spent in acquiring it; much in every way depends upon them; and the more we can make these men feel as *bel)nging to us*, the more we can uphold their situation, the more we can make them feel that they *are officers*, the more we show them kindness and consideration, the more readily they will enter into our views, impart their knowledge, and in the hour of need, the *greater* and the *safer* will be our mutual reliance on each other.
>
> The engineers, whom I have personally known in merchant steamers, were men of a most excellent description, well educated, sober, steady, with a perfect practical knowledge of their business. If such men as these enter into Her Majesty's Service, they will require *consideration*; I will answer for it, they will repay that and kindness a thousandfold. I am not able to speak of the Engineers in Her Majesty's ships, as I have had no opportunity of knowing them; but as they form a very small portion of the whole number in the kingdom, there is no doubt in the event of war, we must recruit our ranks from those employed in the merchant service, and I feel no doubt, that treated well, they will serve us well.

Despite views like these, the engineers in the navy were to have a long and hard passage over many years to achieve accepted social status. Not only were they up against the entrenched seamen, with their almost religious reverence for the masts and yards and shiphandling which had absorbed so much of their lives, they were also up against the Admiralty's contemporary policy of the gentrification of the navy, to which reference was made in the preceding chapter, and they were mostly, to use a contemporary phrase, 'not of the status of a gentleman'. So the advance of the engineer was slow.

The appointment of Captain Sir Edward Parry as Comptroller of Steam Machinery in 1837 has been taken by one naval historian as marking the

8 Robinson, *The Nautical Steam Engine Explained*, London 1839, pp 173–175.

establishment of a real engineering branch,[9] but Parry owed his position more to his strong interest than to any knowledge of naval architecture or steam technology – he was a brother-in-law of Lord Stanley of Alderney, Patronage Secretary of the current administration of Lord Melbourne. Nevertheless, it was in his time that the engineers ceased to be recruited on a casual basis. In 1837 Regulations for Engineers and for Engineer Boys were introduced under which engineers became warrant officers on the same footing as gunners, boatswains and carpenters, but with markedly better pay. Indeed, a first class engineer was paid almost twice as much as a senior carpenter and, when the tropical allowance granted at the same time is added, he was paid more than anybody else on board below the rank of commander.[10] At the same time an apprenticeship system was introduced to ensure the training of future warrant officers. In 1847 engineers at last became officially gentlemen in that a further reorganisation gave the two highest grades of engineer officers the Queen's Commission and, for the most senior, the title of Inspector of Machinery Afloat and a rank immediately below that of commander, senior to all the lieutenants. But they could still never take command. Nor can they today.

A contemporary view of the differences between the terms of service for engineers in the navy and in merchant ships is quoted by Murray.[11] It is also revealing in the attitude shown to the expectation of life.

> . . . the engineers would require better pay than those in the Navy. On board the Oriental [that is, the P. & O.] boats a first class engineer receives £16 to £26 per month. It is true that in the Queen's Service the chief first-class engineers get £17 a month and pensions, but we find our first engineer as good a table as you or I would set down to – in fact, they live like princes. In the Navy they have to find their own table, except the common rations of the ship. As regards pensions, I have heard some of the engineers say, 'What is the use of a pension? Very few of us will ever live to enjoy pensions; if we go on a foreign station perhaps there is not one of us that will return to receive it.' In India we have scarcely kept a complete crew of engineers for more than a year together; we have entire changes year after year, principally from death, and from liver complaints arising from the intense heat of the engine room.

It may seem strange, looking at this situation from the point of view of the late twentieth century, that the first regular service engineers of the 1830s should have been ranked with the carpenter and the boatswain as warrant rather than commissioned, that is wardroom, officers. But to contemporary eyes this was a perfectly natural ranking and appeared so to the engineers

9 Penn, *Up Funnel, Down Screw!* London 1955, p 35.
10 Lewis, *Navy in Transition*, p 200.
11 Murray, *Rudimentary Treatise*, p 176.

themselves, as to the wardroom. All these men, boatswain and carpenter in the age of carpenter and blacksmith technology, engineers in the first manifestations of the new age, were the technicians who looked after the power which made the ship go and, as the quotation from Robinson on page 87 has shown, they were looked on in the same way. Much less easy to understand is the attitude of later generations. The nineteenth century gentrification of the navy, combined perhaps with the contempt for the technical which has been endemic in British society since the 1860s, has meant that the engineer in the navy has never, even today, when not merely the propulsion but the whole fighting capacity of the ship is dependent on him, been accorded full social equality with the executive branch. Early in 1991 the authors listened with wry amusement as two (admittedly elderly) executive officers expressed their shocked surprise that a 'plumber' had been appointed Captain of the Royal Naval College at Dartmouth.

Robinson in 1839 had excellent advice for young officers.[12]

Iron vessels of 1500 tons, engines of five or six hundred horsepower, are constructing to go to India and America. All classes are getting acquainted with steam; both by sea and land it is constantly before us, and we must not fall behind any class of our countryman in the knowledge of that subject by which, in future, our destinies may be guided, our battles may be fought, and it is confidently expected by our country, that our triumphs will be won.

His book is a good account of the working of the contemporary side-lever engines written for the intelligent and involved layman. Many very able young officers acted as Robinson recommended. It is evident from what has been quoted that he had taken his own advice and served in merchant paddle propelled steamships, no doubt during a period on half pay. They saw that, one way or another, the limitations of the paddler were going to be overcome one day and that the future would be with steam. These men, lieutenants soon to be commanders and post captains, often of impeccable social origins, were proud of their technical knowledge which was amazingly extensive as well as detailed. To give some examples, Lieutenant W Gordon, who had served in the steamers *Driver*, *Firebrand* and *Inflexible*, wrote a textbook, *The Economy of the Marine Steam Engine*, published in London in 1845, which gives a very interesting picture of the rapidly developing state of steam technology at the period and of the attitude to steam of a junior officer clearly fascinated by his subject. Among many other things this book contains what appears to be the first description of the engine room telegraph. Direct control of the engines from the bridge or deck had been established as early as 1821 with a remarkably advanced but

12 Robinson, *op cit*, p 172.

simple mechanism with the result that 'it places the engine as much under command as the rudder is, – an undoubted improvement upon the clumsy method of bawling out to the engineer below, who either may not hear, or may chance to be out of the way, – circumstances which may lead to the most serious accidents'.[13]

Lieutenant Cooper Key, later to become Admiral Sir Astley Cooper Key, he who wrote of the salving of *Gorgon*, and to whom reference has already been made (see page 65), achieved post captain's rank at the age of twenty-seven in 1850. Despite the immense knowledge of the technology of wood and hemp which he displayed in his book, in 1844, before he took service in *Gordon*, he wrote '. . . After much consideration and mature deliberation I have come to the determination that the only way to get on in the service by one's own exertions, in these times of peace, is to join a steamer and to follow it up',[14] but the idea that at this period it was possible for an officer to get on in the service by his own exertions alone does suggest a certain naivety. Keppel, youngest son of Lord Albemarle and later as Admiral of the Fleet a close friend of King Edward VII and his Queen, took a house in Greenwich in the mid 1840s in order to be near Penn's Engineering Works and there to be able to study engineering and steam. Henry Codrington, son of one of Nelson's captains at Trafalgar and a post captain at twenty-eight, saw fit when seeking appointment in 1852 to emphasise his steam experience. Codrington in fact had a comprehensive knowledge of steam, revealed in detail in his letters to his family.[15] He showed interest in the welfare of stokers and junior engineers, urging that they should be provided with hot baths at the end of each watch, an unheard of luxury at that period.

There has been a tendency among some naval historians to assert that these men were despised by their contemporaries but, even bearing in mind the strength of their interest, their subsequent careers would suggest the contrary. In the years of the 1830s and '40s before the 'gentrification of the entrepreneur',[16] which as Martin J Wiener has sought to show, was to have a disastrous effect on the development of British society in the latter part of the century, these pioneers were not necessarily inhibited by contempt for technology. Professor Michael Lewis, formerly Professor of History at the Royal Naval College, Greenwich, looking back with the eyes of a later generation saw 'the poor half-pay war lieutenants who accepted the

13 Hall, *An Account of the Ferry Across the Tay at Dundee*, Dundee 1825, Appendix 1, p 2.

14 Vice Admiral P H Columb, *Memoirs of Sir Astley Cooper Key*, London 1898, p 87, letter from Rio, 26 January 1844.

15 See Greenhill and Giffard, *The British Assault*, p 186–187.

16 M J Wiener, *English Culture and the Decline of the Industrial Spirit, 1850–1980*, Cambridge 1981, especially Chapter 7. For a summary of criticism of Wiener's theory see Alan Skead, *Britain's Decline*, Oxford 1987, pp 6–11. Sladen in Smout, ed, *Scotland and the Sea*, has also recently challenged Wiener's thesis.

commands of the early tugs and endured the loneliness of their empty wardrooms'[17] as forced there only by 'dire unemployment'. Yet the subsequent lives of, for example, the three pioneers, lieutenants Evans, Hay and Bullock, in 1828, the first steam commanders to be appointed, do not suggest this sort of image at all. All were posted and set on the inevitable rise through seniority towards flag rank. There is evidence in O'Byrne's *A Naval Biographical Dictionary* (London 1849) which suggests that command of steamers was sometimes given to lieutenants who were regarded as promising officers. The first naval officer ever to take command of a commissioned steam vessel, George Evans of *Lightning*, was not a 'war Lieutenant' but was commissioned in 1821. He was a graduate of the Royal Naval College, Portsmouth, completing his course in only thirteen months and being presented with the first medal ever given by the college. A letter of 15 November 1826 to him from his future father-in-law, formerly the Lieutenant Governor of that institution, Captain (later Admiral) John Giffard, father of Henry Wells Giffard of *Tiger*, gives an excellent impression of the methods used to further the interest of a young lieutenant seeking promotion to commander.[18]

> Portsmouth,
> 15 November, 1826.

My dear Sir,

I am glad to hear that you are at length in a fair way of getting recommended to Lord Melville for promotion, and I should advise you to request your friend to make interest with as many people as he can apply to Lord Melville on your behalf, and get them to state your exemplary conduct while at college, and the short time in which you finished the plan of education at that establishment, for which you had the first medal, which, according to the present regulations, would have ensured you a lieutenant's commission immediately, instead of which you were nearly eleven years a midshipman; that you have been constantly cruising since that time on foreign stations, and given complete satisfaction to the Captains, as will be seen by their certificates, and that from your last Captain, the Hon. Robert C. Spencer, is so strong, that it must be evident the gentlemen urging your promotion are only doing so for a meritorious, good officer, in constant active employment for more than 14 years. I can only add that if I had hoisted my flag I should have nominated you as one of the lieutenants, as proof how fully I am convinced you have conducted yourself with zeal and energy.

I am, very faithfully yours,

J. GIFFARD

17 Lewis, *Navy in Transition*, p 203.
18 G A Guest, ed, *Record of the Services of Admiral George Evans*, London 1876, note 5.

Evans, who had first met *Lightning* at Algiers in 1824, where he had played an active part in the operation preceding the threat to bombard the city, prepared himself for his new responsibilities in *Lightning* by working at the engineering firms of Maudslay, Sons and Field at Lambeth, and Napiers at Glasgow 'where he acquired such practical knowledge of steam engines as to be able to work those of the *Lightning* himself'.[19] There was competition for the appointment to *Lightning* and Evans was preferred for the posting to Captain (later Admiral Sir) Charles Napier, one of the most aggressively self-promoting officers of his generation, who had already demonstrated strong practical interest in steam.[20] This was no doubt due to Giffard's support. Giffard was married to a Bonham-Carter – see the next chapter. Captain Napier was later to stand against Giffard's Whig brother-in-law, John Bonham-Carter, for Parliament in the general election which followed the passing of the first Reform Bill of 1832, as an Independent Liberal for Portsmouth. He was bottom of the poll.[21]

Lightning was at this period employed as the yacht and despatch boat of the then Lord High Admiral, HRH The Duke of Clarence, soon to be King William IV, and the appointment as her commander, far from being a lonely backwater, was one in which the fortunate lieutenant had every opportunity of bringing himself to the attention of the navy's top brass. Evans did just that, and was promoted to commander's rank as a result of initiative displayed, in contradiction to written orders, in towing to sea from Plymouth a windbound squadron of sailing warships whose services were urgently required in Portugal. Evans was appointed to command of HM Steam Vessel *Rhadamanthus*, 800 tons, launched in May 1832, with a 200 horse power engine, and therefore brand new, which was one of the first five paddle steamers to be equipped with sufficient armament to be regarded as fighting ships in their own right. In command of this vessel Evans was involved in a blockade of the Dutch coast with the steamer *Dee* and was then ordered to the West Indies. The passage there in April and May 1833 was the first steam-assisted Atlantic crossing to be made by any British vessel, naval or merchant, which gave Evans yet another distinction. Her log[22] shows that she steamed across the Bay of Biscay and then sailed, with lower paddle floats unshipped, to Funchal, Madeira, where a collier brig awaited her. She then proceeded to Barbados, partly under steam and partly under sail. Evans's career as commander of *Rhadamanthus* in the West Indies provided plenty of opportunities for the display of initiative. He put down a slave mutiny by ordering ten of the captured mutineers to be put

19 Guest, *op cit*, p 5.
20 Smith, *A Short History*, p 84. Greenhill and Giffard, *The British Assault*, Chapter 7. For a more favourable view of Napier, see Lambert, *Crimean War*, Chapters 12 and 13.
21 Williams, *The Life and Letters of Admiral Sir Charles Napier*, *K.C.B.*, London 1917, pp 81–82.
22 Summarised in Smith, *A Short History*, p 35.

into the boiler in full view of two of their companions, who were then released, a charade in which his engineer readily cooperated. The prisoners were, in fact, confined in empty coal bunkers, but the story spread by the two freed men ensured that that particular bit of trouble ashore came to an immediate end.

Evans was employed in 1835–36 in an enquiry into the Post Office Packet Service which revealed among other things that the method of issuing coal to the steamers from the stores was wide open to corruption. He was posted captain in June 1838, having three weeks earlier married Mary, youngest daughter of Admiral John Giffard, who had given him such sound advice and support. A charming description of this couple survives[23] written by Mary Giffard, daughter of the Admiral's second son. Mary Giffard wrote, referring first to her aunt Mary, Mrs Evans

> [She] lives in my mind as the most beautiful woman I have ever seen . . . in her middle age she was indeed beautiful, with her perfect features, delicate complexion, dark eyes and wave of soft white hair, giving much the effect of powder . . . She was exceedingly fond of horses and rode and drove well, and her husband always left the stable department in her hands . . . I have heard her maid say that when dressed to be presented at Court, or for some other great function and looking magnificent, she would go downstairs without once looking in the glass.
>
> Her husband was much older than herself and remarkably ugly – Beauty and the Beast the neighbours used to call them. He was an Irishman and a sailor, a very delightful combination. His name was George Evans . . . He was staying at my grandfather's one day and the conversation happened to turn upon death beds; Uncle Evans in his Irish fashion said that he had been upon his death bed several times and . . . there was nothing so comfortable to remember as any little kindness one had been able to do for a fellow creature. This horrified Calvinistic old Lady Grey who was present and she exclaimed, 'No, no! Captain Evans, all our righteousnesses are as filthy rags'. 'And so they are', quote he, 'but filthy rags will show which way the wind blows . . .'

Evans's flag was achieved in 1857. In the intervening years he had played an important role with the Screw Propeller Company in the development of screw propulsion at sea and its adoption by the navy. We deal with these developments in detail in Chapter 7.

---

23 Mary Giffard, 'What I can remember about the Ancestors', unpublished typescript in private possession.

5

The Making of a Steam
Frigate Captain

The career of Henry Wells Giffard, later to be post captain of the steam paddle frigate *Tiger*, closely reflected the condition of society and of the navy as described in the last two chapters.

His branch of the family could rightly claim direct and unchallenged descent in the male line from one Osbern Giffard who was certainly, with other bearers of the name Giffard, of the first generation of Norman settlers, and appears in the Domesday Survey of 1087 as Tenant in Chief of seven holdings in Wiltshire, in Gloucestershire, and one in Dorset. The vast family tree, even in the simplified form in which it follows the line of descent of Henry Wells Giffard, shows over the centuries the ups and downs of a dynasty: a Chancellor of England, an Archbishop of York, bishops, crusaders, courtiers, knights, peers of the realm, one hanged as a traitor in the ebb and flow of the fourteenth century baronial wars, another an abductor of a nun. The family were beneficiaries of the dissolution of the monasteries; they were granted lands and left a legacy of place names in many of the counties of southern England, settling down as the centuries passed to be country squires and parish priests at Rushall in Wiltshire. There in 1687, William Giffard, an East India merchant, through marriage acquired an estate on which his brother Francis was already rector of the parish. Here they remained as squires and rectors for a century or so.

But Thomas Giffard, William's son, and his wife Mary were incautious enough to have a family of fourteen children and, although at least three died in infancy and the eldest son took his degree at Brasenose College Oxford and in due course became in his turn Rector of Rushall, it is probable that the estate could not provide for an adequate education for the five other surviving sons, let alone the daughters. One son became a farmer, another was apprentice to an apothecary of Devizes, and a third son, James, was apprenticed to Nicholas Smith, 'Citizen Skinner' of London, and in due course became a prosperous provision merchant and chandler in Covent Garden.

James, typically of his age, was widowed and so married twice. The oldest son of his second marriage was baptised as John in September 1766. He joined his father in the Covent Garden emporium. Mary Giffard, a grand-daughter of John who knew John Giffard when she was a child, and he an old man, recorded[1] the circumstances in which this branch of the family began its upward movement back to the status of gentry. Captain the Honorable William Cornwallis, Admiral Lord Cornwallis as he was to be, visited the shop in Covent Garden in connection with the purchase of stores for his then command, *Canada*, 74 guns. Mary Giffard wrote

> . . . seeing the handsome, bright-eyed lad [Cornwallis] said, 'that is a fine boy, Giffard; what are you going to do with him?' Mr. Giffard replied that he did not know, and then Lord (sic) Cornwallis said that he was just going to sea, and if the father approved, would take the boy with him and make a sailor of him. Mr Giffard consulted his [wife] Diana, who approved the prospect for her son, and the lad went down to Portsmouth with Lord Cornwallis and came home no more for eleven years.

Thus began the building of what was to become a powerful interest. Though physically small John Giffard had a good appearance on his side. Mary Giffard records of him in later life

> I remember my grandfather as a very striking-looking old man though small of stature. He had beautiful soft snow-white hair, a very fine head and brilliant brown eyes, 'shining like stars', as I heard Miss Julia Smith describe them. Once when he was travelling by coach, the only other passenger was an old Quaker lady who looked at him much during the journey, and when he handed her out at her stopping place said to him, 'Young man, those eyes were never given thee for thy soul's good'. We, as children, used to be very much amused by his custom of drinking his own health in his first glass of port wine after dinner; 'Your health, John; thank ye, thank ye, Giffard'. This was his weekday toast, his Sunday one was, 'A health to all my friends, and the Devil take the rest of my relations', a sentiment which I must own appeals to me strongly.

John Giffard entered the navy at the right time. O'Byrne summarises his career.[2] He experienced actions against the French and the Spanish in the early 1780s and served again in 1793 with Cornwallis in *Crown*, 64 guns. Here his interest with Cornwallis ensured his promotion to lieutenant. The long wars with the French had now begun. He was made commander in February 1796 and posted by Sir John Jervis into *La Mignonne*, 32 guns, only eight and a half months later. He was then almost continuously employed at sea until 1807.

1 Mary Giffard, 'What I can remember about the Ancestors'.
2 William O'Byrne, *A Naval Biographical Dictionary*.

In November 1802, between appointments in command of *Magnificent*, 74 guns, and *Prince of Wales*, 98 guns, 'lying in Portsmouth', the thirty-six year old post captain took a step which finally ensured his own and his family's future fortunes. He married Susannah, a younger daughter of Sir John Carter of Portsmouth. Sir John Carter through his wife had inherited part of a brewery fortune shared between his wife and her sister Anne who took her portion to the Bonham family into which she married. He was nine times Mayor of Portsmouth, knighted by George III in 1773. The family's power in the naval town was immense. In the words of their historian[3]

> From that date [1782] the Carter influence was paramount. The family controlled the parliamentary nominations almost without exception until the Reform Act of 1832 . . . Between 1747 and 1835 Carters were Mayors of Portsmouth 32 times, while the 35 Aldermen elected between 1778 and 1832 were *all* Carter nominees; likewise the majority of the new Burgesses . . . Their domination of Portsmouth through family influence must have been a record of its kind.

Their achievement was the more remarkable in that they were non-conformists, 'dissenters' and as such statutorily debarred from holding public office. But there were ways round the law which the Carters effectively exploited. Sir John Carter's only son, also John, added the name of Bonham to his after inheriting, in 1826, from his cousin, Thomas Bonham, son of his aunt Anne, the other half of the brewery fortune which his mother had shared. As John Bonham-Carter he was Whig Member of Parliament for Portsmouth from 1816 to his death in 1838. The acquisition of fortune he gained from his cousin enabled John Bonham-Carter to play an active part in national politics. When he was elected to Parliament the Whigs had been out of office almost continuously for some thirty years. The shifting tide of political fortunes, which involved in some degree the slow change in public attitudes towards a more humane society, briefly referred to in Chapter 3, brought the Whigs at last back into power in the 1830s. John Bonham-Carter became deeply involved in the political activities which led to the passing of the Reform Act of 1832, which, although limited in its effects, marked the beginning of a long series of changes in enfranchisement. His work led to an established reputation as a man behind the scenes and he was offered office at least three times, but declining health obliged him to refuse. He died, probably of diabetes, then undiagnosed, in 1838.

John and Susannah Giffard had six sons and two daughters. The sons followed the accepted professions, the law, the church and the armed forces. One son became a barrister, a judge, and in due course was knighted

3 Bonham-Carter, *In a Liberal Tradition: A Social Biography, 1700–1958*, London 1960, pp 18–19.

1. *The loss of* HMS Tiger *under the cliffs south of Odessa,* Vesuvius *far left,* Niger *in the foreground. The lithograph is from a sketch made 'on the spot by Lieut Montagu Buccleuch Dunn,* HMS Niger'. (Private Collection)

2. *The end of* Tiger *as seen by a Russian officer sketching on the shore.* Vesuvius *and* Niger *are offshore.* (Musée de la Marine, Paris)

3. *'Bristol Hot-Wells on the Avon with Steam Packets'. The two steamers are* George IV *of Bristol (left), built there in 1822 and* Saint Patrick *of Liverpool, also built in 1822. The engraving probably dates from the summer of 1823 when these two steamers briefly ran in competition on the Bristol–Cork service.* (Private Collection)

4. *This charming little sketch shows the 'Interior of the Principal Cabin' of a steamer of 1817. It is almost certainly the earliest representation which exists of accommodation in a British steam vessel, showing an elegant, Regency style, apartment. Note the dome roof light.* (Private Collection)

5. Perhaps the earliest photograph of a British-built merchant paddle steamer shows Iris, built by James and William Hall at Aberdeen in 1842 lying in Ålborg Harbour in Denmark in the early 1840s. She has a two-masted schooner rig for sail-assist. In this photograph the topmasts are housed and the single yard lowered. (Handels-og Søfartsmeseet På Kronberg)

6. *Western rivers steamers at St Louis, Missouri.* (Private Collection)

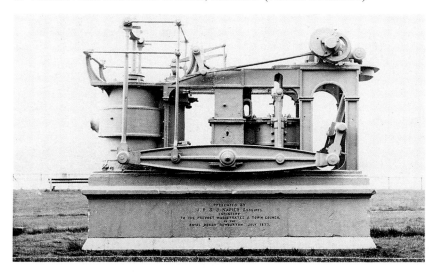

7. *The first marine engine built by Robert Napier in 1824 for the steamer* Leven *in service on the Clyde. Photographed in the 1960s, it is now displayed under cover at the Denny Tank in Dumbarton. An excellent example of the early side-lever engine, it represents the type of machinery fitted to* Lightning, African, *and to all early naval steamers.* (John R Hume)

8. *This model of* Lightning, *the second naval steamer to be built and the first to be commissioned, was made by the late Captain John Rowe, RN, from Admiralty draughts of the vessel and from a lithograph derived from a drawing by Sir Oswald Brierly. The model shows the vessel's gaff rig only diagramatically.* (National Maritime Museum)

9. Great Western *'taking her Departure from Bristol for New York'. Engraved by R J and A W Reeve from a painting by Joseph Walter.* (Private Collection)

10. The cadets' and midshipmens' berth, HMS Caesar, *1854.* HMS Caesar *was a steam screw ship of the line and this quarter is a good deal larger than that provided in the much smaller paddle frigate* Magicienne *in which Owen Daniel served as a cadet.* (Illustrated London News)

11. The steam screw line of battleship Princess Royal *(91 guns, 400 horse power). Commanded by Captain Lord Clarence Paget when Victor Montagu was a cadet on board her in 1854, this photograph was taken at Plymouth in 1864 or 1867.* (Imperial War Museum)

12. The wardroom of the steam screw ship of the line HMS Duke of Wellington *in 1855.* (Illustrated London News)

13. Rhadamanthus, *laid down at Devonport in 1831, 4 guns, 220 horse power. The museum's records show the model to have been built by Mr T Roberts of Plymouth in 1832. Note the absence, at this early date, of paddle box boats.* (National Maritime Museum)

14. *This lighograph, made from drawings by Sir Oswald Brierly, shows the steam screw battle fleet of 1854 with royal poles and topgallant masts and their yards sent down and topmasts housed, anchored and steaming to take the strain off the cables, in a gale in the Baltic.* (Private Collection)

15. *John Giffard, 1766–1855, Admiral of the White, engraved from a daguerreotype made when he was eighty-seven years old.* (Private Collection)

16. *Henry Wells Giffard. From a pencilled note on the original it appears that this watercolour portrait was made in December 1846 when Captain Giffard had been appointed in command of the* Penelope. *He is wearing the full-dress uniform of a Captain.* (Private Collection)

17. *'We heard the* Kite *was wrecked on the coast . . . Lt. Douglas . . . Captain's wife and crew fell into the hands of the Chinese and [were] carried through this country in cages'. Sketch by H W Giffard of Lieutenant Douglas in the cage.* (Private Collection)

18. *Francis Pettit Smith, centre, with officers of* The Great Britain. (Basil Greenhill)

19. Bee, *the little 42 ton steam vessel built under Francis Smith's supervision at Chatham in 1842 and equipped with the screw as well as the visible paddles. An instructional vessel for the Royal Naval College, Portsmouth, she played an important role in familiarising officers with steam.* (Imperial War Museum)

20. The Great Britain *saluting a warship on 26 January, 1845. It is probable that the vessel normally operated as shown here with topmasts on fore, mizzen, jigger, spanker and driver housed. These spars were used in the same way as studdingsail booms and the gaff topsails set flying under conditions when studdingsails would have been used in a square-rigged vessel.* (John Hill)

21. *The paddle box boat and her launching gear are clearly shown in this photograph of a model in the Orlogsmuseet, Copenhagen, of the Danish paddle sloop* Gejser *(8 guns, 430 horse power) built in 1844.* (Basil Greenhill)

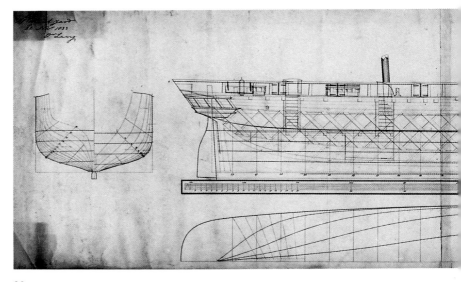

22.

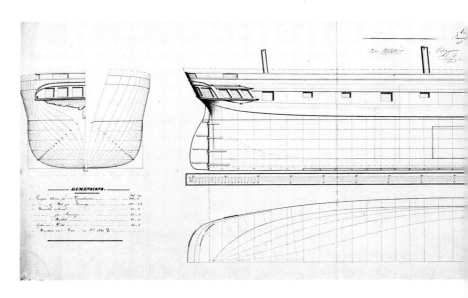

23. *These two Admiralty sheer draughts, the upper of HM steam vessel* Lightning *of 182.*
Royal Navy. (Admiralty draught collection, National Maritime Museum)

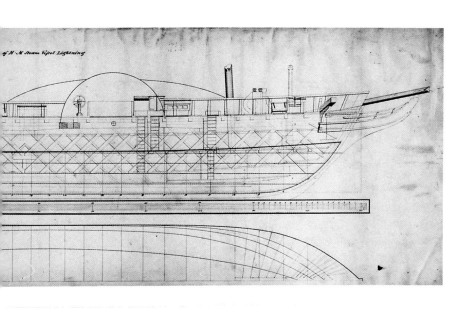

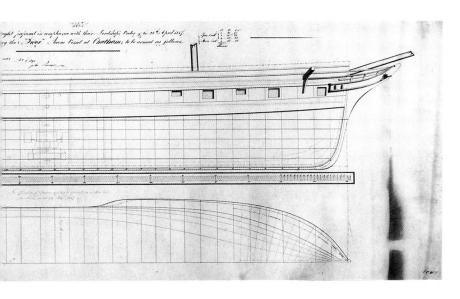

r of the steam frigate Tiger *of 1850, span the development of the paddle steamer in the*

24. *Valorous (16 guns, 400 horse power), the last paddle frigate to be built for the Royal Navy. She remained in service until 1891 and was the last paddle frigate at sea. Note that the port paddle box boat is not in position and that the top of the paddle wheel is therefore visible.* (Private Collection)

25. Terrible, (21 guns, 800 horse power) the most powerful paddle frigate ever built, sketched in the Mediterranean in the early 1850s by the Reverend Calvert R Jones, the pioneer photographer. As she is under steam alone her topgallant and royal yards have been sent down. (Glynn Vivian Art Gallery, Swansea)

26. *The frigate* Unicorn, *46 guns, launched in 1824 at Chatham, was a sister ship to* Penelope *and conveys a good impression of the latter's shape and bulk. Never commissioned, and preserved by the protective housing built over her when she was completed, as she lies in Dundee today she gives a unique impression to the visitor of life in the navy of her period.* (Basil Greenhill)

27. Dragon, *a lithograph by Dutton after Lt W G Masters, Royal Marines. This illustration shows clearly the peculiar combination of a three-masted schooner with a full-rigged ship's masting and rigging with which some paddle frigates and sloops were equipped. The spacing of the masts imposed by the presence of the engines and boilers amidships did nothing to improve performance under sail.* (Parker Gallery)

28. *This drawing of* Njaal *of Mariehamn, built in Norway in 1881, shows the normal masting and rigging of a barque in contrast with the rigging of* Dragon. *She was sketched by Henry Bush, R.O.I. at Yarmouth in 1914.* (Private Collection)

29. *Contemporary model of* HM *steam paddle frigate* Tiger. (National Maritime Museum)

30. The 'heavy turnery', Penn's engineering works at Greenwich. Here the compact engine of Arrogant *and the oscillating engines of* Tiger *were built and here a number of enterprising young naval officers worked to learn steam engineering.* (Private Collection)

31. Detail of the paddle sponsons and paddle box boats of the model of Tiger. (National Maritime Museum)

32. Tiger. Note the two brailing sails set from standing gaffs on the fore and main lower masts. These, together with the mizzen, comprise a three-masted schooner rig for steaming closer to windward when the squaresails would be taken in and the upper masts and spars perhaps sent down. (Illustrated London News)

33. Constantinople and the entrance to the Bosphorus in the nineteenth century. The typical Turkish local small sailing vessels are of types described in Sir Alan Moore's The Last Days of Mast and Sail *(1926).* (Private Collection)

34. Odessa in 1854. From Nolan's History of the Russian War.

35. 'At the arrival of Furious two guns were fired without ball, in consequence of which the vessel hoisted its national flag . . . Immediately a boat was sent out with a white flag in the direction of the mole . . .' Note the Odessa steps behind the mizzen of Furious. (Musée de la Marine, Paris)

36. *The great fortress of Kronstadt in 1854.* (Illustrated London News)

37.   The paddle frigate Leopard *(18 guns, 560 horse power) built at Deptford in 1850. This pencil sketch was made by Sir Oswald Brierly off the coast of Finland in 1854 when the vessel was a unit of the Baltic Fleet. Note, again, the awkward spacing of the masts. Of the fore and main Brierly has noted on the drawing 'masts not rake much and same height'.* (Private Collection)

38.   *The steam screw battleship,* HMS Duke of Wellington, *(131 guns, 780 horse power) laid down at Pembroke in 1849 and converted to steam in 1852, flagship of the Baltic Fleet in 1854, in dry dock in Devonport in March, 1854.* (Photograph by Linnaeus Tripe (1822–1902) in the Plymouth City Museum)

39. *The bombardment of Odessa. The vessels from left to right are* Sampson, Retribution, Mogador, Descartes, Vauban, Tiger *and* Terrible. (Musée de la Marine, Paris)

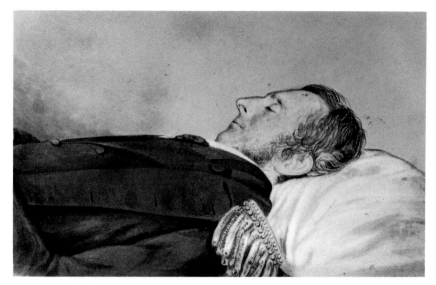

40. Captain Giffard's 'body was dressed in uniform, and laid for the inspection of visitors. The likeness was taken by photography, and kept by many as a souvenir' . . . This illustration is from one of these souvenirs, which appears to be a carefully drawn copy of a photograph. (Private Collection)

41. Ella Emelia, widow of Captain Giffard, who offered to share captivity with him, drawn in old age. (Private Collection)

as Lord Justice of Appeal in Chancery. One became a major in the 60th Rifles, another a captain in the East India Company's military service. One daughter, as has already been noted, married George Evans of *Lightning*, the other married a lawyer. The oldest son to survive infancy was named Jervis, after his godfather, Sir John Jervis, by whom his father had been posted captain. Sir John Jervis later became Lord St Vincent and the Giffards had a double connection with him, and thus with the Whig naval élite, their own and through the Carters. Mary Giffard wrote[4]

> All the naval people habitually went to Sir John Carter's house, including old Lord St. Vincent, who was a great friend of both my grandmothers, as well as of their husbands. 'He was like a good brother to me, when my husband was in Spain', I have heard my grandmother Evelegh say of him, and I think of it when people say that Lord St. Vincent was such a very hard man.

Jervis Giffard did not follow a naval career but took holy orders and was rector of a Surrey parish and fellow of his Oxford College. He was also, in those days when the medical profession was still ill-established, something of a doctor. Indeed, he studied medicine for a short time in Paris and gave his master's published work on the treatment of gunshot wounds to Florence Nightingale, daughter of another influential Portsmouth family, with which the Bonham-Carters were linked by marriage, before she left for the Crimea.

The Naval Academy at Portsmouth had by the beginning of the nineteenth century fallen on bad times. John Giffard's connection with St Vincent took him to the heart of the Whig naval establishment. In 1806–07 there was a short break in the long era of Tory rule during which, in what was contemporaneously called 'the Ministry of All the Talents', Charles James Fox and Thomas Grenville were in turn First Lords of the Admiralty, but the real power rested with St Vincent. As Commander in Chief of the Channel Fleet he had great influence over the Board of Admiralty and he took the opportunity to bring about the reform and enlargement of the Naval Academy, which he described in a letter to Grenville as a 'sink of vice and abomination'.[5] In these circumstances it is perhaps not surprising that Giffard, known to St Vincent as a steady man, broad-minded and of wide experience and associated with a prominent Whig family, should have been appointed lieutenant governor in March 1807 with the very responsible job of rebuilding the institution. In this, as has already been seen, he was highly successful in that under his command the reputation of the college became established and its influence increased out of proportion to the actual numbers it trained. John Giffard remained lieutenant governor of the

4 Mary Giffard, *op cit*.
5 Rodger, 'Officers, Gentlemen and Their Education'.

college until his advancement on the seniority list to rear admiral in 1819. In the long years of contraction of the navy and relative peace he was never employed in flag rank, although he sought appointment vigorously from time to time, but automatically advanced to vice admiral on half pay in 1830 and to full admiral in 1841.

Mary Giffard has a delightful description of his wife Susannah in old age.[6]

> She is said not to have been pretty in her young days, though her portrait as a child is charming and in her old age, I thought her beautiful with her soft white skin and delicate wintery bloom and the sweet calm benevolence of her expression. Unlike most of her contemporaries she eschewed 'fronts' and wore her own white hair and with the rich dark silk dresses she habitually wore and the folds of spotless white net coming up to her slender throat, she looked the very picture of what an old lady ought to be.

The third son of John and Susannah was Henry Wells Giffard born in June 1811, and as is clear from the foregoing he was born into the right family at the right time to have good prospects, should he join the navy. He did so through the Royal Naval College in 1824. At that time the sons of naval officers, up to thirty in number, were admitted free of the normal fees of £100 per year and £10 per month for broken periods.[7] He joined on 1 April 1824, and left on 1 March 1825. The lieutenant governor, then Captain J W Loring, reported to the Admiralty Secretariat[8]

From Royal Naval College Portsmouth 18th March 1825:

Sir,

I request you will inform the Lords Commissioners of the Admiralty that the Reverend Dr. Inman has this day reported to me that the following students have finished their education at this Establishment. Mr. Henry Wells Giffard in 378 days less than the days allowed.

Mr. William George Hayden   In 197 days less than
James Thomas Caldwell   the time allowed
Mr. Alexander Boyle   In 169 days less than
Thomas Stevens   the time allowed

Messrs. Giffard, Caldwell, Boyle and Stevens wish to go to sea in His Majesty's ship *Aurora*, and Mr. Hayden in His Majesty's ship *Glasgow*. I am, Sir, your obedient humble servant (Capt.) J. Wentworth Loring Lt. Governor.

J. W. Cooker

6 Mary Giffard, *op cit.*
7 PRO ADM 1/3516.
8 PRO ADM 1/3517.

Henry Giffard was awarded the 'First Medal', the much esteemed prize given to the volunteer who completed the course in the shortest time. His career as a midshipman lasted from 1825 to March 1831. He served in HMS *Aurora* for his first year. His midshipman's log[9] shows a passage to the Tagus via St Helena. *Aurora* then lay in the Tagus from 17 June 1825 to 10 March 1826 when she was ordered to prepare for sea to carry the news of the death of the King of Portugal to Britain. This must have been a somewhat frustrating experience for a keen and able young midshipman but his next ship, *Blonde* (Captain Lord G Byron), took him to Bermuda, and then on 6 December 1826 he joined *Asia*, a ship of the line of 84 guns (Captain the Honorable E Curzon), flag ship of Vice Admiral Sir Edward Codrington, who had been one of Nelson's captains, in command of *Orion*, 74 guns, at Trafalgar. This was the 'old navy' with a vengeance and in *Asia* Giffard had his baptism of fire in the last great battle ever to be fought between sailing warships. This was the battle of Navarino, still a matter of controversy among historians, fought in a bay on the south-west coast of the Peleponnese, the peninsula which comprises the southernmost part of mainland Greece. The battle was a major incident in the struggle by which the Greeks eventually gained their independence from the Turkish Empire, of which they had been part since the 1400s.

The course of this war of independence was made the more complex by the attitudes of the major European powers. The Austrian and Prussian authorities were hostile to the establishment of an independent Greece, the French and the British nominally indifferent, although the idea of Greek independence was attractive to many European romantics who volunteered by the hundred to fight with the Greek insurgent forces. Most famous of these, of course, was Lord Bryon, whose death in 1824 ensured fresh waves of support in Britain for the rebellious Greeks. Gradually, the European powers became more deeply involved, largely through prolonged diplomatic negotiations conducted in Istanbul between the ambassadors of Britain, France and Russia. At this period, with the slowness of communication and the fact that the ambassadors themselves were men of considerable political influence in their own countries – Stratford Canning, the British Ambassador, was a cousin of George Canning, at first Foreign Secretary and then, after April 1827, Prime Minister – ambassadors could and did put a stamp of their own views upon their actions. This was especially true of Stratford Canning, a man of strong personality and undisguised pro-Greek sympathies.

From early 1827 pressure was brought to bear on the Turkish authorities to encourage them to make peace with the Greek rebels. Meanwhile, both French and British naval commanders in the Mediterranean were men of inclination sympathetic to the Greeks. This was true of Sir Edward Codrington, who succeeded as Commander in Chief, Mediterranean, in

February 1827. He had, for instance, subscribed to the Greek Committee in London.[10]

In July 1827, a treaty was signed in London between the British, French and Russian governments under which mediation was to be offered to the Turks through the ambassadors in Istanbul, and the Greeks were to be informed by the naval commanders in chief of this offer. At the same time, an immediate armistice was to be demanded of both the Greeks and the Turks, 'previously to the opening up of any negotiation'.[11] Should the Turks fail to respond favourably to the initiative taken by the three powers, the instructions issued to the three naval commanders in the Levant of 12 July 1827 were specific.[12]

> The measures to be adopted . . . will exist in an immediate communica-
> tion with the Greeks, and the union of the squadrons of the High Powers
> for the purpose of preventing all Turkish and Egyptian succours men,
> arms, vessels and war-like stores, from arriving in Greece or in the
> islands of the Archipelago.
>
> These squadrons from that time shall treat the Greeks as friends,
> without, however, taking part in the hostilities betwixt the contending
> parties.

The instructions went on

> You are aware that you ought to be most particularly careful that the
> means which you may adopt against the Ottoman Navy do not
> degenerate into hostilities . . . Every hostile proceeding would be at
> variance with the pacific ground which they have chosen to take, and the
> display of forces which they have assembled is destined to cause that wish
> to be respected; but they must not be put into use unless the Turks persist
> in forcing the passages which they have intercepted.

The Russian contribution of naval forces comprised four ships of the line and four frigates of the Baltic Fleet from Kronstadt. These vessels amounted to a formidable armament and were in command of a very able officer, Count Heiden, a Russian citizen of Dutch extraction who had experience in the Royal Navy. This force reached the British fleet in mid-October and an order of battle was agreed for the combined fleets,[13] although the jealousy of the French made difficult the establishment of a good working relationship between the commanders. The Turks refusing

---

9 NMM Log/N/A/21.

10 Woodhouse, *The Battle of Navarino*, London 1965, p 34.

11 Bourchier, *Memoirs of The Life of Admiral Sir Edward Codrington*, London 1873, Vol 1, pp 508–510.

12 Bourchier, *op cit.*, pp 510–511.

the call to armistice, there followed a complex series of events which culminated in the combined fleets entering the Bay of Navarino where the Turkish fleet was lying. In Admiral Codrington's own words[14]

> I felt myself justified in concluding that the imposing spectacle of the whole Allied Squadrons (that force which the government had deemed ample for the purpose) anchored in the bay of Navarin, where we could be eye witnesses of his proceedings and ready to punish any infraction of his agreement, would awe Ibrahim at once into submission, and thus obtain without bloodshed the *objects of the Treaty*.

After further objections from the French admiral had been overcome the combined fleets entered Navarino, in total ten ships of the line, ten frigates, four brigs and three cutters. Anchored in a defensive formation within were three ships of the line, seventeen frigates, thirty corvettes, twenty-eight brigs, five schooners, and six brig-rigged fire ships.[15] One of the boats of the British ship *Portsmouth* was fired on with small arms, which naturally produced a response which very rapidly developed into a general conflict. This continued for four hours, and the Turkish and Egyptian fleets were effectively destroyed, those vessels which were not damaged beyond repair being blown up by their own crews. A number of British ships were severely damaged, including *Asia* herself. The British force lost seventy-five killed and 197 wounded, but not a single allied ship was lost in a battle in which the general melée which followed the first shots constituted less a planned action than a series of conflicts between individual ships.

Young Henry Giffard's account of the battle in his midshipman's log[16] is brief and somewhat stacatto but tends to confirm other accounts of this controversial battle.

18 Oct. Russian Admiral came on board
19 English, French & Russian Squadrons in company. Standing in for Navarino
20 6.30am made all sail making for Navarin. PM moderate breeze and fine standing in for the entrance of Navarin. 1.30 beat to quarters
WIND come on board a Turkish boat observed the Fort hoist Turkish
SSE colours and fire a blank gun. 2.20 let go the S.B. [stb'd bower] under all sail about one cable's length on the *Captain Bey's* larb'd bow ran out to 60 fathoms let go the B.B. [best bower] and ran to

13 Bourchier, *op cit*, Vol 2, p 63.
14 Bourchier, *op cit*, Vol 2, pp 64–65.
15 Bourchier, *op cit*, Vol 2, p 71.
16 NMM Log/N/A/23.

30 fathoms clewed up & furled sails. *Genoa* anchored ahead of line of battleship next to *Capt. Bey* & the *Albion* passing the *Genoa* closed to the next ship in succession. The *Syrene* between the first ships of the Turkish line the Russian Admiral bore down to his station at the bottom of the harbour. 2.30 observed the *Dartmouth* which ship anchored close to a fire vessel sent a boat to board her who fired on the boat which was returned by the *Dartmouth* with musquetry. Sent a boat with a flag of truce to *Moharem Bey*. On going away Mr. Mitchell the pilot was shot in the breast by a man on board the frigate while her Capt. was speaking to Lieut. Dilke on the gangway. 2.40 observed the *Brulot* on fire about this time a shot was fired at the *Syrene* which she returned with a broadside. The action now became general having hove in on the larb'd spring we opened our starb'd broadside on *Capt. Bey* and some few other guns on a frigate. 3.15 having completely silenced *Capt. Bey* hove in on the spring and opened our broadside on *Moharem Bey*, a frigate, and some other vessels which had been raking us astern. 4.40 the mizzen mast went by the board and all the rigging was cut to pieces by the raking fire to which we were exposed. 5.20 having silenced every vessel our guns would reach ceased firing entirely run a hawser to the *Genoa* to be in readiness to haul clear of a frigate which was on fire under our bows. At 6 she blew up with about 200 of her crew with a tremendous explosion. Found the number killed to be Mr. Smith (the master) Cap. Bell of the Marines, Mr. Lewis boatswain & 16 men and marines and 53 wounded. A Russian frigate firing occasionally at a Fort.

11.30 observed 3 frigates and several smaller vessels blow up and several on shore. Mid't Moderate breeze and fine the boats rowing guard.

The action led to a good deal of criticism of Admiral Codrington for destroying a Turkish fleet which might conceivably one day have been a useful force against the Russians. It was followed by episodes of seamanship of the type referred to in Chapter 3 (on page 67). *Asia* was given jury rig by her own hands, using the main topmast as a mizzen, and sailed to Malta, where she was given a more complete jury rig under which she sailed to Portsmouth. She spent eleven weeks completely refitting and then returned to the Levant via Malta, anchoring at Corfu on 17 June 1828. Henry Giffard's log naturally takes for granted all these manifestations of the highest skills of seamanship of a type now completely lost.

Giffard was detached from *Asia* to *Pelican*, Commander W A B Hamilton, later to be Second Secretary (in modern terms effectively the Permanent Under-Secretary) of the Admiralty during the War with Russia, which was to begin in 1854. He returned to Navarino where he contracted 'bad marsh fever', the contemporary term for malaria, and 'my life was despaired of'.[17] He was first sent to Malta.

> The surgeons determining to send me home for a change of air, I rejoined *Asia* on 1st March at Malta, and on the 25th . . . *Dryad* homeward bound . . . I joined *Victory* at Portsmouth in June, 1829 and was belonging to her until the 17th Oct: I was the greater part of the time on leave recruiting my health and only did a few days duty on board. I was appointed on the above date to the *Winchester* (Captain C.J. Austen,) Flag of Vice Admiral Griffith Colpoys at Chatham. On my appointment to the *Winchester* I passed my examination at the Royal Naval College for Navigation obtaining full numbers and was complimented by Sir Robert Stopford on giving me my certificate.

Giffard's experience on *Winchester* had once again involved completely remasting and rerigging the vessel at Chatham in October – December 1829, and then in January completing the running rigging and bending the sails while lying at anchor in Gillingham Reach. But with *Winchester* came his first contact with the new world in which his future was to lie. The vessel was towed to Gillingham Reach by the steamer *Comet* which a fortnight later brought to her '50 cases of specie containing £500 each'. Moreover, *Comet* escorted *Winchester* to sea, staying with her during 20–22 January 1830, and leaving her only when she was anchored in the Nab Channel from which she sailed, the wind serving, for Port Royal, Jamaica, via Spithead, where the admiral embarked on 22 January, and immediately 'passed an East Indiaman towed by two steamers. Wind N running S. AM shorten sail and come to in Downs 4.40pm with best bower in 9 fathoms'.[18]

After a brief spell on loan to HMS *Hyacinth* 'for the purposes of keeping watch',[19]

> I passed my examination for seamanship before Captain Austen[20] and Commanders Jackson and Cavendish and returned to the *Winchester*.
> On the 4th October (1830) I received an acting order as Lieutenant of the *Shannon*, and took my passage to Jamaica in the *Victor* to join her. I was so young-looking the tailor at Halifax [Nova Scotia which *Winchester* was visiting] made enquiries to find out if I was not doing him, before he made my clothes.

---

17 NMM JOD 30, p 5.
18 NMM Log N/W/7, pp 4–5.
19 NMM JOD 30, p 6.
20 Captain Charles Austen (1779–1853), Flag Captain of *Winchester*, was a brother of Jane Austen.

Superficially, the appointment to *Winchester*, the rapid taking of examina-
tions and the promotion which followed seem to the eye of the end of the
twentieth century to be the result of a normal procedure of vacancies,
seniority, qualification, and more or less automatic promotion. In the 1820s,
in the closed, heavily politicised world of the navy, this was very far from
the case, even at the apparently humble level of the first commission as
lieutenant. On 22 April 1827 Admiral Giffard had written to Sir Francis
Baring, then, with John Bonham-Carter, one of Portsmouth's two Members
of Parliament.

> Petersfield,
> April 22nd, 1827

> Dear Baring,
> You are a most worthy colleague and I thank you for all your
> communications. I can foresee already that some of the new appoint-
> ments will expose you to certain applications for your good Offices, and
> if Denison be one of the Lords of the Admiralty, I have no doubt you will
> shortly hear something about a good word for one of my naval relations.
> I don't mean from the quarter where I now am.[21]

Winchester, as has already been noted, was the flagship of Vice Admiral
Griffith Colpoys. During the great naval mutiny at Spithead in 1797, Sir
John Carter had used his considerable influence in Portsmouth to negotiate
an arrangement by which the mutineers were allowed to pass through
Portsmouth in procession, Sir John accompanying them, in order to bury
three of their comrades who had been killed on board HMS *London*, flagship
of Admiral Colpoys, father of the man whose flag was carried by
Winchester, in Kingston churchyard. The whole incident passed off
peaceably and a violent confrontation was avoided. An interesting sequence
of events followed. In the words of an early nineteenth century account[22]

> When the sailors returned and were sent off to their respective ships, two
> or three of the managing delegates came to Sir John to inform him that
> the men were all gone on board, and to thank him for his 'great goodness
> to them'.
>   Sir John seized the opportunity of enquiring after their Admiral, as
> these delegates belonged to the *London*: 'do you know him Your
> Honour?'. 'Yes, I have the greatest respect for him and hope you will not
> do him any harm'. 'No, by G-d Your Honour, he shall not be hurt!' It
> was, at that time, imagined that Admiral Colpoys would be hung from
> the yardarm and he had prepared for this event, by arranging his affairs,

---

21 The *Winchester* Papers, F12.
22 In the monthly magazine *Athenaeum*, July 1808.

and making his will . . . The next morning however, the Admiral was privately, unexpectedly and safely brought on shore . . . the delegates brought him to Sir John Carter and delivered him to his care; they then desired to have a receipt for him, as a proof they had safely delivered him into the hands of the civil power; and which receipt he gave.

Sir John Carter, who had saved the life of Vice Admiral Griffith Colpoys's father, was of course Henry Giffard's maternal grandfather. Henry Giffard's uncle, John Bonham-Carter, was Perpetual Whig Member of Parliament for Portsmouth and, although the Tories still held the reins of government, the Whigs were on the verge of assuming power. It is perhaps not surprising that Henry Giffard served only five years as a midshipman, less than the minimum statutory period of six years, and without any service in the intermediate rank of mate (sub-lieutenant after 1861). How good his interest was is best perhaps illustrated by a few words of quotation from professor Michael Lewis.[23]

A well backed youngster might reach his Lieutenancy in well under six years. But he was an exception. After 1815 a midshipman was very lucky if he emerged to the quarterdeck in six years. The average time lag for this step was a good deal more than this: more like twelve years.

In *Shannon*, Henry Giffard continued on the West Indies station, being confirmed in rank as lieutenant on 4 March 1831. Then, in the summer, in his own words[24]

as the *Shannon* was going home [and would be paid off, leaving him as a very new lieutenant without appointment] the Admiral gave me an appointment to the *Hyacinth*, 11th July, 1831 . . . I went across to Panama with the Captain and some others and on my return was laid up by the yellow fever which very nearly finished me, on my return to Jamaica I was some time in the hospital.

Hyacinth returned to Portsmouth in November 1832, carrying three-quarters of a million dollars in specie, and was paid off. In Giffard's own words again[25]

I was five months before I could obtain employment, during part of the time I went with Jervis [his elder brother, in holy orders] to Dittisham, a beautiful village on the Dart . . . At length on 14 May, (1833) after having made great interest I was appointed to a ship, the *Volage* (28 guns, Captain Byam Martin) fitting out at Portsmouth.

23 Lewis, *Transition*, p 156. See also Austen, *Mansfield Park*, esp. Chap. 31.
24 NMM JOD 30, p 6.
25 NMM JOD 30.

Giffard obtained this appointment at a time when seventy-five per cent of lieutenants in the Royal Navy were unemployed, although of course many of them were over age for further service.[26]

In *Volage*, he served first as second and then as first lieutenant for four years and two months, his longest uninterrupted period of service in a single vessel to that date. After service in the Mediterranean, Giffard was transferred back to *Hyacinth* in September 1837 as first lieutenant. On 9 May 1838, when sailing from Trincomalee towards Penang, the vessel was struck by lightning. She had no lightning conductor and so lost her main topgallant mast and topmast. They anchored to effect repairs – another example of the skills and also the materials available as a matter of routine on board a naval vessel of the period – and arrived, after a difficult passage involving much anchor work, at Singapore on 29 May.[27]

As has already been noted, Henry Giffard's maternal uncle John Bonham-Carter, Member of Parliament for Portsmouth since 1816 and a considerable force behind the scenes in the Whig government, died of the effects of diabetes in February 1838. There followed what is perhaps the most blatant example of political interest at work which has yet been noted in the case of an officer not of the nobility. It was probably a belated response to pressure exerted by John Bonham-Carter on the Admiralty through Sir Charles Wood, First Secretary to the Admiralty and very much the right-hand man of Lord Minto, the First Lord. John Bonham-Carter was on very familiar terms with Sir Charles Wood and was himself probably under continuous pressure from Admiral Giffard, his brother-in-law. Only a few days after John Bonham-Carter's death the First Lord of Admiralty, Lord Minto, wrote to the Prime Minister, Lord Melbourne.[28]

Private   Admiralty
                                                    21.2.38

My Dear Melbourne,

I have long been watching for some opportunity to promote Lieutenant Giffard, and I think it may now fairly be done as a just compliment to poor Carter's memory. The commission shall therefore be made out tomorrow and I will announce it to Admiral Giffard by this evening's post.

Yours Ever,
Minto.

---

26 Lewis, *Transition*, p 87.
27 NMM JOD 30, p 9 and PRO Log N/H/3, Lieutenant H W G Pb.
28 PRO Melbourne MS 859 9–13, R Archive.

Thus, Henry Giffard became a commander (to be in charge of a small vessel or chief executive officer of a large) after only six years and eleven months' service as a lieutenant. Thereby he fell into a trap. For at this period there were many more commanders than posts for them. Giffard therefore found himself on arrival at Spithead as a passenger in *Wolf* a year later, on 26 February 1839, without employment. But with the sort of interest demonstrated by the circumstances of his promotion, he was not in much danger of being long ashore. In his own words[29]

> Nothing in particular occurred during my stay at home and on 2nd May I got an appointment to the *Cruizer* in the East Indies.

As Lord Minto no doubt foresaw, no officer of commander's rank could have hoped for a better, more fortunately timed posting than that to the brig *Cruizer*, 18 guns, lying in Singapore in September 1839.

29 NMM JOD 30, p 8.

6

The Steamers' War

The war between Britain and China of 1840–42 was the first conflict in history in which the mobility and power of the steamer played a large part in determining the outcome. The war also appears to have been the theatre for the playing out of a piece of entrepreneurial enterprise towards the marketing of the iron steamer, which comprised salesmanship dramatic even by the standards of that most enterprising period in the history of industrial development.

The steamers concerned were not vessels of the Royal Navy. The only way a naval paddle frigate or sloop could reach Indian, let alone Chinese, waters was by the long route round the Cape of Good Hope. As yet the steamers which had done this had been on a one way passage to India or Australia for delivery for subsequent local use and they had made much of the passage under sail. To send a squadron of paddlers to China from Britain would have been a vastly expensive business, even if it had been at all practical, and factors of engine maintenance, bunkering and so forth were decisively against any such action. It was to be several years yet before the first steam-assisted vessel to circumnavigate the globe, the paddle sloop *Driver*, set out on a commission which was to last five years and during which much of her time was spent under sail. The steamers which were to make such a mark in the war were, therefore, the locally available vessels of the Indian Navy and the Bengal Marine.

Considering the great advantages steam conferred in Indian waters it is not surprising that its development seems to have been rapid. India at this period was governed by the East India Company with the aid of its own very large army and two maritime forces, one on each coast of the sub-continent, the Bengal Marine, based in Calcutta, and the Bombay Marine. In May 1830, the Bombay Marine acquired the title of The Indian Navy, by order of the Court of Directors of the East India Company,[1] and although the principal effect of this development may have been to enhance the morale of the service, the change of title was also followed by its speedy conversion into a steam-driven force. The great incentive to development was the

1 Low, *History of the Indian Navy, (1613–1863)*, London 1877, 2 vols, Vol 1, p 532.

necessity of increasing the speed of communication between London and Bombay and Calcutta. The development of steam propulsion meant that the route via the Mediterranean, an overland stage to Suez, and through the Red Sea, could be used. The Red Sea could not be navigated with any speed or regularity by sailing vessels while the north-east monsoon precluded their use between Bombay and Aden for several months each year. The pioneer steam vessel on the east side of the land barrier was *Hugh Lindsay,* built in Bombay, which made her first passage to Suez in 1829.

In the 1830s, with the development of marine steam engines powerful enough to deal with the north-east monsoon, the service developed rapidly. The paddle sloop *Atalanta* of 617 tons, 210 horse power, 4 guns, was built in London in 1836 for the Bombay Marine or Indian Navy, as it was now called. She was followed almost immediately by the Glasgow-built *Berenice,* of 756 tons, 220 horse power, 4 guns. Each of the vessels made well-recorded pioneering voyages to the east.[2] They were employed in the mails and passage service to Suez from Bombay and with *Hugh Lindsay* settled down to a regular service that continued unbroken from 1837. They were soon followed by *Semiramis,* 750 tons, 300 horse power.

The employment of Indian naval vessels on the essential duties of the Suez Packet Service was the subject of much contemporary controversy. It was argued that the efficiency of the Indian Navy as a fighting force, which might be needed at any time should hostilities break out on either the east or west side of the sub-continent, was much reduced by the concentration of the greater part of its tonnage and personnel on essentially civilian work. Be that as it may, by 1839 the Indian Navy had become essentially a small steam navy, some of the vessels of which were employed purely as fighting vessels, some as armed packets, and some on survey work of the great rivers of Bengal and in the Middle East. Engineers were recruited in Britain and a building and maintenance yard for steam vessels and their machinery was established at Bombay.

Commander Henry Giffard used this route when he travelled to Singapore to take command of *Cruizer* in 1839, and his account of his journey is an illustration of the state of development of communications with the Far East which came with the application of the paddle steamer.[3] Giffard began his journey at Falmouth on 10 June by taking passage in the East India Company's steam vessel *Royal Tar*, an iron paddle steamer of 141 tons which had been built at Glasgow in 1837. She arrived in Gibraltar on 17 June. This appears to have been his first long passage under steam. At Gibraltar he trans-shipped into HMS *Acheron* on 19 June (it looks as if she was waiting for service passengers from *Royal Tar*) and sailed for Alexandria via Malta, where he again trans-shipped into a steamer arriving

---

2 See Low, *op cit*, Vol 2, pp 50–52.
3 The account appears in NMM Log N/H/3, Lieutenant H W Giffard.

in Alexandria on 2 July in the early morning and recording himself 'very well satisfied with the feeding, etc. on board'. On the evening of the same day he embarked in a boat to travel by the 48 miles of the Mahmoudieh Canal to Atfeh on the Nile. These large boats were towed by horses[4] and the journey took sixteen hours, after which he trans-shipped again into a Nile vessel. This was before a river paddle steamer service was inaugurated in 1842 and Giffard's onward journey to Cairo by river boat took him from 10 am on Wednesday 3 July 1839 to 7.30 pm on Friday 5 July. He described the passage as a 'pretty prosperous voyage'.

He left Cairo for Suez at 5.30 pm on 6 July in 'a kind of covered wagon on springs, two horses', the baggage following on camels. This was a journey of 70 miles across the open desert at the hottest time of the year, deliberately scheduled to be made overnight. He arrived at Suez at 12.30 pm the following day, Sunday 7 July, and on the Monday embarked in the Indian Navy's paddle steamer *Atalanta* (the camels with the baggage having arrived just in time) for a passage to Aden down the Red Sea which took seven days to 15 July. One of the present authors can say from personal experience that the heat in the Red Sea as felt in a 7 knot paddle steamer in July must have been appalling but Giffard makes no mention of hardship or discomfort of any kind in his log.

At Aden, Giffard shifted next day to the East India Company's brig *Taptee*, which he describes as 'a horrid little gun brig of 160 tons', and which took ten days to sail to Bombay, arriving on 27 July. On 28 July – Giffard's journey seems almost incredibly fortunate in its timing since no part beyond Gibraltar can have been arranged beforehand – he took passage in the former East India Company ship, now privately owned and an opium carrier, *Thomas Coutts*, at 1334 tons a very large vessel by the standards of the times. She was also a very fast ship. In 1826 she had made the shortest round voyage to China ever known. The year before Giffard sailed in her she had been involved in a blockade running exploit into Canton which had been highly embarrassing for the local British administration at a time of difficult relations with the Chinese, but this did not inhibit Giffard from using her as the quickest means of reaching his new command.

Thomas Coutts took nearly four weeks to sail to Singapore, arriving there on 23 August. Here Giffard found that *Cruizer* was at sea. He had taken seventy-five days to reach Singapore from Falmouth. Because of the very fortunate timing this had been an unusually fast journey, but it was to be eighty-nine days before his commission was read on board, and he took over command of *Cruizer* from Captain King on 4 September, recording himself as 'very happy to be in command'.[5]

After Henry Giffard has assumed command on 4 September 1839,

4 Maber, *North Star to Southern Cross*, Prescot 1967, p 1.
5 NMM JOD 38.

Cruizer was employed on routine duties round the coasts of what is now Malaysia until mid April the following year. War with China now being imminent she was refitted at Singapore between mid April and the end of May. She then took part in the assembly of the British fleet at Singapore.

The origins of the war, like those of most wars, were complex, but the main strands which led to the opening of hostilities can be simplified. The principal causes of the conflict were economic. China, like Japan, at the time, did not recognise the rest of the world as comprised of powerful independent states with their own cultures. With one-third of the world's population – seven times that of Russia, twenty-seven times that of the United States – she was potentially an enormous market for an industrialising Britain. But China had no diplomatic relations with other countries, although she had a long history of foreign trade of various kinds. At the time the war began her officially strictly controlled foreign trade was conducted, as far as Europeans were concerned, only through Canton under terms and conditions decided by the Chinese authorities. South-east Asian vessels had a wider range of ports open to them and Chinese vessels could go where they wished.[6]

The conflict has been described as 'Palmerston's War'.[7] Lord Palmerston was then Foreign Secretary of the Whig government, and it has been asserted that his chief aim was to open up China to British commerce. At the height of the war he wrote to Lord Auckland, then his appointee as Governor General of India.[8]

> Will the navigation of the Indus turn out to be as great a help as was expected for our commerce? If it does, and if we succeed in our China expedition, Abyssinia, Arabia, the countries of the Indus and the new markets of China, will at no distant period give a most important extension to the range of our foreign commerce.

At this period British commerce with China was principally involved with tea. Although in those years before the development of the Indian tea industry tea was still an expensive commodity, the demand for it in Britain was steadily growing. In 1757 the central administration of China at Peking had designated Canton, the most southerly of Chinese cities, as the sole port in the country open to European traders. Since 1815 Britain had had a permanent factory, or trading enclosure, in Canton. Canton is about 40 miles up the estuary of the Canton river from the open sea, and the East

---

6 Din-tsun Chang, 'The Evolution of Chinese Thought on Maritime Foreign Trade from the Sixteenth to the Eighteenth Century', *International Journal of Maritime History*, Vol 1, 1989, p 57.

7 Ridley, *Lord Palmerston*, London 1970, p 258.

8 Palmerston to Auckland, 22 January 1841, quoted in Ridley, *op cit*, p 260.

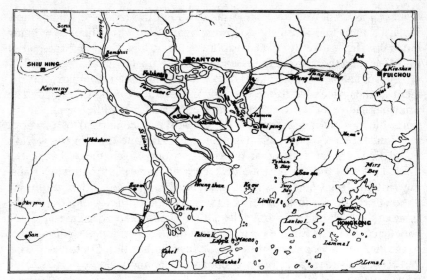

Map of the Canton – Hong Kong area.

Indiamen from Britain could relatively easily reach Whampoa, 12 miles downstream from the town. As Professor Gerald Graham wrote,[9]

> . . . year upon year, lighters from the newly arrived Indiamen at Whampoa continued to unload their cargoes at Canton – woollens, lead, Cornish tin, raw cotton from Bombay (later on calicoes), and the usual array of clocks and musical boxes . . . Generally in April the restless Company Ships weighed anchor . . . Most of them carried raw silk and nankeens, porcelain ware, lacquered cabinets, rhubarb root, and above all else tea. By the late 1820s, Britain was drinking some 30 million pounds of tea a year.

This tea had to be paid for and the trade was not balanced by the value of the outward cargo. This was not a modern credit economy in which a trading deficit could be met by the ready movement of funds from an area in trading surplus, nor could a pattern of debt be built up as part of a complex of financial operations. This was still a cash economy. The supercargoes of the East India Company's ships had to buy the cargoes for export with local currency, or some internationally recognised medium of exchange. This meant gold bullion, which already in the early nineteenth century was moving in relatively large sums each year from Europe to China.

The development by the Chinese of a taste for opium in the early nineteenth century was to solve the balance of payments problem and it led

9 Graham, *The China Station*, Oxford 1978, pp 5–6.

to a situation very familiar in the late twentieth century. The drug barons, Chinese, British and American, took over and because their trade was unlawful in the Chinese state, corrupted parts of the administration and became at times stronger than that administration itself. The Indian sub-continent produced the opium, as it still does today. The Chinese administration placed a ban on imports. Because it was essential to retain its locally privileged trading position the ships of the East India Company itself, and those more numerous vessels on charter to the company, did not themselves carry the drug as part of their official cargoes, but the company was inevitably closely linked with private traders who did carry the drug. The production of opium in India was not merely legal, it increasingly provided, through the duty payable upon it, a substantial part of the revenues of the government of India, increasing, according to Professor Graham,[10] to comprise nearly one-seventh of the government's total income. The smuggling of opium into China became a vast industry in which the Indian and, at one remove, the British governments had a double vested interest.

This situation contained the seeds of conflict between Britain and China. Alone it would not necessarily have led to official hostilities. But it was complicated by two further factors. The first involved the structure of the Chinese administration. The contact of the foreign merchants with that vast and complex organisation was limited by the Chinese government to a group of Chinese merchants in Canton, known to the British as the Hong Merchants, who alone could conduct commercial and, indeed, any other kind of relations with foreigners. There was no machinery for diplomatic representation, either locally in Canton or nationally in Peking, and the chances of getting redress for, or even of discussing, the numerous small frictions which inevitably arose in the trading relationship were slight, the process of attempting to do so very prolonged. The British lived in their close claustrophobic factory area on the bank of the Canton river completely cut off from the teeming life of the city. That life was incomprehensible to them. Chinese culture, the structured society, its values and ideas, were in almost every way alien and, inevitably, regarded with a contempt as great as the Chinese had for Western culture. There was no way of breaking down the barrier, even had there been the will on either side to do so.

On the Chinese side the foreigners were regarded, in graded categories, as barbarians from uncivilised and upstart societies, to be treated as such. Until the eighteenth century there had been some reason for this attitude. What the Chinese authorities did not take account of, because of their own side in the mutual isolation, was the effects of technology, and it was to take twenty years and two wars to bring the message home.

10 Graham, *op cit*, p 6.

As is so often the case, economic factors finally determined the course of events. The trade with China, both licit and illicit, was highly profitable to the foreign merchants. It was also profitable to different elements in Chinese society, but the Chinese, especially the local authorities in Canton and the provincial authorities, were in control and the foreign merchants had to operate on their terms. For many years it was worth adopting a realistic and pragmatic approach, tolerating the resultant complex of corruption and appeasement, sometimes of humiliation, to keep the profitable business going, even to the extent that British warships did not enter Chinese waters for fear of giving provocation which might lead to the disruption of trade. As long as the East India Company had the monopoly of the trade, long established channels of communication, official and unofficial, could be used to oil the wheels of commerce. The company was prepared to put up with the assertion of supremacy over all mankind made by the Peking authorities in the interest of the maintenance of lucrative business. The Chinese placed East India Company officials in a higher category of Western foreigner than the free traders who openly moved in when the company's monopoly of the Chinese trade was ended in 1833. The ending of the monopoly meant the break up of a reasonably stable situation. In the resultant tension there were the seeds of an armed conflict which in the event was, as Professor Rawlinson has pointed out,[11]

not really . . . an 'opium war'; it was a clash between cultures.

Britain with her rapidly expanding economy, sought to destroy the age old tribute system, by which China had incorporated into the trading process a strong element of ritual designed to demonstrate barbarian veneration of the Son of Heaven – the Emperor of China.[12]

Since it was obvious that any attempt to influence relations between Britain and China by force could only be made by sea it might be imagined that the Chinese administration would have made every effort to provide itself with ships and weapons and trained men to oppose an attack by a Western navy. But the cultural and linguistic barriers worked both ways, and the Chinese were as ignorant of developments in the West as the West was of China. Rawlinson quotes from a Chinese source the Governor General of Nanking who in 1842, when he saw a paddle steamer's engine room, was finally convinced that the vessel was not driven by oxen.[13]

China's seaborne armed forces comprised sailing vessels of war, built in the Chinese tradition and generally referred to by English speaking people as 'junks' – as they will be here, for convenience of reference, and without

11 Rawlinson, *China's Struggle for Naval Development, 1839–95*, Harvard 1967, p 3.
12 Rawlinson, *op cit*, p 12.
13 Rawlinson, *op cit*, p 23.

respect, in this context, for their numerous varieties. These vessels comprised part of what was intended to be a kind of provincial constabulary, rather than a navy in the Western sense. They were meant to be used against Chinese pirates – piracy was endemic on the coast – not against European warships, of the powers of which the Chinese had little or no experience. Much less were they intended to be used against steamers, the full possibilities of which in river warfare were still not fully appreciated, even by the Royal Navy. Moreover, the organisation of the Chinese waterborne forces was not one designed for all out war. It was extremely elaborate, with broken chains of command, which did not encourage efficiency, even had the weapons available been remotely adequate for the mid-nineteenth century situation. There was no strategic tradition, and no experience of fighting on deep water. Training was inadequate and the navigation methods of the officers often rudimentary, depending largely on local knowledge of the coastline. There had been a sad decline since the years between 1405 and 1433 when in a series of seven government-organised voyages large Chinese fleets had explored the Indies and even reached the coasts of East Africa. The Chinese were dependent virtually solely on their land fortifications for their defence against waterborne attack.

The occasion for the outbreak of hostilities followed a determined effort by the Chinese central administration to end the opium trade because of its socially destructive effects. The Emperor himself appointed Lin Tse-hsii, one of his ablest and most formidable officials, to be the Imperial Commissioner with instructions to suppress the business of the smugglers. Lin effectively besieged the Canton factory and made prisoners of its inhabitants. He then confiscated 20,000 chests of opium, estimated to be worth some £5,000,000, and had it destroyed. All British subjects left Canton for the Portuguese trading port of Macao on the coast. The total value of the opium in ships lying in the river awaiting smuggling in 1990s currency was perhaps £500 million.

Commander Giffard later recorded his own views on the origins of the war.[14]

There had been various misunderstandings between us and the Chinese for a length of time past, and now this expedition is bound to settle differences by an appeal to Force . . . Our trade with the Chinese has never been on a very respectable and firm footing, when the company had the monopoly they had ways and means of settling disputes, but since the trade has been thrown open, there has been nothing but squabbles. Various and conflicting were the opinions at our little settlement of Singapore about the merits of High Commissioner Lin (the

14 NMM JOD 38.

Chinaman) and High Commissioner Elliot (the Englishman). There had been many and numerous courses to give us dissatisfaction, quite sufficient for the appeal to arms, but the present case, though they have no right to imprison our Authorities and merchants and for which we must and aught to have satisfaction, yet most unfortunately it was brought on by the Opium trade; and this has rather given the appeareance that although having just cause our Government would not stir until they were forced by such a large revenue being in danger that it was not justice, so much as money they were seeking.

This is a fair statement of contemporary opinion. Whatever followed later in the century, there was in the late 1830s little or no opposition to the opium trade on moral grounds. The use of opium, which was readily available at apothecaries' shops, insofar as it was thought of at all was regarded much in the way the use of tranquillisers, so widely used and liberally prescribed by the medical profession, is regarded in Britain today. For instance, the *Quarterly Review* was very doubtful whether 'the evils of opium were worse than those of gin and whisky'.[15] There was some feeling in Britain against waging an expensive war for purely economic reasons, but much of the expense in fact fell on the government of India. The British government was determined to obtain compensation for the opium destroyed in order not to have to meet the merchants' bills itself, which, particularly, would have been extremely difficult. Moreover, it was not difficult to persuade public opinion that, having been affronted by the Chinese, the nation's honour was at stake. In Parliament the opposition concentrated on allegations of government incompetence rather than on the iniquities of the opium trade.

After somewhat prolonged preliminary moves, by no means hastened by the difficulty of communication between the Indian authorities in Calcutta, the commander in chief of the China station (who was based at Trincomalee in Ceylon, now Sri Lanka) and the British government in London (which had the final say if major action against China was contemplated), Lord Palmerston informed Captain Elliot, Royal Navy, the chief superintendent and plenipotentiary at Canton who had a strong interest (he was the son of Palmerston's closest friend of his university days) that a British naval force with army support would be sent to arrive in the spring in 1840.

It is an indication of Chinese attitudes that when he learned that a British fleet had sailed to blockade Canton, Commissioner Lin Tse-hsii did not wish to believe that such an impertinence could be perpetrated.[16] The British

15 Hibbert, *The Dragon Wakes*, London 1984, p 135.
16 Rawlinson, *op cit*, p 25.

fleet which fought this war comprised a somewhat motley collection of British sailing warships, steamships of the Indian Navy and of the Bengal Marine, chartered civilian transports, many Indian owned, and at least one vessel which appears to have been a privately promoted mercenary without status as a ship of war, the iron paddle steamer *Nemesis*. In their wake came the inevitable camp followers, and in this case opium laden vessels as well, hoping that the disturbed situation would give enhanced opportunities for illicit trade.

The principal British naval vessels initially engaged were *Wellesley*, 74 guns, bearing the broad pendant of Commodore Sir J J G Bremer, the 16 gun brig *Cruizer*, Commander H W Giffard and the 10 gun *Algerine*, Commander T H Mason, which vessels escorted the convoy comprising the principal part of the transports, which themselves carried some 4000 soldiers and their equipment. These vessels arrived off the Canton river from Singapore in the second part of June 1840. In the following weeks they were joined by *Melville*, 74 guns, bearing the flag of the commander in chief, Rear Admiral the Hon George Elliot, *Blenheim*, 74 guns, *Druid*, and *Blonde*, 44s, *Conway*, *Volage* and *Alligator*, 28s, *Modest*, *Pilardes*, *Nimrod*, *Larne* and *Hyacinth*, 20s, and *Columbine*, variously given as 16 and 18 guns.

Besides these vessels there was a most interesting fleet of an entirely different kind. *The Bombay Times* summed up the strength of the Indian Navy in the beginning of the 1840s.[17] It comprised fifteen sailing vessels of from 70 to 400 tons, carrying between them 128 guns, seven paddle frigates and sloops of from 700 to 900 tons, and two new steamers of 900 tons plus which were almost ready for service. Most significantly perhaps for the future history of the steamship, there were already seven iron built armed river steamers on the Indus and four on the Euphrates of from 40 to 70 horse power each. In fact *The Bombay Times* does not seem to have taken account of older vessels still in service and still available to the Indian Navy on charter, and the potential steam strength of the service for employment in the China War appears to have been even greater than this list suggests. In addition there were a number of steam vessels of the Indian government's Bengal Marine.

There was therefore a squadron of armed paddle steamers, manned by officers and men familiar with Eastern conditions and subject to the disciplines of an established naval service. This force was under the control of the government of India, available to fight in a war which was being conducted from Indian bases.

These steamers of the Indian Navy and the Bengal Marine were diverted from their normal duties and, for the first time in history, a substantial squadron of armed paddlers was brought into action to fight as one of the principal elements in a fleet. This was to be a war in which the disadvantages

17 Quoted in Low, *op cit*, Vol 2, p 137.

of the paddle steamer – her vulnerability, her inability to mount a broadside of guns, her poor qualities as a sailing vessel and her strictly limited range under steam – were of little importance, and her advantages, above all mobility against adverse currents and winds, manoeuvrability and speed, were to be demonstrated. Moreover, paddle steamers generally were of shallower draught than sailing vessels of comparable fighting potential and this was to prove invaluable on the rivers. This advantage applied especially to the iron vessels employed, which, because of the relative lightness of the material of which they were constructed, carried an even smaller draught than their wooden counterparts with the same fighting capacity.

For this was to be a river war. It was a war fought largely in restricted channels with strongly flowing adverse currents, a war of attacks on land forts, requiring the exact placing of attacking vessels under fire and in adverse conditions, and a war against an enemy whose organisation of armaments was not strong enough to take advantage of the paddle steamer's fatal vulnerability.

The paddle steamers of the Indian Navy, those chartered for service in that navy, and the steam vessels of the Bengal Marine proved to be a vitally important factor in the more or less successful completion of the campaign. Altogether there were at least eighteen of them engaged in hostilities with the Chinese from time to time during the two years of the war. Such was to be the demonstration of the steamers' power that the Duke of Wellington was moved to write to the Governor General of India, Lord Ellenborough, at the end of 1841, that the armed steamer was indispensable on the coasts of China.[18] Nevertheless, the steamer was a rare commodity and a highly valuable military asset on the Indus and the Irrawaddy. Threats to British India could come from either side of the sub-continent and not all available steamers could be released, even for the potential furthering of British interests in China.

The steamers' role began when *Atalanta* and *Madagascar*, a Bengal government steamer pressed into war service, escorted *Wellesley*, H W Giffard's *Cruizer*, *Algerine* and the transports which arrived off the Canton river on 20 June 1840. With the main fleet a week later came *Queen*, a steamer built at Northfleet for the Bengal government which was also pressed into service.

The British fleet, which had been cobbled together from stations around the globe, was initially under the command of Commodore Sir Gordon Bremer, in the absence of the commander in chief, Rear Admiral George Elliot, a younger brother of the second Earl of Minto, who at the time was First Lord of the Admiralty. They assembled off the mouth of the Canton river on 28 June 1840 and declared a blockade (which could not be very effectively enforced because of the maze of creeks and channels through the

18 Wellington to Ellenborough, 29 December 1841, Wellington Papers.

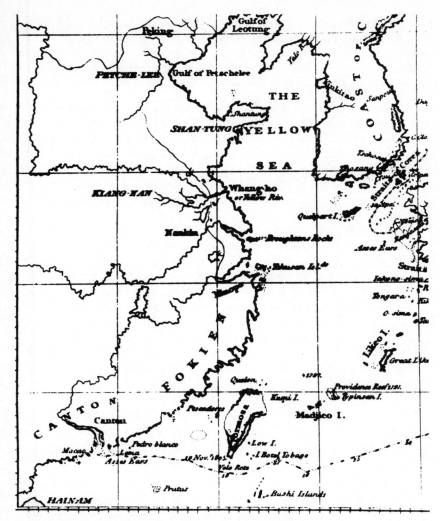

Map of the coasts of China from Canton to the Yellow Sea.

countryside) and then, instead of invading the river in force the fleet sailed northwards, first capturing the island of Chusan, or Tchusan (see map), in pursuit of the policy of exerting power directly on the centre of the Chinese administration. Because of adverse weather and the shallow bar across the mouth of the Peiho river (control of which was the key to the establishment of pressure on the government in Peking) and because the health of Admiral Elliot was failing, the commander in chief and Captain Elliot, the Superintendent of Canton (on whom a great deal of responsibility fell throughout the first part of the war), allowed themselves to be persuaded by

Chinese emissaries into accepting friendly words and promises of negotiation at Canton. These, however, led to nothing except in due course to rebukes to the two Elliots from Lord Palmerston for their negative approach and the failure of the fleet to present a real threat. Giffard summarised these events in his journal.[19]

> 28th September. The Admiral arrived. We heard there was a kind of truce established, that we were to hold Chusan for the present, and a high officer to be sent to Canton, I do not think anyone in the expedition but the heads put the least confidence in this, we only thought they wished to gain time. To my disgust I was ordered to Calcutta with dispatches and to take up my old Station in the Straits of Malacca.
>
> We had heard the *Kite* was wrecked on the coast, she was an armed transport. Lieut. Douglas, twelve marines (the Captain was drowned) Captain's wife and the crew fell into the hands of the Chinese and were now at Ning-po having been carried through this country in cages.
>
> We sailed on 1st October and arrived at Calcutta on 13th November. Here we were docked – on the 5th December Lord Auckland, Miss Eden and the Nabob of Bengal paid the brig a visit, we manned yards, saluted &c. and on the 10th sailed for Madras to take Sir Hugh Gough, the new Military Commander in Chief to China, where affairs did not appear to have been progressing very favourably, the negotiations dragging their length along slowly and much sickness among the troops. A new climate, our provisions bad and the water not very good had all doubtless conduced to the sickness.

Giffard's passage to China with Sir Hugh Gough on board from Madras was broken by an event which had nothing to do with the war. A British whaler, *Pilot*, had run into a situation by no means unique in the history of South Sea whaling.

> 29th December, we observed a boat at sea, picked her up, she had 3rd Mate, Doctor and eight men belonging to the *Pilot*, whaler, they had been a week out having escaped from Nou Cawry harbour where the natives had captured their vessel and murdered the rest of the crew, they had had no sustenance but a few cocoanuts; we immediately altered course and on the 31st in the evening arrived at the Island, I had intended to have been there before daylight but the wind failed us, and I had not time to spare to make other arrangements, we found the vessel not in Nou Cawry as was supposed, but in a small harbour close to it, the natives immediately deserted and took themselves off, we burnt upwards of seventy huts and all the canoes we could find and refitting the vessel sailed on the 4th day, there were marks in the vessel of bloodshed.

19 NMM JOD 38.

The story as related to us was this; they had come to these Islands, to recruit and refit after a long whaling cruise, the natives piloted them into the harbour, they supposing it to be Nou Cawry. There were three villages one at the narrow entrance and two others on the opposite sides, the first day they tried to get the natives to trade, but could get but little from them, the Captain incautiously spread a quantity of different things he had to trade with the South Sea Islanders, in hopes they would bring poultry &c. to exchange, the second afternoon the 3rd Mate with the Doctor and boat's crew went on shore to the village at the entrance of the harbour, the Captain would not give them any arms, because the inhabitants were a peaceful race (which was their character, apparently a false one) when there they saw another boat load go to the village on the opposite side, leaving very few on board and some of them sick, the vessel at the same time being crowded with natives. Soon something strange about the natives made them retire to their boat, they heard a yell from the ship and were attacked at the same instant, two men speared and killed, they shoved off pulled towards the ship the natives had possession and armed themselves with the whale spears and harpoons, they pulled out of the harbour and were chased in canoes for upwards of two hours, the darkness served them, but when I picked them up they could not have lasted much longer. I asked if they had given any provocation, they assured me not, the mate said there was no fear of that until, at all events, they were ready for sea – and the Doctor was a simple man; therefore I do not think they had given any provocation. We had to beat up to Canton against the monsoon and arrived there on the 1st March.[20]

Giffard continues his account of the conduct of the war.

We heard negotiations had gone on a long period, we had given up Chusan, Captain Anstruther, Lieut. Douglas, the woman, Mrs. Noble and several prisoners had been delivered to us, the poor marines had died; Admiral Elliot had gone home sick and Sir Gordon Bremer was again Commander in Chief and Captain Elliot the sole plenipo. – They

---

20 The barque *Pilot*, 418 tons, was a former British warship, built at Northam, Hampshire, in 1807 as an 18 gun brig of the same class as Giffard's *Cruizer*. She was sold out of the navy in March 1828, and henceforth employed by successive owners as a South Seas whaler out of London. This particular voyage had begun when she cleared London on 31 January 1840, under a master named Wheeler. The next report of her after the incident described by Giffard was in the Timor Strait in August 1841 when she had taken seventy barrels of oil. She continued whaling voyages and was finally condemned in December 1844 after having gone ashore in Algoa bay.
Sources: *Lloyd's Register*, 1840; Colledge, *Ships of the Royal Navy*, vol 1; Parliamentary Papers, *Return of Wrecks in South Africa*; Jones, *Ships Employed in the South Sea Trade, 1775–1861*, Canberra 1986.

had just captured the Boyne, the first base and we joined the Squadron about two miles below Canton off a Fort called Howaua's, Flags of Truce were flying.

The Chinese had broken faith with us in everything, they had only been amusing us to gain time and make preparations and had now thrown off the mask.

As Captain Elliot's negotiations at Canton were getting nowhere an attack was mounted on the forts at Chuenpi and adjacent islands. These were easily destroyed by the guns of the ships; the Chinese, with no knowledge of the weaponry available to the fleet, had thought them impregnable. This small victory led to the Convention of Chuenpi, under which trade was to be resumed at Canton, an indemnity was to be paid by the Chinese, and Hong Kong was ceded to the British. In return, the occupying force at Chusan withdrew. Again the Chinese procrastinated and the reluctant Captain Elliot brought British forces to Canton, during which operation new navigable channels were found in the river by the shallow draught steamers. There was a truce on 21 March 1841 under which trade with Canton was reopened and tea once again flowed out to the British markets.

But the Chinese were moving troops, hoping to drive out the British once and for all. Learning of this, Captain Elliot ordered the fleet now at Hong Kong to move upstream to Canton again. A combined operation was launched under the command of General Sir Hugh Gough and very soon Canton was at the mercy of British forces which commanded the heights all around the landward side of the city. At this moment Captain Elliot, in his capacity as plenipotentiary, arranged for a further truce under which the British forces withdrew from their position of strength, indeed withdrew from the river altogether, in return for an indemnity of $6,000,000 and a resumption of trade.

This decision of Captain Elliot was greatly criticised by his fellow officers of the time and, although the matter has been the subject of a good deal of controversy, in the view of some historians it led to the unsettled period in Anglo-Chinese relations which followed and which was ended only by the second Chinese war of the late 1850s. It is probably true to say that Captain Elliot, whose understanding and knowledge of the Chinese was greater than that of most of his contemporaries, nevertheless made an error of judgement with profound consequences. He was in search of a political settlement which would lead to satisfactory long term trading relations. Like many men and women with deep specialist knowledge of an exotic society, he may have found it difficult to take a realistic view of the forces at work in that society. Canton could have been destroyed by the British forces, or forced to surrender on terms which made it unavoidably clear to the Chinese that they were faced with a culture materially more powerful than their own, with which they had better do business on equal terms. As it was, the British withdrawal was seen in China as a great victory for Chinese arms and became the principal inspiration of renewed and reinforced anti-foreign movements, which were to lead in the end to the sacking of Peking in 1860.

Whatever historical view may be taken, Lord Palmerston as Foreign Secretary was not at all satisfied with the way in which substantial (and very expensive) forces sent to China were being used. He recognised something which Captain Elliot, for long submerged in the local scene at Canton, had lost sight of, that is, that the reality of power in China lay in Peking, and only by the convincing display of military power in the north could the Chinese administration be persuaded to open up their country to foreign trade and contracts. Not surprisingly, Captain Elliot was recalled (but, equally unsurprisingly, survived to become a knighted admiral)[21] and replaced as plenipotentiary by Sir Henry Pottinger. Commodore Bremer was ordered to retake Chusan, and a new commander in chief, Sir William Parker, was directed to penetrate the River Yangtse Kiang towards Nanking and make a conspicuous demonstration of power as a base for the resumption of negotiations with the central government of China.

Given the slowness of communications, even with the fast paddle steamers as despatch boats – the paddle steamer *Sesostris* of the Indian Navy played her part in carrying Sir Henry Pottinger to Hong Kong in the record time of fifty-seven days from London – the actions which followed had already been initiated when the new orders arrived. Although delayed by the effect of typhoons on 21 and 26 July 1841, and by epidemics of dysentery, the fleet was underweigh to the north in time to conduct its operations before the break up of the weather which could be expected in October. Amoy was taken in late August and Chusan reoccupied in early October. Chinhai on the nearby mainland was occupied on 10 October, with the loss of seventeen killed and thirty-six wounded. The Chinese losses were estimated in thousands. Linpo, up river, was occupied without opposition on 13 October.

The British force settled down for the very cold winter and soon found itself under psychological and physical siege. Meanwhile, changes of government and ministers in Britain and a change of Governor General in India led to much discussion of the policies to be pursued. In the event a strengthened British combined force, despite being hampered by lack of hydrographic information, proceeded to the far north to impose a direct threat on the central government. It did not proceed in the direction of Peking but up the Yangtse to Nanking, where a treaty was signed on 29 August 1842. Under this imposed agreement Hong Kong was leased, four ports in addition to Canton opened up to world trade, and an indemnity of $21,000,000 was to be paid by the Chinese in bullion. British Consuls were

21 Blake, *Charles Elliot, R.N., 1801–1875*, London 1960, pp 122 and 125.

to be appointed to the treaty ports Foochow, Ningpo, Shanghai and Nanking, and there was to be equality between Chinese and British officials of corresponding ranks. It seemed that a solution to the troublesome and economically important problem had been achieved. In fact, the heart of the Chinese illusion in Peking had still not been touched, and much was to follow before this happened, twenty years later.

For his various parts in the campaign Giffard was mentioned three times in his commander in chief's despatches to Admiralty. As a consequence of the opportunities to perform conspicuous service provided by the China War (and with a Whig government, still in power) he was promoted Post Captain on 8 June 1841, that is before the attack on Amoy in which he played a leading role. Now too senior to command a small brig, he left *Cruizer* to return to Britain in the early part of 1842.

The China War showed that the paddle driven steamship, in the special circumstances of river warfare against an enemy not similarly armed, had a war potential over and above the roles in which she had become established in the British navy. The steamers again and again played a vital part in the campaign. Indeed, it is difficult to see how it would have been conducted without them. To summarise their roles: both *Atalanta* and *Madagascar* played an active part in the capture of Chusan in July 1840, *Atalanta* towing the flagship *Wellesley* into position. *Queen* and *Madagascar* were also in action in the capture of the Chuenpi forts on 7 January 1841, as was *Nemesis*, which with other steamers was frequently employed on sounding the shallow channels of the rivers and seeking new routes through the labyrinthine deltas. The steamers, particularly the iron *Phlegethon* and *Nemesis*, drew much less water than sailing vessels. Quite apart from their manoeuvrability, this gave them great value in the peculiar circumstances of river warfare.

Atalanta with *Nemesis* also performed conspicuous service during the advance on Canton in May 1841, *Atalanta* earning herself a special mention in despatches and for her captain, Commander Rogers, in due course a Sword of Honour from the East India Company Court of Directors and, 'the lucrative post of Master Attendant at Calcutta'.[22]

It was the Indian Navy's steam frigate *Sesostris* which brought the new commander in chief, Admiral Sir William Parker, and the new 'Plenipotentiary, Minister Extraordinary and Chief Superintendent of British Trade in China', Sir Henry Pottinger, to the Canton river from Bombay in July and early August 1841. When the fleet sailed to recover Chusan a fortnight later the weather division was led by *Queen* and the lee division by *Sesostris*. The steamers *Phlegethon* and *Nemesis* accompanied. In the attack on Amoy *Sesostris* received the first shot and she and *Queen* were in the heart of the

22 Low, *op cit*, Vol 2, p 142.

action. *Phlegethon* and *Nemesis* landed the assault troops. In the recovery of Chusan in the second half of September 1841, *Sesostris* provided covering fire for the landing troops. It was the four steamers which took the troops to Ningpo. *Sesostris* again played a leading part in saving the British forces from attack by fire rafts, while she and *Phlegethon* and *Queen* played a major part in defeating a land attack on the city.

The reinforced fleet which advanced up the Yangtse to capture Nanking contained the Royal Navy's steam vessel *Vixen*, 8 guns, the Indian Navy's steamers *Auckland*, *Ariadne*, *Medusa*, *Sesostris* and *Phlegethon*, and four steamers from the Bengal Marine, *Tennasserim*, *Hoogli*, *Pluto* and *Proserpine*. *Nemesis* was also with the fleet. These steamers were lashed alongside the sailing ships of war to tow them into action on the Yangtse. They reconnoitred the complex river system, and they landed the troops for the assault on the various settlements which had to be neutralised on the way up the river towards the Nanking.

Right at the end of the war two paddle sloops of the Royal Navy arrived in Chinese waters having steamed and sailed round the Cape of Good Hope. They were *Vixen* (mentioned above; 280 horse power) and *Driver* (6 guns, 280 horse power). *Driver* continued her voyage by way of Borneo, New Zealand, Cape Horn and South America and thus completed her historic first circumnavigation by a steam-and-sail vessel.

The China war also provided a theatre for the staging of what appears to have been a piece of vigorous, almost dramatic, marketing of the use of iron for ship construction.

Before the war the use of iron for the construction of the whole fabric of ships, as opposed to the use of iron for the fastenings of wooden ships – and the metal fastenings of a wooden vessel made up a surprisingly high percentage of both her weight and her cost, 300 to 400 tons of metal going into the construction of a large wooden ship – was being promoted by several engineering companies. Perhaps the most enterprising of these was the firm William Laird and Sons of the Birkenhead Iron Works who launched three small iron vessels in 1829–30, and then in 1831 built the first iron vessel to make an ocean voyage, *Elburkah*, which was used with great success in the exploration of the River Niger. This vessel was followed by five more iron steamships built in 1833 and 1834, including *Garryowen*, 263 tons, 80 horse power, which was steamed to the Shannon river in Western Ireland, then operated there by the Dublin Steam Packet Company for thirty years, and two vessels which were to play an important part in the early surveying of the Euphrates. This survey was a necessary part of the work towards the establishment of fast communication with India. The

Aleppo–Euphrates–Persian Gulf route was a possible alternative to that via the Red Sea.[23]

These two vessels were *Tigris* and *Euphrates*, which were respectively of 109 and 179 tons and of 20 and 50 horse power. Built in Birkenhead they were dismantled, shipped out to the Middle East and re-erected. Colonel Francis Chesney, the commanding officer of the Euphrates Expedition of 1833, for which the vessels were built, reported on them most favourably.[24]

> It is but right to tell you that the iron vessels constructed by you far exceeded my expectations, as well as those of the naval officers employed in the late expedition, who would one and all bear testimony anywhere to their extraordinary solidity; indeed, it was often repeated by Lieutenant Cleaveland, and the others, that any wooden vessel must have been destroyed before the service was one half completed – whereas the *Euphrates* was as perfect when they laid her up in Bagdad as the first day she was floated. As I am now occupied in preparing a work on the expedition, I shall have better opportunities in the present of doing justice to the subject of iron vessels, for it is my belief that they will entirely supersede wood, on account of their comparative strength, cheapness, and durability, whenever people are satisfied that their only disadvantage – the free working of the compass – has been overcome.

In the article quoted above it was asserted (in terms which might suggest the inspiration of a handout from Laird and Sons) that

> there are boats built by Mr Laird in both north and south America – in all parts of India and on the Euphrates and the Indus – in Egypt, on the Nile – in the Mediterranean – on the Vistula, on the Shannon and on the Thames. One of these boats on the Savannah has been constantly at work for these last six years without any repairs; which is a great test, if we consider the constant caulkings required to preserve a timber ship.

The claim that Laird's contacts were more or less world-wide is substantiated by his correspondence, part of which has recently become available.[25] This correspondence does indeed show that the company was vigorously promoting the iron steamer at a time when iron was becoming available in quantities, qualities, and at a price which made the building of iron ships a reasonable commercial proposition. With a number of other companies, Lairds were in the forefront of the promotion of this second stage in the development of steamships. The wooden paddler, at least as a

23 Sutton, *Lords of the East*, London 1981, pp 133–134.
24 Quoted in an article by Augustin F B Creuze in the *United Services Journal*, May 1840, pp 98–99.
25 Laird correspondence – in private hands.

merchant vessel, had reached her plateau of development. The absorbing of cargo space by engine and bunkers, the inherent weakness of the structure of wooden vessels, made all the more apparent by the necessity of carrying heavy engines, boilers and fuel, as well as cargo, had the result that the demands of constant maintenance, always a continuing cost, became even greater unless the vessel was built, like a warship, to standards which required an investment excessive in the face of likely returns. All these factors indicated that the wooden paddler had not much further to go as a merchant vessel.

The iron steamer, once iron became an economic proposition, had great advantages. Inherent in the economic proposition was the fact that by the late 1830s and early 1840s, it was possible to build in iron more cheaply than wood. Because iron vessels required far less maintenance than wooden vessels, and because iron-working facilities were rapidly becoming more and more widespread world-wide, maintenance was cheaper. Iron ships were lighter and could offer more cargo space with the same tonnage and dimensions. They were not subject to the endemic leaking of wooden vessels and therefore delivered their cargoes in better condition, which was good for shipowners and cargo insurers, if not for lawyers. Iron ships could be and were from the very beginning built with effective watertight bulkheads and double bottoms which made them better insurance risks. *Lloyd's Register* began the classification of iron vessels as early as 1837.

In the face of all these developments it looked as if the paddle steamer, even with her strict and predictable limitations, might be susceptible to a degree of commercially profitable further development. But three factors in particular stood in the way. The first was the difficulty of fouling. Iron ships did not need protection against the marine life which in warm (and some cold) seas destroyed wooden planking by drilling into it for food and shelter. But iron ships did need to be protected against the accretion of seaweed and shellfish growth on the hull which provided a continuous drag on its progress through the water. Wooden ships had, since the preceding century, been protected by thin copper or yellow metal plates but these could not be applied to an iron hull because electrolitic action produced rapid corrosion of the iron – the process was the same as that which takes place in an electric torch battery. It was to be a long time before chemical anti-foulings protected the steamer, but in the meantime the economic advantages of iron and steam outweighed, generally, this disadvantage.

The second difficulty was that of the compass, which was thoroughly put out by an iron environment. This difficulty, referred to by Colonel Chesney in his report quoted above, was overcome, at least to the degree which made iron vessels on deep sea an acceptable insurance risk at this early stage, by a series of experiments originally initiated by the Lairds, who were concerned that the problem of compass error might inhibit the marketing of iron ships. Trials were carried out by Commander Edward Johnson on board the Laird-built *Garryowen* in the River Shannon in 1835. These experiments (which established Johnson in a successful career as an authority on the compass) led to a further series of trials in 1838 by Professor Airey, then Astronomer Royal, of a system of magnets and soft iron correctors placed within and around the binnacle. Airey's work was done on board *Rainbow*, an iron paddler built by Lairds for the General Steam Navigation Company (which proved in fact so fast on the London–Antwerp service that the company's competitors paid the General Steam Navigation Company £2500 per annum not to employ her on that route).[26]

Airey's work had grave flaws[27] but it proved seminal. The decision to build *The Great Britain*, the first modern ship, now restored in Bristol, of iron stemmed from the demonstration of the Airey system on board *Rainbow* to Christopher Claxton, managing director of the Great Western Steamship Company, *The Great Britain*'s owners, after which he wrote to Professor Babbage of the Royal Society and the father of the computer, on 27 November 1838.[28]

> Great Western Steamship Office
> 35, Princes Street
> Bristol
> Nov. 27th 1838

My dear Sir,
    I hardly know whether keeping my word passed to you at the Bath Hotel may not expose our company to some injury, for if I see most right you expressed yourself as connected or intimate with some of the Directors of the *British Queen* company with whom we are unhappily at issue. I say unhappily because the glorious efforts of companies like both of ours to exalt science and settle disputed theories ought not to suffer either check or hindrance from trifling considerations. Their conduct to us has been such as to bar reconciliation without ample explanation from them, apology I ought to say. My business with you is to fulfill a promise which I do with pleasure. We have settled to build an iron ship – and mean to construct her ourselves. If you wish for the full particulars it must be with the clear understanding that they are not to be given to the enemy. I made a voyage in the *Rainbow*, took the bearings and distance, worked the course & perfectly satisfied myself of the perfect adjustment of Professor Airey's Apparatus. Took some of my own on board & made many interesting experiments, found my compasses correct in his

26 The Laird Papers – in private hands.
27 Fanning, *Steady As She Goes*, London 1986, pp XXXII–XLII.
28 Babbage MSS. BL Add 37, 191 p 39.

Binnacles, which goes to prove the adjustments will suit ordinary cards. Found both his & mine *wild* when removed from the Binnacles. The Professor explained them fully to me & so satisfied am I of his having conferred a vast benefit on seamen that I would have no hesitation in crossing any sea or latitude with his correctors. The only doubt appears to be in the length of time the magnet will retain its' power, or rather the exact degree of power necessary for the occasion. Should it wear off *practice* will detect it, it is well wrapped up in tallow, flannel & wood.

Your very faithful serv't

Chris P. Claxton
Managing Director

Professor Babbage FRS
Dover St.
Manchester Square

From now on the building of ships principally of iron was thought to be freed from the crippling incubus of compass deviation, although in fact many losses followed from the placing of undue faith in Airey's methods.[29] The reference to the 'enemy' is to the British & American Steam Navigation Company, which had been set up in rivalry to the Great Western Steamship Company and which, in the determination of its directors to gain the possible marketing advantage of priority, had chartered the small steam paddle vessel *Sirius* to make a crossing to New York with passengers a few hours ahead of *Great Western* on her maiden voyage, an exploit in public relations which cost them an operating loss of £3500. The company failed after the loss with all hands of its second steamship, *President*, in 1841.[30]

The third difficulty was of a different kind. Because of uncertainties as to cost, the effectiveness of Airey's compass correction and also the effect of shot on hull structures built of contemporary iron, the naval authorities in the 1830s and early 1840s were still cautious of building in iron.[31] This meant that Admiralty contracts for iron vessels were slow in coming forward, although the Lairds worked vigorously to promote them. It also meant that the paddle steamer postal packets which ran from Falmouth to the Mediterranean and which at this time were Admiralty controlled, and the subsidised merchant ship services which, as a condition of the mail contract, had to be vessels acceptable to the navy for possible war service, were also mostly of wooden construction, although *Dover*, a Laird-built packet of 1840, was perhaps the first British government-owned iron steamer. This limited the number of possible future orders for iron ships.

29 Fanning, *op cit*.
30 Pond, *Junius Smith*, New York 1927, esp p 127.
31 Brown, *Before the Ironclad*, London 1990 pp 79–82.

In this situation *Nemesis*, which, as has already been recorded in this chapter, played an active part in the war with China, was built at the Birkenhead Iron Works by the Lairds under conditions of some secrecy. Her origin is obscure. It has frequently been stated[32] that she was built to the order of the East India Company but in fact on completion she was registered under the current Merchant Shipping Act as of the Port of Liverpool, No 6 of 1840,[33] on 13 January 1840, as the sole property of John Laird of North Birkenhead, Shipbuilder. Both the Laird Papers and East India Company papers have been searched without, so far, revealing any indication of negotiations between Lairds and the East India Company over the construction of the vessel. The Register contains the notation 'Sold to Indian Navy', but no date is given for the transaction. The earliest listing of the vessel as belonging, not to the Indian Navy but to the Bengal Marine, occurs in the India Register for 1843.

In the light of the foregoing it could be that *Nemesis* acted as a kind of privateer. Creuze's article in the *United Services Journal* in 1840[34] describes *Nemesis* as a 'private armed steamer'. On board her during the war was W D Bernard, 'A M Oxon', who, perhaps as part of the whole arrangement with the Lairds, wrote 'from notes by Captain W.H. Hall, R.N. and personal observations', a piece of more or less instant journalism,[35] as soon as the war was over. According to his account, *Nemesis* 'was sent to sea as a private armed steamer'.[36] Bernard goes on to say that she

> was built in England and for the service of the East India Company, went to sea as a merchantman, although heavily armed; she was never commissioned under Articles of War, although commanded principally by officers of the Royal Navy; neither was she classed among the ships of the regular navy of the East India Company.[37]

This is a somewhat obscure statement.

This evidence suggests that it is by no means impossible that *Nemesis* was built by the Lairds at their own risk as a promotion vehicle for the iron paddle steamer, in great haste to take advantage of the heaven sent marketing opportunity provided by the coming war with China, in a piece of inspired salesmanship to demonstrate beyond reasonable doubt that as

32 For a very recent example see Brown, *op cit*, p 75.
33 PRO BT 107/268.
34 Creuze, *op cit*.
35 Bernard, *Narrative of the Voyage and Services of the Nemesis from 1842–3*, London 1844, 2 Vols. Hall was at this period an acting lieutenant. Later in the Baltic as Captain of *Hecla* he was always referred to as 'Nemesis' Hall. See Greenhill and Giffard, *The British Assault*, numerous references.
36 Bernard, *op cit*, p 2.
37 Bernard, *op cit*, p 1.

regards seaworthiness iron construction had nothing against it, and as regards maintenance every advantage. Weight is perhaps lent to this theory by the secrecy which accompanied her voyage to China, the longest passage ever made to that date by a steam-assisted vessel. When she left Liverpool she cleared for Odessa, and after grounding on the north Cornish coast she was repaired at Portsmouth. She cleared again for Odessa when she left Portsmouth on 20 March 1840.

But in fact she made a steam-assisted passage to Table Bay, arriving on 1 July whence she cleared for a port in Australia, actually sailing to Ceylon [Sri Lanka], where she was ordered to the Canton river. There would seem no need for all this secrecy if she had been built to the order of the East India Company which, as we have seen, already had several other iron steamers in position to take part in the coming war with China. As it was, it appears likely that she fought the war as a mercenary with a mercenary crew, albeit certainly with the blessing of the East India Company. Be that as it may, *Nemesis*'s performance showed, moreover, as did the performance of the other iron steamers in the campaign, that iron construction had advantages over wood for special purposes, in that vessels could be built of shallower draught and greater mobility. Undoubtedly, the much publicised *Nemesis* played a role in familiarising the world with the possibilities of iron construction of ships but the ready availability of Bernard's somewhat excessive account of the exploits of *Nemesis* has led historians to give undue emphasis to her role in the campaign, as opposed to that of other iron and wooden paddle steamers. This was, for the first time in history, a steamer's war. The peculiar circumstances in which it was conducted enabled the paddlers to display their powers to the maximum advantage, and called forth little challenge to their weaknesses and limitations. It convinced a number of officers, including the newly posted Captain Giffard, of the power and future importance of steam.

7

The Birth of the Screw
Propelled Steamship

It is ironic that the paddle steamer proved herself at war, in the special circumstances prevailing in China, in the same years as *Archimedes* was demonstrating, and selling, the advantages of screw propulsion which was to render her obsolete. It is ironic also that the vessel which is sometimes described as the first steam paddle frigate, *Penelope*, and the navy's experimental screw propelled steamship *Rattler*, which was to show the way to break through the dead end into which the paddler had led the steamship, were commissioned in the same year, 1843. Only one year later the merchant shipping industry gave birth to *The Great Britain*, the first fully powered, big, iron, ocean-going (within Samuel Seaward's twenty day passage limit) steamship. In the late twentieth century she is often referred to as the first modern ship.

Thus the ultimate development of the paddle propelled steam warship, and the gestation of the screw propelled warship which was to succeed her, were simultaneous. It is true to say that the first paddle frigates, like *Cutty Sark* and her contemporary tea clippers a generation later, were obsolete before they were launched. But it was not apparent until late in the 1840s that the manifold problems of screw propulsion were going to be solved at all, and certainly not as rapidly as they were.

The limitations of the paddle steamer for both commercial and naval purposes have been rehearsed at length in Chapter 2. As far as the navy was concerned, year after year the size of steamers grew. And with the size, the cost of construction and maintenance increased so that the question, in the words of one historian,[1] 'pressed itself more clearly – what was the naval utility of such expensive and lightly armed vessels?' They could and did serve very successfully as deep sea tugs, as raiding and troop landing vessels, and in river warfare, as the war with China had shown. They served very effectively on anti-slavery patrol, in the bombardment of some less formidable land fortifications, as survey vessels – they were to prove supremely valuable in this role in the so-called Crimean War – perhaps

1 Robertson, *The Evolution of Naval Armament*, p 232.

132

above all as fast despatch vessels. They were now being regarded as essential units of the fleet. In the words of Sir William Laird Clowes, in the Syrian campaign of 1840 they had 'first convincingly demonstrated their great utility in this war'.[2]

But still the paddle steamer was neither capable of entering competitively into the world's carrying trade nor of being a ship of the line, or indeed a really satisfactory naval vessel, except for the specialised purposes listed above. A contemporary, Fincham,[3] summed up just two of the reasons very nicely when he wrote of the paddle frigate *Odin* of 1845.

> as the position of the machinery and boilers is partially above the water line, and the propellers are exposed to danger in broadside fighting, the ship is necessarily imperfect in these two conditions, as well as in the position of the sails; for in this case the proper place of the mainmast was occupied by the boilers, and consequently the centre of effort of the wind on the sails is in the wrong place.

These difficulties were never to be overcome.

Both *Rattler* and *The Great Britain* were the children of *Archimedes*. For many years schemes had been put forward for overcoming the disadvantages of the paddle steamer by the use of propulsion by some kind of rotating screw in the stern, or projecting from the bows, of a vessel. Dr Ewan Corlett, the engineer and naval architect who was most responsible for the salving and subsequent restoration in Bristol of *The Great Britain*, has commented orally to the authors that there is no such thing as an invention. There is a time when the circumstances arise, because of the availability of materials at commercial prices, qualities, and quantities, of developments in support technology, such as, in the case of the use of power propulsion at sea, in lubricants and seals, gearing techniques, in boiler-making and furnace design, when ideas long discussed in theoretical terms become sufficiently practical to justify the investment of risk capital in their experimental application, whether that risk capital be in the private sector or in public monies. In the former case the final ingredient will be the entrepreneur. If the results of entrepreneurial application are successful, then you have an invention. Whether that invention is successfully applied, commercially or in the public sector, depends on a further mixture of events in which the working of the market, together, often, with political forces of varying complexity and with personalities, determine whether the application ever achieves widespread use.

The screw propeller had many 'inventors'. Bourne[4] lists no less than 470 men in one way or another associated with the development of screw

---

2 Laird Clowes, *The Royal Navy*, Vol VI, p 318.
3 Fincham, *History of Naval Architecture*, London 1851, p 335.
4 Bourne, *Treatise on the Screw Propeller*, London 1852.

propulsion over many years. No less a person than the first James Watt wrote to his friend Dr Small as early as 1770,[5] 'Have you ever considered a spiral oar for that purpose, or are you for two wheels?' Watt, to make his meaning clear, made a rough sketch of a screw propeller. Americans, Britons and Frenchmen all devised ideas for screw propulsion of vessels. Robert Wilson, as we have already pointed out in Chapter 2, in fact solved the basic problem in the early 1820s with an efficient screw propeller placed, as the successful screw was eventually to be, between the sternpost and the rudder of a vessel. There were practical experiments with screw propulsion in Sweden as early as 1816 with the little 30 foot *Stockholmshäxan*. In Italy, *Civetta* may have operated successfully with a screw for a short time in 1829. But very little is at present known about these early vessels and it was not until the mid 1830s that technology and industrial development finally came together, with entrepreneurship motivated by the potential financial advantages to be gained from the breaking of the paddle barrier, to bring about the successful development of the screw.

In doing this, industry and marine engineering had to overcome a number of major technical problems, each of which was fundamental to the success of screw propulsion, each of which was being met for the first time. To give only a few examples of these problems, it had to be demonstrated that a suitable engine could be developed. Hitherto, all marine engines had been, as we have seen, of the slow running type, suitable for the direct drive of paddles and mostly of the side-lever type. In fact, even by 1840 no really large marine engine running at more than 20 rpm had ever been built.[6] It had to be shown that the theoretical idea of the screw would work at all in practice and if so, in which of the various forms of screw advocated by different engineers and theoreticians, from one which resembled a short length of an auger to one comprising a cylinder fitted on its outer side with skewed plates at angles to its surface or, as eventually proved the case, something in between these two extremes. It had to be demonstrated that it was practical to transmit power from an engine amidships, where the development of the paddle steamer had necessarily put it, or perhaps in the after part of the vessel, where the propulsion unit of the first large, screw driven steamship to be built in the United Kingdom, *Great Northern*, was placed. It had to be demonstrated that industry could produce a shafting which could take the stresses involved, and that the stresses and the torque of the shaft and the screw would not be such as to tear the vessel slowly to pieces and shorten her life to a degree which meant that she could not represent a profitable investment for merchant shipping. In fact, it soon became apparent that for this very reason of the stresses involved in transmitting hundreds of horse power down a rotating shaft, and because

5 Smiles, *Lives of the engineers Boulton and Watt*, Popular Edition, London 1904, pp 157-158.
6 Corlett, *The Iron Ship*, London 1990, p 61.

wooden ships constantly change shape in a seaway when laden with heavy cargo and when taking the ground in a drying harbour (and at this period most harbours in Britain were tidal), the screw driven wooden merchant ship was not a commercial proposition. But this restriction on the development of the wooden, screw driven ship did not apply to the navy because naval hulls were built to higher standards of strength than vessels which had to earn their living at sea and the cost of maintenance did not have to come out of revenue earned. Nor did naval vessels usually take the ground, except by accident, or carry cargoes of constantly varying weight and distribution inside the vessel. Thus it was that in 1853, when the navy was completely committed to a wooden steam screw battle fleet, of the 187 merchant steam vessels which appear in *Lloyd's Register* for that year only six were wooden screws as opposed to 74 iron screw propelled steam vessels.

A stern bearing had to be developed which would not corrode excessively as a result of galvanic action with the copper sheathing with which wooden ships were clothed below the water line to protect them from the marine boring organisms which destroyed unprotected wooden ships in warm (and sometimes cold) waters and from the accretion of marine growth, barnacles, seaweed, and such like on the vessels' underwater body. Brass and copper bearings wore excessively under the continuous friction of the propeller shaft. In the screw sloop *Malacca* the brass stern tube is reported to have been worn away at the rate of 5 pounds each working day.[7]

How was the thrust exerted by the end of the propeller shaft, which comprised the force driving the vessel forward and represented the continuous pressure from a rotating surface of over one hundred pounds per square inch, to be taken up and transmitted to the vessel as a whole? How was such a bearing to be designed and lubricated so that the metals involved did not eventually weld together? It is to be borne in mind, for example, that the engine of *The Great Britain* of 1844 was the most powerful steam unit of any kind existing in the world at the time[8] and that with an indicated horse power of 1800 it had to push a load draught displacement weight of 3675 tons through the water at 12 miles an hour.[9] The forces involved, about 10 tons on the 18-inch diameter shaft end under normal working conditions and about twice that when accelerating, were taken up on

> a circular steel plate 2 feet in diameter supported by a block attached to the engine beds, against which a gunmetal plate, also 2 feet in diameter and attached to the shaft itself, pressed. Water under pressure was fed to

7 Smith, *Naval and Marine Engineering*, p 79.

8 Oral communication from James Richard, Engine Consultant to the SS *Great Britain* Project.

9 Corlett, *op cit*, especially Appendix 6.

a cavity in the centre of the two plates, escaping rapidly; this, according to Guppy 'very satisfactorily lubricates them'.[10]

Indeed, the problem of lubricants was absolutely fundamental, for without them theoretical development could not be given practical application. The history of lubrication is fundamental to the history of the application of power at sea, as on land.

The design of the propeller itself was entirely a novel challenge. There was no background of experience and knowledge on which to draw and the understanding of the forces involved was consequently limited. Many and varied were the solutions proposed to the two problems of hydrodynamic efficiency and physical strength. For many years it was not understood that a rotating propeller derives its thrust principally from the effect of the hydrofoil section of the blades, rather than from a screwing action. Johnson's encyclopedia of 1853[11] has forty-two types of screw propeller which had already been proposed at the time of the publication of the book. Even Brunel had difficulty in designing a screw which combined the virtues. His first propeller for *The Great Britain* was, modern tank tests have shown, remarkably efficient hydrodynamically but, as its behaviour in service showed, it was not mechanically strong enough to take the stresses of 4½ tons per square inch experienced at the roots of the blades when the vessel was steaming at full speed.

The matter of the positioning of the screw was in the event to prove very important in the early history of the steamship, and in several different ways. The first patents for screw propulsion were taken out within six weeks of one another in the early summer of 1836. The second of these was in the name of a Swedish engineer and inventor, Johann Ericsson, whose biographers have shown him as an eccentric genius.[12] Ericsson's patent concerned the design of the screw itself, a complicated arrangement of what would now be described as contra-rotating propellers. In his early experimental installations, including one demonstrated in 1837 to Admiral Sir Charles Adam, the First Naval Lord, Sir William Symonds, Sir Edward Parry, and Sir Francis Beaufort, this complex propulsion unit was placed abaft the rudder and there is evidence that the result was detrimental to the steering of the vessel.[13]

At any rate, the naval authorities had other sufficient reason not to

10 Corlett, *op cit*, p 63, quoting Guppy, Mins Proc Inst Civil Engineers, iv (1845) p 160.
11 Johnson, *Imperial Cyclopedia of Machinery*, London 1853.
12 Notably, White, *Yankee from Sweden*, New York 1960.
13 See, for instance, Lambert in Fisher, ed, *Innovation,* pp 61–88. The research project, the results of which were embodied in this paper, was sponsored by the SS *Great Britain* Project of Bristol. The present authors are greatly indebted to Dr Lambert for drawing their attention to material used in this chapter and for his help in its interpretation.

pursue trials with the Ericsson system. At a time of not infrequent financial stringency they were ready to interest themselves in a well financed development project in the private sector and there was one to hand in Britain, well backed by prominent figures and with bankers' and engineers' support. The man who had filed the first patent application, on 31 May 1836, was Francis Pettit Smith, an Englishman born in 1808 at Hythe, who had settled as a farmer, first on Romney Marsh and later at what was then the village of Hendon. He had developed an interest in screw propulsion for ships, although how this came about is still something of a mystery, and his patent application followed trials with models. The wording[14] showed that he had realised, as Robert Wilson had done before him, the essential problem of efficient screw propulsion and found a solution to it. The propeller was to be placed 'in a recess or open space formed in that part of the after-part of the vessel commonly called the dead rising, or deadwood of the run'. In other words, the propeller was to be forward of the rudder with the result that, in the words of Dr Corlett,[15]

> The propeller is able to pick up the so called 'wake' of the hull. This is water which has been slowed down by friction with the hull and acts to increase the efficiency of the screw. The screw also generates a solid, fast moving stream of water which is directed on to the rudder and greatly improves the steering capabilities of the ship . . . This is also a very advantageous position as regards shafting and the ability to transmit power to the propeller.

The registering of this patent was followed by an example of entrepreneurial enterprise, of promotion and marketing, and of the interaction of private and public sectors, which would not have been out of place in the late twentieth century.

Francis Smith appears to have succeeded in interesting a banker, Mr Wright,[16] whose support may have been crucial in getting the whole project off the ground. Lord Sligo, who seems to have been Smith's principal 'interest', involved himself in Smith's work and in *Francis Smith*, a 34 foot launch which ran successful trials on the Thames and in the estuary in 1837. These successes led Lord Sligo to consult the then Captain George Evans. This officer, as we have seen (Chapters 2 and 4), in 1827 as a lieutenant had been appointed to command *Lightning* and had become the first commissioned officer of the Royal Navy ever to be appointed to take charge of a commissioned steam vessel. He later commanded *Rhadamanthus*, one of the first five steam vessels actually built as fighting ships and the first British

14 As quoted by Smith, *Marine Engineering*, pp 69–70.
15 Corlett, *op cit*, p 46.
16 Wilson, *Screw Propeller*, p 38; Bourne, *op cit*; *London Mechanics' Magazine*, No 830.

steam-assisted vessel to cross the Atlantic. George Evans briefly recorded the incident.[17]

> On the 18th Lord Sligo drove me down to the East India Docks to get my opinion of a screw attached to a boat of Mr. F. P. Smith, whose father was tutor to Lord Sligo. I examined the boat and highly approved of its construction, and told Lord Sligo it would be a good investment to have a small vessel built on the same principal, which was done . . .

A private company, the Screw Propeller Company (or the Patent Screw Propeller Company – there seems to have been more than one name in use) was registered, which included Lord Western, Lord Sligo, and Henry Wimshurst, the Blackwall shipbuilder. According to the *London Mechanics' Magazine*, [18] the chief promoters were Mr Wright, the banker, and the Rennie brothers. Their political influence may well have been decisive in encouraging the Admiralty's interest in Smith's patent. At a meeting of the Institution of Naval Architects on 25 July 1888, Mr G B Rennie made an intervention in discussion which, even after making due allowance for the bias imparted by family loyalty, casts some light on the process of decision taking. Mr Rennie said,[19]

> Mr. Smith had very considerable energy, and he asked Mr. Wright. the banker, to take the matter up as a very important subject in steam navigation. All the leading engineers were consulted, and they all gave an opinion adverse to it, with the exception, I may say, of my father, Mr. George Rennie, who made a report upon it to Mr. Wright, and stated that the adoption of the screw propeller would be a great improvement in steam navigation, and offered, provided he could get the money, to have a vessel built and design machinery suitable for the purpose, and a vessel was eventually built, called the *Archimedes*. The *Archimedes* was built on the Thames, and was engined by the firm in which my father took an interest. This was the first engine of any size at all used for steam navigation with the screw propeller. Those engines were of the vertical type, and the screw propellers were worked by gearing. The experiments made eventually led to the introduction of the screw propeller into the Navy and Mercantile Marine. My father and my uncle, Sir John Rennie, at that time knew Sir George Cockburn very well, and strongly recommended that the screw propeller should be introduced into the Navy. I may say at that time the officials were strongly against it. Sir George Cockburn, who was then senior Sea Lord, said, 'If you

17 Guest, ed, *Admiral George Evans*, p 30.
18 *London Mechanics' Magazine, op cit.*
19 Transactions of the Institution of Naval Architects, London 1889, Vol 30, p 106.

recommend this as practicable, and recommend us what to do, we will see what can be done in the matter'.

Smith's patent was purchased from him, but, in modern parlance, his services were retained by the new company. The company's objects were to demonstrate, improve and, through the sale of licences under Smith's patent, especially to the Admiralty, to exploit the financial possibilities of the patent. They financed and arranged the building of the *Propeller*, soon renamed the *Archimedes*, a screw steamer designed to be a floating advertisement, demonstration ship, vehicle for sales promotion, and a test bed.

Launched in November 1838, and costing her promoters £10,500, she was the world's first sea-going screw driven steamship. With an overall length of 125 feet, a beam of nearly 22 feet (the length to beam ratio of 6 to 1 reflected contemporary paddle steamer practice) and a displacement of 232 tons, she had an engine, by Rennie, of 80 nominal horse power. She was big enough for the results of her trials to be relevant for larger and more powerful vessels. The company used various methods to promote her. On 16 October 1839, she was demonstrated to a party of naval officers and others in the Thames. These included Captain Sir Edward Parry, Comptroller of Steam Machinery (see Chapter 4), and Captain George Evans. These officers put in somewhat conflicting reports of the demonstration. Parry wrote to Charles Wood, Secretary of the Admiralty.[20]

On Wednesday we had a trial of the 'Archimedes' by special invitation. None of the Board could go, but there were on board, Symonds, Shirreff, Ewart, Basil Hall, Austin, Evans, Miller (of M. and Ravenhill) and Rennie's man, – not either of themselves – a dozen gentlemen who are Screw Proprietors (i.e. shareholders in the company), and a few idlers besides.

The first thing that strikes you, is the abominable annoyance created both by the sound and the vibration. It is like the most noisy flour-mill, as regards the former, and the shaking very great. In the cabin it was not easy to converse comfortably across the table, and I should envy the nerves of the man or woman who could ever get a wink of sleep there, – i.e. in any part of the only cabin.

The whole vessel is occupied by the cabin, the machinery and boiler, and a small place forward for the crew. I do not see that she can carry anything else but Passengers.

We had the Master of the *William and Mary* with a proper log line, glass, &c. – that no 'passenger's Log' might impose upon us. Her utmost speed thus measured under Steam alone was 7¾ knots; but very soon

20 Parry, *Parry of the Arctic*, London 1963, pp 203–205.

after starting it became obvious that the steam could not be kept up. You are aware, I believe, that, after the bursting of Rennie's Boiler, and the notoriety of that fact occasioned by the Coroner's Inquest on the man who was killed by it, the Company insisted on not allowing Rennie to repair his boiler, not even to put in a new one at his own expense, which he offered to do, – but they employed Miller and Ravenhill for this purpose. The question now arose, why cannot the steam be kept up? and this question was very naturally put to Mr. Miller, who assured us that there must be something very wrong about the Engines, as the boiler was precisely the same as that which they furnish for Cylinders of the same diameter, and with the same length of stroke on the ordinary construction, and it is found amply sufficient in producing steam.

Rennie, who came to me yesterday, asserts, on the other hand, that the Boiler is too small, – for my own part I do not believe it. The two Manufacturers must, however, settle between them how it was that poor Mr. Smith's screw had no fair trial, the power applied being so much below what the Engines ought to have produced, that instead of 30 revolutions of the crank per minute, only 22 to 22½ could be produced by the most careful 'firing' with very good coals; and when half a dozen watches were produced near the measured mile, it was in vain to proceed with the experiment, the steam being so deficient that no fair result could have been obtained. So far, therefore, as the principle of the screw is concerned, it must be considered no experiment at all.

As the screw revolves 5⅓ times for each revolution of the crank, it is obvious that the speed of the screw was never much above 130 in a minute, – generally as little as 127. If, therefore, it had been driven at the rate of about 170, which 32 of the crank would have given it, I should think the vessel's speed might have increased to 9 or 9¼ – but this can scarcely be calculated.

I do not think the vessel should have had so much immersion – her draught being 10¼ feet, – her tonnage being under 200 tons, – a certain depth is necessary for the immersion of the screw, but 7ft. draught would I believe, have been enough, as it has turned out; since they have very much decreased the original radius of the screw. She is a nice little vessel, and a pretty model for sailing, which it seems they were anxious to combine with the screw-experiment, – two things not altogether compatible. They are about to take her over to Holland. Some large Steamers are said to be building for a communication between Amsterdam and London, and, in connection with this scheme, they (I know not whether the Company or private Individuals) think the *Archimedes* will do to put upon the North Holland Canal, a navigation of about 60 miles.

I thought you would like to know the real facts of this experiment, which will doubtless be stated somewhat differently in print.

By way of contrast, Captain George Evans reported to Admiral Sir William Parker, Second Naval Lord.[21]

> In my trip on board the *Archimedes* I observed that the screw possessed the following advantages over the common paddle-wheels:–
>
> 1st. By its immersion it is secure from the effects of shot.
>
> 2nd. Its action and power are not materially affected by the inclination of the vessel.
>
> 3rd. When the vessel is deep in the water the power is increased, as the screw moves in a denser medium.
>
> 4th. It admits of guns being placed on the broadside.
>
> 5th. Its motion, from being under water, is silent, and well adapted to surprise an enemy during the night; and during the day it is difficult to distinguish the *Archimedes* from a sailing vessel.
>
> 6th. It does not add to the breadth of the vessel, a circumstance of great importance, not only in navigating crowded rivers, but particularly in entering docks, basins, canals, etc.
>
> 7th. It does not agitate the water so as to injure banks of rivers, canals, or passing boats.
>
> 8th. There is no risk in passing close to buoys, or floating bodies, during the night.
>
> 9th. Sail can be carried as in any other ship, which must reduce the expenditure of coal, and increase the speed.
>
> 10th. The strain on the engines being steady and uniform, diminishes the wear and tear of both engines and vessel, and in all probability engines of a slighter construction will be found sufficiently strong, thus reducing, not only their weight and expense, but the space they occupy.
>
> 11th. Considerable more speed is to be obtained by the screw, as a propeller, than by the wheel or paddles; for that segment of all wheels or paddles, revolving out of the water, has to overcome the resistance of the atmosphere, and of course the greater their velocity, the greater this resistance becomes.
>
> In thus stating the advantages of the screw, under circumstances which render the common paddle-wheels lamentably deficient, I have now to draw your attention to what I consider one of the most important results of this excellent invention, namely, its effect on the steerage. The screw being placed immediately before the stern-post, forces the water against the rudder with such velocity, that the slightest motion of the helm is sufficient to turn the vessel. This motion of the water against the rudder commences the moment the screw revolves, and causes the vessel to

answer her helm, before she gets headway! In backing the engine a similar effect, in the opposite way, is produced on the rudder.

You can easily imagine how desirable this great power over the steerage of a vessel must be in crowded rivers, towing ships, and in frequently getting under weigh in a confined harbour, or on a 'lee shore', for however slowly the vessel may be going, the screw will force the water against the rudder with sufficient velocity to make her answer her helm.

When I take into consideration the probability that ere long an engine will be adapted to give the screw any velocity required (such as Lord Dundonald's rotary engine now in the course of trial at Portsmouth), I have no hesitation in declaring it to be my firm conviction that the screw will supersede every other means hitherto adopted for propelling vessels, except in 'very shoal water'.

As events were to develop, this was perhaps the most important single document in the development of the screw steamship. It is perhaps small wonder that it was Captain Evans's opinion that the directors of the Screw Propeller Company sought to publicise. On 31 December 1839, Lord Western wrote to Captain Evans at his London address.[22]

Our *Archimedes* Directors are beginning to show a little business-like activity by the spur of necessity, and are about to prepare a prospectus, to be put before the public; and I am desired to ask you if you will allow your letter to Sir William Parker to be introduced into it – of course with Sir William Parker's consent. I need hardly add that it would be, in my estimation, and, indeed, everybody's else, of the greatest use to us, and operate essentially to our success. An office is now opened in Cornhill (No. 71), where a Clerk and, I should hope, a Director, will be always in attendance, and that we may eventually open to the public the formation of a powerful Company. I am sure you will pardon my request, which you will of course unhesitatingly decline to acquiesce in if you do not like it.

A complex series of events followed. First, Commander Edward Chappell, RN, an experienced steam vessel officer who had been by his own claim in his *The Reports relative to Smith's Patent Screw Propeller* (London 1841) for thirteen years superintendent of the Post Office steam packets at Milford and Liverpool, and who was to be deeply involved with the Screw Propeller Company, conducted a series of trials with *Archimedes* in working conditions against paddle packets of the Dover Mail. These trials were

22 Guest, *op cit*, p 29.

made in early 1840. *Archimedes* was steamed against four packets, including *Widgeon*, the fastest of these vessels. Commander Chappell reported[23]

It is evident that in this vessel the propelling power of the screw is equal if not superior to that of the ordinary paddle wheel. Mr. Smith's invention may be considered completely successful.

Archimedes, still in charge of Commander Chappell, was then sent off on a cruise round Britain and a passage from Plymouth to Portugal which constituted a sales and marketing tour, the object of which was to familiarise the merchant shipping industry and the navy with the advantages of the screw as applied under the Smith's patent. During these trials, various changes were made and several different types of screw were tried. The results completely vindicated Francis Smith's placing of the screw between the sternpost and the rudder.

How the company worked is well illustrated by a letter from Commander Chappell to William Laird, at Birkenhead, the builder of *Nemesis*, whose entrepeneurial initiative was described in the previous chapter.[24]

> 17 Queen St.
> Mayfair
> London
>
> 11th July 1840

My dear Laird,

I should have replied to your kind letter earlier, but that I have been whirled along at such a rate as left me little time or quiet to sit down to correspondence. Our whole march round the Kingdom was a splendid triumph rather than a trial. At Glasgow we were enthusiastically received and I am under much obligation to you for the letter you sent, as well as for the attention and assistance received from your friends in Scotland. No doubt you saw the Glasgow, Greenock or Paisley papers giving accounts of our experiments in the Clyde. At Aberdeen, Leith, Newcastle and Hull our reception was equally warm and our exhibition equally satisfactory. I will send you one of the Edinburgh papers: and I can pledge my honour that from the beginning to the end of the expedition, not a line was written or dictated to any of the newspapers by any person on board *Archimedes*. The published accounts therefore shew the unbiased opinion of the Press. I have not at hand at this moment your letter with the accompanying note of your friend of Waterford but will you be so good as to tell him, if he will take the pains to draw up a series of questions upon the subject of the Screw, and address them to me, I

23 Fincham, *op cit*, p 347.
24 The Laird Papers – in private hands.

shall have great satisfaction in replying to them one by one, so as to give him information upon every point where he may feel at a loss.

The Directors of the Patent Screw Propeller Company, acting upon my suggestion have decided upon the immediate appointment of agents of all the out-ports of the Kingdom. At their request therefore I have undertaken to negotiate with parties willing to act on their behalf at all the places lately visited by the *Archimedes*. Should you be desirous to accept the office for Liverpool and the Mersey, I know of no person so competent to advocate the adoption of screw Propellers, nor so likely to keep a sharp watch over the interests of the Directors in protecting them against invasions of their patent by piracies, or otherwise. You would oblige me therefore by letting me know if I am at liberty to name you to the Directors for the appointment of their agent in the River Mersey.

It is not yet determined how the agents are to be remunerated; but I believe it will be by a percentage upon the Licences they may dispose of.

Should it not be convenient for you to undertake the Agency will you point out any person whom you think would be able and willing to undertake the office.

Yours very faithfully
E. CHAPPELL

Brunel, Claxton & Co are very seriously debating upon adopting the Screw in their large iron ship. [*The Great Britain*]

The Screw Propeller Company was not financially successful and it collapsed in the mid 1840s when Wright's bank failed. *Archimedes* was sold, her engine was taken out, and in 1849 she was metal-sheathed against marine borers and marine growth on the hull and put as a three masted, schooner rigged sailing vessel into what appears to have been regular trade to California, which opened up during and after the gold rush of 1848–49. She appears to have been sold in American waters and was last reported in trade between Chile and Australia in 1856. But she had done her job. Francis Smith himself proved not very competent in managing his financial affairs and passed through some vicissitudes before being appointed director of what is now the Science Museum and, eventually knighted. Commander Chappell was posted for his work with *Archimedes* and, although not re-employed by the navy in his captain's rank, went on half pay and became Secretary of the Royal Mail Steam Packet Company.

The whole concept of the use of steam in warships, which could be effective instruments of global policy, depended at this stage in the development of steam power on the use of steam as an auxiliary to sail in vessels capable of long range operation, firing broadsides from heavy guns. Once it was apparent, as it was from the earliest days of *Archimedes*'s trials, that this was probably now achievable through the use of the screw, the navy pushed the new idea as hard as its limited resources, (the early 1840s were a time of deep recession and cuts in government spending) politics, and the limitations of the bureaucracy would allow. In fact, the revolutionary steps towards the adoption of this entirely new concept of the ship as a weapon were taken more quickly than new developments of old weapons have been introduced in the last years of the twentieth century. At the same time, the development of the paddler continued for eight more years.

For reasons which have been discussed, the navy with its particular requirements for world operation was to adopt the screw much more rapidly than did the merchant shipping industry. As already mentioned, the private sector was interested in the fully powered steamer, but until the introduction of high pressure boilers and the compound engines of the mid 1860s her range of operations limited her to relatively few trades. The result was the predominance of the small, square rigged sailing ship, usually built of wood, as the normal vehicle of world trade until the early 1870s.

A further result was the creation of some confusion, from time to time, in the relationship which was to develop between the great engineer Isambard Kingdom Brunel and the Admiralty over the application of the screw in the navy's own experimental vessel, *Rattler*, when in due course Brunel was appointed consulting engineer to the project – a very natural development, bearing in mind his association with the Great Western Steamship Company and the building of *The Great Britain*. Naval thinking throughout was in terms of the steam screw auxiliary. Brunel, neither a naval nor a merchant ship naval architect, saw the screw as the answer to the problem of the fully powered steamship within the limits of the technology of the age. He was also, it would appear, impatient of bureaucracy and, accustomed to promoting and selling his ideas in the private sector at a time when risk capital appears to have been readily available, impatient of those whose political and public responsibilities imposed caution in the spending of public funds.

In May 1840, as part of her combined further trials and promotional voyage around Britain, *Archimedes* paid a visit to Bristol, where the Great Western Steamship Company was already building *The Great Britain*. The results of this visit were to be far reaching and the first of them is perhaps best summarised by quoting from the report in the *Bristol Press* of the annual meeting of the proprietors of the company, held in the company's offices in Prince Street.[25] The Report of the Directors presented at that meeting and 'unanimously received and adopted', *inter alia* stated that

> The Directors having satisfied themselves that it would be for the interests of the Company to get rid of the paddles in their iron ship, and to substitute a propeller upon the principle of the *Archimedes* screw have

25 13 March 1841.

taken the necessary measures for that purpose; the slight alterations required to her frame were easily affected, and at a trifling cost. The published reports of Captain Chappell made by the order of the Commissioners of the Admiralty, supported by the opinions of men of the highest classes in the naval service, and the careful examination of the performances of the *Archimedes* whilst in Bristol, excited the anxious attention of the Directors. Mr. Brunel, the Company's Consulting Engineer, entered closely into the investigation, as one most important to science and to their interests; the owners of the *Archimedes* most liberally placed her at his disposal for the purpose of experiments, and the Directors were allowed to send several confidential persons to see her to register observations on some points of primary importance in steam navigation, in reference to which, the performance of the *Great Western* had already possessed them of invaluable data. The result of a most elaborate report by Mr. Brunel, left no doubt in the mind of the Board, and they congratulate the proprietors on circumstances having allowed them to avail themselves of this great improvement in science, which will still enable them to maintain the advantages gained by the hitherto unequal character of their first ship. Had the last meeting empowered the Board to raise temporary loans, the completion of the Company's second ship in 1841 might have been effected, but this without unduly hurrying her work could not now be accomplished. By this period next year, she will, the Directors anticipate, be perfect for service.

But *The Great Britain* was not 'perfect for service' in March 1842. She was not in fact ready for sea until 12 December 1844. In the meantime, Brunel's exhaustive and carefully argued report of October 1840,[26] on the trials with *Archimedes* and on the application of the screw, which showed him now an ardent convert to this means of propulsion, was copied to the Admiralty, possibly by Christopher Claxton, Harbourmaster of Bristol since 1834, a director of the Great Western Steamship Company and close friend of Brunel for many years. Claxton, although usually described as 'captain', was, in fact, a half pay lieutenant who after 1819 was never again employed by the Service, although the rank of retired commander was to be conferred on him in June 1842. Born in the same year (1790) as Sir Edward Parry, a naval contemporary, he was in correspondence with Parry. As early as July 1838, Parry wrote to 'Lieutenant C. Claxton, R.N.' thanking him for a copy of the published logs of the first voyage of *Great Western* and sending good

26 The report is in the Wills Memorial Library of the University of Bristol. It is admirably summarised in Corlett, *op cit*, pp 50–52, and is doubly valuable for what it reveals of the state of knowledge of ship design and engineering in the early 1840s.

wishes for the success of the vessel.[27] While on 6 November 1840, he again wrote (addressing this time Christopher Claxton, Esq) saying *inter alia*[28]

> I shall feel particularly obliged by any information you can give me respecting the hull or machinery (including the *Screw*) of your large iron ship. What kind of engines have you finally determined on and when do you expect her to be ready?

In May 1841, in company with Peter Ewart, first chief engineer of Woolwich Dockyard, Parry visited Bristol to inspect 'the Establishment of the Great Western Steamship Co., and their large Iron Steam Ship now constructing'.[29]

Brunel in his report had listed the advantages of the screw propeller, all of which were particularly relevant to the navy's problems with paddle vessels. He concluded that they were a great saving in weight and the transfer of the weight of the engine and transmission from well above to well below the water line, the fact that the screw was unaffected by the trim or rolling of the vessel and allowed the free use of sails, the freedom from shocks to the engine caused by irregular immersion of the paddles, the greatly improved steering and the reduction in overall breadth were additional advantages. Also, the hull design could be improved.

During the latter part of 1840 and the year 1841, there was a great deal of discussion inside the Admiralty, some of which can be read in the minuting and correspondence. The first action appears to have been to build at Chatham in 1842 a small vessel of 42 tons as an instructional vessel for the gunnery training ship HMS *Excellent* and as such also for the RN College at Portsmouth. She was therefore to play an important role in familiarising officers with steam and thus generally steaming up the navy. Francis Smith was employed to supervise the construction of this vessel,[30] named HMS *Bee*, which was equipped with a screw as well as paddles. Both means of propulsion were powered by the same side-lever engine. *Bee* in her early days (she was to last until 1873) was also used for experimental work with different screws.

The first proposal for the building of larger vessels as a floating test bed for naval applications of the auxiliary screw came from Captain Chappell, who had continued his work with the Screw Propeller Company. He put forward two suggestions. The first was that a steam engine should be installed in a paddle sloop then building, *Shearwater*. Peter Ewart was of the

27 Parry to Claxton, 12 July 1838. ADM 92/4 236.
28 Parry to Claxton, 6 November 1840. ADM 92/4 420/1.
29 Parry to Secretary, Bristol, 8 May 1841. ADM 92/4 437/8.
30 Surveyor to Admiralty, 10 August 1841. ADM 92/10 106.

view that this could be done,[31] but Sir William Symonds did not like the proposal for the modification of the stern of the vessel.[32] The second proposal was that a frigate might be fitted with an auxiliary steam engine and screw. On this proposal Sir William Symonds commented

> nor do I see any objection to the screw being adopted according to Captain Chappell's second proposal, as such a frigate might be rigged as usual, either fitted for a troopship, storeship or armed with heavy guns.[33]

Parry followed up this opinion less than a month later with a firm proposal to the Board.[34]

> Mr. Ewart is of the opinion that there can be no doubt of the gearing of the screws being practicable, and capable of being effected conveniently and without noise to any objectionable extent in a vessel built and fitted for the purpose.
>
> I submit that a sister ship to the *Polythemus* be built for this purpose, and that Messrs. Seaward and Capel be directed to furnish drawings and an estimate for engines of 200 horsepower precisely similar to those of the *Polythemus*, but adapted, in the gearing to the driving of a Screw instead of Paddle Wheels. To communicate with the Surveyor, Mr. Ewart, Captain Chappell and myself as to the form etc. of Screw to be adopted in the first Instance.
>
> The aperture for the Screw may be so contrived as to form and size, as to allow the application of any of the numerous modifications of Blades, Propellers etc., so as to ascertain their relative advantages.
>
> W.E. Parry.

With regard to the noise created by the gearing of the transmission in *Archimedes* in her early days, Brunel had shared Parry's opinion (see page 139), saying in his report on screw propulsion that 'the noise and tremor caused by the machinery is such as to render the vessel uninhabitable and perfectly unfit for passengers, I should almost say for a crew'. But this difficulty could be easily overcome by the use of straps instead of gearing, the method Brunel used both in *The Great Britain* and in *Rattler*. The problem was, of course, that the slow running engines of the time, working at 15 to 20 revolutions per minute, had to be geared up to provide the minimum of 50 to 60 revolutions demanded by the screw propeller. Throughout these exchanges there is no sign of opposition to the

31 Admiralty to Surveyor, 4 November 1840. ADM 83/25 S.5055.
32 Surveyor to Admiralty, 12 February 1841. ADM 92/9 432.
33 Surveyor to Admiralty, 16 November 1840. ADM 92/9 p 330.
34 Parry to Board, 14 December 1840. ADM 92/4 423/4.

development and application of auxiliary screw propulsion from Sir William Symonds in his part as Surveyor of the Navy, nor is there any sign of anything but enthusiasm by the Board of the Admiralty as a whole. On the contrary, everything was moved forward relatively energetically.

It was shortly afterwards that Parry appears to have decided to bring in Brunel. He may well have felt the need for the support of so prestigious and knowledgeable a figure in his dealings of detail with Sir William Symonds, a man of powerful personality and great experience. It will be remembered (page 88) that Parry himself owed his position more to his interest than to his knowledge of steam vessels and naval architecture. The backing in matters technical of the consulting engineer to the biggest and most sophisticated shipbuilding project ever conceived to that date, *The Great Britain*, a screw propelled vessel a third as big again as the largest warship afloat, was likely to be very useful at times. Be that as it may, Brunel received a letter dated 22 April 1841 from Parry as follows.[35]

My dear Sir, I am desired by Lord Minto to say that he would be glad if you could make it convenient to attend the Board of Admiralty on the subject of the Screw Propeller, on Monday at 2 o'clock or on Tuesday at ½ past 10.

W.E. Parry.

I.K. Brunel, Esq., 18 Duke Street, Westminster.

Whilst this progress was being made in the Admiralty the private sector remained interested in the small, fully powered steamship for short range operations, limited to the twenty days rightly foreseen by Samuel Seaward (page 48). It was not until the 1860s, when technology and industry had developed to the point where the compound engine became commercially practicable and its operation in steamships profitable that the twenty day barrier was really overcome. But, in the meantime and within these limits, even at this very early stage at the beginning of the 1840s, the private sector was moving rapidly. According to a list, probably put out as part of the Screw Propeller Company's sales drive, and reproduced in a number of journals,[36] there were already in service by July 1842 the fully powered screw steamers *Bedlington* (270 tons, 60 horse power), *Princess Royal* (101 tons, 45 horse power) and the auxiliary *Novelty* (328 tons, 25 horse power). Under construction at the time were *The Great Britain* and *Great Northern*. In addition, two packets for the French Postal Service and a French naval

---

35 Parry to Brunel, 22 April 1841. ADM 92/4 436.
36 Such as *The Nautical Magazine*, Vol XI, 1842, p 850 and *The Shipping Gazette* of 9 December 1842.

vessel named *L'Orient* were claimed to be fitted with screws as patented by Smith.

Bedlington was a twin screw barge built of iron for service on the short run between Blyth and Shields with coal. She was plagued by mechanical faults and, although the world's first twin screw steamer, must be judged a failure.[37]

Novelty was built by Henry Wimshurst for the Screw Propeller Company at Blackwall in 1840 as a test bed for further experiments to demonstrate the potential of the auxiliary screw steamer. She started life with a 25 horse power 2 cylinder engine working at a pressure of 60 pounds per square inch, probably the highest pressure ever used in a marine engine up to that time. She was soon modified, and in 1843 Wimshurst described her as follows.[38]

> The *Novelty* is a very burdensome vessel, built as I have said by myself, with a view of testing the application of steam, in combination with a screw as an auxiliary power to merchant ships. She is a three masted vessel with a capacious hold, and as her funnel forms the mizzen mast, and she is of course without the clumsy appendage of paddle boxes, she differs in no respect in her external appearance from that of an ordinary sailing vessel.
>
> She is fitted with a pair of non-condensing engines, the cylinders are 30 inches in diameter, and the length of a stroke 3 ft. 4 ins; the effective force of the steam on the piston is 20 pounds mean pressure, being cut off at half stroke. The engines make about 55 double strokes per minute, and the power is applied direct to the crank or cranks from the screw access without the intervention of gearing or any kind of multiplying motion.

Novelty in her external appearance looked, in fact, like any single topsail barque of the period. In 1841, she was chartered to take 421 tons of mixed cargo from Liverpool to Istanbul. This was the first long commercial voyage made by a screw auxiliary steam vessel.

Great Northern was the largest screw propelled steamship in the world at the time she was launched at Londonderry on 23 July 1842. She was a wooden auxiliary screw full rigged ship of 1111 tons, measuring 217 feet overall, and she appears to have been the first steam vessel to have carried her machinery in the after part of the vessel instead of amidships, thereby seeking to overcome the problem of transmitting power down a rotating shaft to the screw from an engine placed amidships, a process which resulted in stresses few wooden merchant ships could withstand. Of 360 horse power, she was not only the largest but also the most powerful screw vessel

37 Martin and McCord, *Maritime History*, No 1, April 1971, pp 46–64.
38 Wimshurst, 'The *Novelty* Steamship', *Nautical Magazine*, 1843, pp 107–110.

ever built. Constructed on speculation and financed by local merchants, Francis Smith himself and the Screw Propeller Company were deeply involved in her construction. It appears evident that she was built in the belief that there was a reasonable chance of a lucrative Admiralty charter for her, or outright sale as a floating test bed. In fact, the naval authorities took considerable and continuing interest in her construction. William Blessley, foreman of Sheerness Dockyard, was sent to Londonderry on the instructions of Sir John Barrow, Second Secretary to the Admiralty, in May 1842[39] to survey the vessel. His examination revealed that although well built in many respects she had softwood beams, shelves, waterways, decks, and the greater part of her planking. This damned her from the start. Sir William Symonds commented[40]

> From Mr. Blessley's report she appears strongly put together, and that she is very capacious as to room; But I fear that some of her materials are of doubtful durability.

Moreover, before *Great Northern* no big engine had been built specifically to drive a screw propeller at sea and, for reasons already explained in this chapter, it may have been on the outer limits of the technology of the late 1830s to do so. Even Brunel was to side-step the problem with the solution for *The Great Britain* of an adaption to a screw propeller of a power unit for paddle propulsion, designed many years before by his father, which gave good and commercially viable service until it was ruined by a winter on the beach after the vessel had grounded in Dundrum Bay. The engine of *Great Northern* was designed and built in the yard at Londonderry from parts assembled from different makers in the British Isles. From contemporary accounts[41] it is apparent that it was a ramshackle affair which was still inadequate even after it had been partly rebuilt by the London engine builders Miller and Ravenhill.

Great Northern sailed to London in December 1842, experiencing some difficulties with her engine on the passage, and on arrival in dock, on the instructions of the First Naval Lord, Admiral Sir George Cockburn, she was visited by Parry himself, accompanied by Thomas Lloyd, Inspector of Steam Machinery at Woolwich. It is apparent that she was taken very seriously by the Admiralty and this interest was to be demonstrated again when in October 1843 she made a demonstration trip, with her refurbished engines, in the Thames with Thomas Lloyd, Captain Sir Francis Collier, superintendent of Woolwich Dockyard, Francis Smith and Captain Chappell on board. But her defects were too great to be overcome. The Admiralty were looking for a purpose built floating test bed, and in June

39 Barrow to Symonds, 3 May 1842. ADM 1/5522 3143.
40 Symonds to Admiralty, 13 May 1842. ADM 1/5522 No 397.
41 See, for instance, *The Artisan*, January 1843, Vol 1, p 28.

1843 they very wisely bought *Mermaid*, to be renamed HMS *Dwarf*, built of iron on the Thames by Ditchburn and Mare, of 164 tons displacement, a fully powered vessel ideal for their purpose as a test bed for George Rennie's propellers. *Great Northern*, after languishing for some years in the London river, was broken up.[42]

With *Dwarf*, technically the first screw steamer ever to be commissioned into the Royal Navy, full scale experiments were carried out, at the suggestion of Thomas Lloyd, to determine the interaction of the shape of a vessel's after body and the various types of screw propeller. These showed the great influence of the underwater body in the efficiency of screw propulsion.[43]

★ ★ ★ ★ ★

The outcome of Brunel's interview with Lord Minto was that he was appointed consulting engineer with, as Parry expressed it in a letter to Brunel of 31 July 1841,[44]

> sole responsibility and consequently the sole direction of the mechanical arrangements for making trial of the Screw Propeller in a vessel to be built as a Sister Ship to the *Polythemus*, and so far as I am aware this understanding is still in full force . . . I am quite sure that there neither was, nor is, the smallest intention of allowing any interference with your own views on the part of the Admiralty Engineers, and you; and you may depend upon it that there will be none.
>
> All that the Engineer Officers will have to do is to assist in carrying forward your views and I do not recollect that their report or opinion has been called for, except in the question which you referred for a decision to the Admiralty. I mean the question as to what manufacturer should be called upon to make the Engines. The result has been that two of the three named by you have been invited to tender, and there I think the matter rests. No tender will be accepted without reference to you. At least if my views are followed, I do not see how, under the circumstances, you need apprehend any interference whatever.
>
> At all events I wish to venture to say that, if anything occurs approaching to such interference, I hope you will mention it to me, and I will do everything in my power to set the matter right, and in so doing I am sure I shall be acting in the full spirit of Their Lordships' intentions in this matter.

42 For a detailed study of *Great Northern*, see Greenhill, in Fisher, ed, *op cit*, pp 43–59.

43 Engineer Vice Admiral RW Skelton, 'Progress in Marine Engineering', Sir Thomas Lowe Gray, Memorial Lecture, *Proceedings of the Institute of Mechanical Engineers, 1930*, Vol 1, p 9.

44 Parry to Brunel, 6 July 1841. ADM 92/4.

The inference may be that Brunel's intolerance of the public sector had been at work, and also that there had perhaps been some personality clash between him and Symonds, despite the latter's sympathy for the development of the screw. Both men were at the top of their professions, both strong personalities and both would seem, from the records they have left, inclined on occasion to arrogance. Before Brunel's position, and that of Francis Smith and the Ship Propeller Company, were finally clarified there was a further conference at which all the men principally involved, that is Brunel, Symonds, Smith, Captain Chappell and Peter Ewart, met under the chairmanship of Lord Minto in September 1841.

It is almost needless to say that there followed political complications. The Whig government headed by Lord Melbourne was replaced in the same month by a Tory ministry under Sir Robert Peel. Brunel's sympathies were well known to be with the Whigs and there followed a period of uncertainty during which the new Admiralty Board considered adapting an existing vessel, the paddle steamer *Acheron*, for screw propulsion trials, rather than building a new vessel especially for the purpose. There was a great deal of sense in this proposal. As has been seen, the navy's interest was in the development of screw propulsion in existing ships which would retain a full sailing performance and range. Brunel, as always, was thinking of the fully powered steamer with its very limited range at the time. Naturally, Brunel opposed the idea strongly in a letter of 10 Feburary 1842 to Sir James Barrow, Second Secretary to the Admiralty, on the technical grounds that the vessel's afterbody was quite wrongly shaped, being too full for screw propulsion, that the presence of the paddles' sponsons presented an insuperable problem, and that the new engines prepared for her were too powerful to allow a proper comparison with her performance as a paddler. Brunel ended[45]

In conclusion I must beg strongly to urge upon Their Lordships if they are still desirous of determining whether the screw is equal or superior to the paddles for all or any of the objects required in Government Steamships, that this point can be determined only by building and rigging a vessel expressly adapted to the Screw, and as nearly as possible of the same dimensions with the same power as some of the best paddle Steam-boats with which her different qualities under different circumstances can be tested – that this mode of making the experiment will be the only effectual one and will eventually cause much the least waste of time and as a very good Steamboat will at all events be obtained, it cannot be considered as involving any waste of money or any expense for the mere experiment.

45 Brunel to Barrow, 10 February 1842. ADM 83/25.

Sidney Herbert, now Chief Secretary to the Admiralty, endorsed Brunel's letter as follows,

> 'Feby. 18, Send this to Sir W. Symonds and desire him to report any Steamer now in progress of building he considers fit to receive the engines ordered for the Screw, and he thinks can be adapted or altered for that purpose and to communicate with Sir E. Parry and Mr. Brunel. Sidney Herbert.

No vessel under construction suitable for adaptation could be found in February 1842. It was finally approved that a new vessel would be built, at Sheerness. She would be built in place of a paddle sloop which was to be called *Rattler* and which had been scheduled on paper for construction.[46] The new vessel would also bear the name *Rattler*.

> Surveyor of the Navy, noted 25th.
> Their Lordships are pleased to approve of your proposition dated the 22nd Inst. for building a Steam Vessel at Sheerness not larger than the *Prometheus* for the reception of the Screw Propeller and that she be substituted in the Scheme for the ensuing year for the *Rattler*. By Command of Their Lordships, John Barrow.

From now on the work proceeded very rapidly, although there were inevitably some further hiccups. Symonds reported on 9 September,[47]

> Having in my recent visit to Sheerness observed that the work on *Rattler*'s afterbody is suspended on account of the indecision of the Engineers who are to provide the Screw Propeller for her – I recommend that Mr. Brunel and Mr. Smith be informed thereof and urged to give their final directions immediately.

Here it would appear that Brunel rather than the Admiralty[48] was dragging his feet.

Whilst *Rattler* was being built, and in the two or three years immediately following, developments in screw propulsion were taking place in the United States. Ericsson and his screw were taken up by Robert F. Stockton, an influential American politician and naval officer, and after a long political process the USS *Princeton*, propelled by Ericsson's screw, was launched at Philadelphia on 7 September 1843. Launched five months after

46 Barrow to Surveyor, 24 February 1842. ADM 83/25.
47 Surveyor to Admiralty, 3 September 1842. ADM 92/10 377.
48 For a blow by blow account of Brunel's relations with the Admiralty at this point and of the various stages in the building of *Rattler*, see Lambert, *op cit*.

Rattler, she appears to have been the second screw propelled steamship of war and the first with all her machinery below the water line. The competition, to some degree commercial, between the Ship Propeller Company and the sponsors of Ericsson's screw system led to the publication of some extensive misinformation. An excellent example of pseudo-scientific denigration of *Archimedes* and her work is provided by a pamphlet[49] published in London and New York in 1841.

Of great interest was *Bangor II*, a small iron twin screw steamer, built at Wilmington, Delaware, between October 1843 and May 1844. She was of 231 tons, 131 feet in length and rigged, like *The Great Britain*, with loose-footed sails set from standing gaffs and brailing in to the weather of the sail, in her case as a three masted schooner. Her machinery comprised two separate horizontal engines, each driving a screw. Owned in Bangor, Maine, and registered at Frankfort, Maine, she was managed in Bath on the Kennebec which was her operational base, and she ran between Boston and Bangor with passengers and freight. She was sold to the United States government in December 1846, and employed, as the USS *Scourge*, as a unit of the United States Navy during the Mexican War. She took part in a number of actions and after the war she was sold again to owners in Lafayette, Louisiana. She became a merchant ship once more and continued as such until she went missing in 1856 on a passage from Pensacola, Florida, towards New Orleans.

Little *Bangor II* would appear to have been the second iron sea-going screw steamship to enter commercial service, after the British *Bedlington*, the first successful sea-going twin screw steamship and the first screw driven warship successfully involved in action. Her engines operated at the then high pressure of 46 pounds per square inch and it would appear that they were locomotive units operating on fresh water. Her sea-going ability was therefore limited to the regular passage of 170 miles or so from Boston to the freshwater of the Penobscot river for which she was designed. For naval service she appears to have been refitted with low pressure marine engines and boilers using salt water.[50]

Rattler was launched on 12 April 1843. *The Times* reported the event the next day.

> Yesterday, about an hour before high water, at half-past 10 o'clock, the steam frigate *Rattler* was launched from the slips at the Royal dockyard,

49 Byrne, *On the Best Means of Propelling Ships at Sea*, London and New York 1841.

50 Bradlee, *Some Account of Steam Navigation in New England* in the Essex Institute Historical Collection, Vol IV, Oct 1919, Salem, Mass 1919, pp 266–269. *Dictionary of American Naval Fighting Ships*, Vol VI, Washington 1976, p 388. Heyle, *Early American Steamers*, Buffalo, NY 1953, p 47–48. *The Bath Independent*, Bath, Maine, 1 Aug 1929, p 4, col 1. For a detailed study of *Bangor II*, see Greenhill and Corlett, 'The Iron Screw Steamship *Bangor II*', *International Journal of Maritime History*, II, No 1 (June 1990), pp 213–226.

Sheerness, into the waters of the Medway. This vessel is built on the principle of the invention of Mr. Smith, the patentee of the screw propeller, and will be immediately fitted up with boilers and engines and the necessary apparatus for working the screw. She is of a remarkably fine model, and from what can be judged of her appearance, will be a most efficient and warlike craft, when her masts, rigging, and guns are placed on board. She is of the same tonnage as the *Polythemus* steam frigate, and of the same dimensions; that vessel has portable wheels in boxes, and is built in that respect upon the old principles of construction. The fact of this frigate, the *Rattler*, being now afloat, and about speedily to be fitted and completed for service, is important, because it will test the principle over the screw-propeller effectually. The great advantages of this principle over the paddle-wheels and boxes, hitherto made use of in steam navigation, are that in vessels to be used as men-of-war the whole length of deck is uninterrupted, so that what is going on at the bows of the vessel can be seen from the stern, and vice versa; and the whole battery of her guns can be worked uniformly, and under the direction of the captain. In short, the view is not broken by paddle-boxes, and the deck, as it were, divided into two distinct parts. Another advantage is that the screw being under water is out of the way of mischief, and not liable to be damaged by shot; and a further advantage is, that she is capable of being turned about in a much smaller space than a steamer propelled by paddle-wheels, which, as everybody knows, takes an immense space in the water to perform her evolutions. Neither, it may be added, does the screw-propeller retard the sailing powers of the vessel, which paddle-boxes must unavoidably do, from the awkwardness of their position and their largeness of dimensions. The *Rattler* was laid down about 12 months ago, she is built of oak, and constructed with great strength, which may be judged of from her deflexion or expanding upon the strain of launching being only half an inch. She does great credit to Mr. Atkins, the builder, who has shown his perfect professional knowledge in the building of this noble vessel. Her dimensions are as follows:

	Feet.	In.
Length extreme	195	
Length on the deck	176	6
Length of the keel for tonnage	157	9½
Breadth extreme	32	8½
Breadth moulded	31	10
Depth in hold	18	7½

The *Archimedes*, the well-known original screw-steamer, the property of the Ship Propeller Company, conveyed a party of gentlemen connected with scientific and nautical pursuits early in the morning from Blackheath to Sheerness, to inspect the *Rattler*. Mr. Atkins, the builder, kindly explained to them her principle, and the party afterwards returned to London in the *Archimedes*; on board which vessel a cold collation, supplied by Mr. Pritchard, of the East India Dock-house, was served up, and 'Success to the new steam-frigate' drunk with the usual honours by all present.

This account bears all the hallmarks of a handout from the Screw Propeller Company.

Rattler was fitted by Maudslays at their Thames yard with a 200 horse power engine driving the shaft through straps instead of gearing. The engine under operational conditions turned at 25 revolutions per minute, the shaft rotating at 112 revolutions. Her displacement was 1112 tons. She took until October to engine and fit out. Her first trial trips were made as soon as she was handed over to the navy and before she was coppered at the Royal Dockyard at Woolwich. The whole history of her construction and trials shows the Admiralty as anxious to do all it could to further as rapidly as possible the development of the application of the screw to vessels of war.

The Admiralty's close interest in the technology and performances of screw propelled vessels is shown by their continued involvement with *The Great Britain*. When she finally went on her trials in January 1845, Thomas Lloyd and Commander Crispin, formerly commanding officer (according to O'Byrne's *Biographical Dictionary* of 1849) of the 'Steam Cruizer' *Vulcan* and, from 1 June 1845, commander of the Royal Yacht *Victoria and Albert*, were on board by the Admiralty's order. Both reported on their experience. Commander Crispin's letter to Sidney Herbert has survived.[51] Writing from *Victoria and Albert*, he reported in most glowing terms on the screw and on the speed, handiness, and seaworthiness of *The Great Britain*.

> H.M.S. Yacht *Victoria & Albert,*
> Portsmouth,
> 29 Jany 1845.

Sir,

   In obedience to the orders of my Lords Commissioners of the Admiralty, I beg to inform you that I proceeded to Bristol on the 23rd Instant, and on my arrival on board the Iron Steam Ship "Great Britain" in King Road, found her ready to go to Sea, which we did about 7.30 P.M. on the same day. . . . At 5 A.M. on the 24th the wind which hitherto had been from the S.W. blowing strong, suddenly chopped round to the N.W. and blew very hard. At 9 when off Lundy, we found a very heavy nasty cross Sea, occasioned by a spring Ebb Tide running against the Gale. I had therefore a fine opportunity of judging, both the

---

51 Crispin to Herbert, 29 January 1845. ADM/87.

qualities of the Ship and screw. The former I found to have all the quickness of Motion and a Vessel of 500 tons, more particularly in regard to her rolling, which certainly surpassed any thing I had ever before witnessed, having timed her frequently during the passage to roll from side to side 7 times in a Minute, and on some occasions even as many as 9 times in the same period. – This quickness no doubt arose from her exceeding light draught of Water, at the same time I must observe, that her very wonderful stability when pressed with canvas was astonishing! – Her pitching was very easy, and although so light I watched most particularly the keel of the Ship from over the Stern, to see how far she rose and lifted the Screw out of the Water, and to my great surprise she never on any one occasion, had less than 6 feet of it immersed. –

The Screw far surpassed my most sanguine expectations on all points connected with it as a propeller, for, with all the disadvantages above related, against this heavy Sea and Gale, it propelled this large body of 3500 tons at the rate of 4 knots. – At 10 we were enabled to set the Fore Staysail, the wind having come round to N.N.W. steering West. –

We then went 4 and 6, and what now struck me as most astonishing, was that although this Sail – 320 feet from the Propelling power, with this heavy Sea on her bow, that the Rudder had perfect command of her, and that she did not fall off in the slightest degree from her course, and that *one* Man was sufficient to Steer her. – Shortly after this the Foresail was set, which increased her speed to 5 and 2, from this time more Sail was gradually increased until the whole of her Trysails and Jib were set, at this period she had reached a speed of 8 and 2. – I again went into the Engine Room and found, although this speed was acquired, no more Steam was used, but was still working with 9 tenths of the Throttle Valve shut and expansively cutting off the Steam at one sixth of the stroke, thereby proving the immense advantage of the Screw as a Propeller over the Paddle Vessel, and I am quite sure that had a Paddle Vessel been similarly situated she could not have attempted to carry such a press of Sail: for had she done so, her lee wheel would have been so deeply immersed, and her weather one so much out of water, that her speed would have been greatly retarded. – Another vast advantage of the Screw was this, that although there was so much Sea, and the Ship pitching considerably, yet the Machinery worked with almost the same regularity that a Paddle Vessel would have done had it been in the smoothest Water, and I am convinced that with the Screw as a Propeller, no Engineer will ever have the slightest dread of his Engines overrunning themselves at one moment, and being as suddenly checked the next. – To conclude my observations on the Screw, my only dread of its use rests in this, that from its immense power always acting on the Ship, in all weathers the same, that should not greater caution be observed by the officer in charge of the Watch, the Ship might be forced with too much impetus against a head Sea, but this I need not remark is a good fault, and can easily be avoided by proper judgement.

At 8.45 P.M. on the 24th we rounded the Longships, when the wind died away and the Sea smooth, the sails of no use but notwithstanding the precautions obliged to be used from working with new Machinery, having 11 out of the 12 Engineers unfit for duty from *Sea Sickness*, the Stokers in the same state and almost refusing to keep proper Fires, and the Steam consequently seldom up, we passed the Needles at 1.45 on the 25th thus under Steam alone, running a distance of 174 miles in 16 hours, and obliged all this time to work expansively, cutting off the Steam at one sixth the Stroke.

We anchored in the Downs at 1.30 A.M. on the 26th and at 8 A.M. we started, and although it was blowing a furious Gale from the N.W. right ahead, reached Woolwich at 3.3 P.M. this speed in such weather, far surpassed anything I had ever witnessed, to prove which I produce this one fact. –

At noon a Steamer 3 miles ahead, at 1.10 we passed her, and had anchored off Blackwall, one hour and ten minutes ere she reached that place this Vessel was the 'Water Witch' a Hull Boat and generally supposed to be a very good one.

The quick manner in which this immense body answered her helm surprised me, and is one of the great recommendations of the Screw as a Propeller, in proof of which I will only mention that she came through the Needles passage against the strength of a Spring Ebb Tide at full speed, and did not swerve from her course so much as I'd seen the *Vulcan* do when similarly situated. – I am therefore decidedly of opinion, that the Screw Propeller is in every way beyond comparison superior to the Paddle Wheel and I am led to this conclusion from the very great attention to its working in the *Rattler* in smooth water, as well as to its still better qualities, observed most minutely in a rough Sea during this Voyage in the *Great Britain* under the most unfavourable circumstances.

The experiments with *Rattler* as a floating test bed continued through the mid 1840s. Within a year of her completion, the Admiralty had ordered the conversion or construction of large vessels fitted with auxiliary steam machinery. *Rattler* still had her engines high in the vessel, in a position as vulnerable to shot as those of a paddler. This problem was solved by a new development introduced by the indefatigable Francis Smith and the Ship Propeller Company.[52]

---

52 Back (Secretary Ship Propeller Company) to the Admiralty, 11 June 1844. ADM 87/14.

Ship Propellers Office, 15, Fish Street Hill, 11 June 1844.
To the Secretary of the Admiralty,
Sir,

I am instructed by the Directors of the Ship Propeller Company to request the favour of your laying the following statement before the Lords Commissioners of the Admiralty. They beg leave to inform Their Lordships that a new Crankshaft has been invented which in the opinion of able Engineers is capable of superseding Cog Wheels, Straps or other gearing in combination with the Screw, and with the permission of the Board of the Admiralty, Mr. Smith will do himself the honour of exhibiting a model, explaining its use in simplicity and peculiar fitness to confine all the Machinery within a few feet above the Keelson of any vessel.

The Directors are confident that this invention will be a most valuable acquisition in H.M. Naval service by affording the means of employing auxiliary steam power for large men-of-war. Within a space infinitely smaller than has ever been contemplated and without interfering with their sailing qualities or their armaments. Should therefore Their Lordships be disposed to entertain the subject and will favour Mr. Smith with a cross and longitudinal section of any large ship, he will annexe a capital drawing, which will duly exhibit the exact space the whole Machinery will occupy in such ship. I have the honour to be Sir, Your very obedient Servant,

W.M. Back (Secretary)

Endorsed June 12, Surveyor to send him a longitudinal section of the *Amphion*
20th Section sent to Mr. Back.

After the appointment of Sir Baldwin Walker as Surveyor of the Navy in 1848, progress was very rapid.[53] As early as September Lord Auckland, First Lord of the Admiralty from 1846, had declared[54]

I am satisfied that the whole theory of shipbuilding will be directed from the old notion of sailing ships to the manner in which the screw auxiliary may best be combined with good sailing qualities.

The whole technique of ship handling had to be reassessed, slowly and painfully, as the Baltic campaign of the coming War with Russia was to reveal. But that same campaign showed the steam auxiliary screw frigate and ship of the line to be, by their very potential, the most formidable weapons which had ever put to sea.

53 See particularly, Lambert, *Transition*, pp 31–40.
54 Auckland to Napier, 7 September 1848, British Library Add Mss 40, 023 + 278 (Napier mss).

Meanwhile, the development of the paddle frigate was vigorously pushed forward towards the limits of which steam vessels propelled by paddles would ever be capable. Despite all the work going forward on the development of screw propulsion, she was, as far as she went, at this time in the 1840s the only effective steamship of war. Paddle frigates continued to be built until 1851 when *Valorous* was launched, and she was to last in service until 1891 and to be the last paddle frigate in the navy.

The scene is set, socially, politically, economically, and in terms of industrial and technical development. The paddler, for all her disadvantages, had her strong advocates and uses which made her essential as part of any grouping of naval ships of the 1840s. She was the subject of much controversy and much experiment in armament in engines and in new construction. Paddlers were built at all the royal dockyards and some ten different firms built the engines. Because of her deficiencies and the nature of the services for which she had proved most valuable – towing, reconnaissance, survey work, anti-slavery patrol, troop transport, above all as a fast dispatch vessel – she had always tended to be fully powered and, as bigger and bigger vessels had been built, so had their power increased. By 1842, the designs of vessels which were to be first-class paddle frigates were approved for construction. At the same time, as a result of the work of the Ship Propeller Company, of Brunel, and of *Archimedes*, the Admiralty in the early 1840s were beginning their large scale experimental work on screw propulsion with the launch of *Rattler*.

So the evolution of the paddler into the paddle frigate and the beginnings of experimental work on screw propulsion through the navy took place in the same year. Some seventeen or eighteen vessels, usually contemporaneously described as paddle frigates, were commissioned in and after 1843, together with some fifteen sloops.

The screw was finally proved at a series of trials conducted off Lisbon in 1850. These showed that the auxiliary screw steamship, represented particularly by the screw frigate *Arrogant* of 1846, could have all the virtues and broadside fighting power of the sailing vessel plus the greater mobility and safety of the steamer. She was built under the supervision of John Fincham and given a compact engine by Penn of Greenwich. There is a reproduction of this type of engine on board *Warrior* at Portsmouth today. Machinery breakdowns with the early screw frigates were frequent, but the trials with *Arrogant* and a number of 'blockships', coastal defence vessels of limited sailing range, showed the potential of the screw when more reliable engines were developed. It was fighting power, not speed under steam or sail, which was the ultimate determinant. The much publicised trials in which *Rattler* towed the paddler *Alecto* stern first against the full power of her engines merely demonstrated the superiority of the screw for towing purposes. Thus, for the time being, 'the riddle of the age', as Dahlgren had described the conundrum of the design of a truly effective steam warship, was solved. The new construction of large purely sailing ships was stopped in 1849.

Some indication of the rate of adoption of the screw by the navy and the merchant shipping industry up to 1852 is given by Murray and by Parliamentary Papers.[55] The latter record fifty-eight screw driven steamships as registered under the Merchant Shipping Acts in 1852, nearly all under 1000 tons. Murray lists thirty-nine 'screw steamers in Her Majesty's Navy' of which a dozen or so were at the time completed, rigged and equipped in varying degrees. These twelve vessels included four or five which might be considered to be screw frigates. His list of paddle steamers of all kinds in 'Her Majesty's Navy and Post Office Service' totals 116.

The useful if somewhat arbitrary selection of the world's merchant tonnage which appears in *Lloyd's Register* for the following year, 1853, is revealing. Of the 187 steam vessels listed seventy-four are iron screws, six are wooden screws, fifty-four are iron paddlers and fifty-three wooden paddlers. In that year there were 9934 vessels listed in the register book. Merchant steamers of all kinds therefore represented less than 2 per cent of all vessels by number and screw steamers 0.8 per cent of this selection of the world's tonnage.

But in August 1852, the first really successful steamship of the line, *Agamemnon* (91 guns, 600 horse power) was launched. She was designed from the start as a steam auxiliary, with fine lines at the bows and a long run and fine stern lines. In 1852 also a further French invasion scare, based partly on their construction of the steam screw line of battleship *Le Napoléon* (the vessel's performance did not justify the commotion caused – see Chapter 12) led to the decision of a short lived Tory administration under Lord Derby late in that year to create a steam screw battle fleet.

Fifteen months later, under the pressure of the War with Russia which broke out in March 1854, it proved possible to provide eighteen screw propelled vessels of 60 guns or more, four steam screw frigates and four smaller screw driven vessels together with at least eighteen paddlers for the Baltic Fleet, which began the build up of the threat to St Petersburg which was to prove decisive in the outcome of the war.[56] This was, for the first time in history, a predominantly steam driven fleet. At the same time three vessels of 60 or more guns, eleven smaller screw driven vessels and twenty-one paddlers were sent to the Black Sea. Here, among other functions, the paddlers represented the towing power for a predominantly sailing fleet.

55 Murray, *Marine Engines*, pp 202–12, Return of the Whole of the Registered Steam Navy, BPP, 1852 (XLVIX).

56 O'Byrne's *Naval Annual* for 1855, London 1855, p 20–32 and 58–68. These figures may not be complete but they indicate the situation.

8

The Employment of the Paddle Frigate: 1 *Penelope* on Anti-Slave Trade Patrol

The steam paddle frigate had a life of only about eight years, in the sense that only for eight years were vessels built or converted to be of this class. The definition of a paddle frigate was not always clear, as we have seen with some references to *Gorgon* (see Chapter 2, page 53) and the designations of the different types of paddle propelled vessel changed over the years. Usually, they were associated with the nature and distribution of the armament, but the situation was not made simpler by the fact that this was often changed in the search for maximum effectiveness. In 1844, after the commissioning of *Penelope*, the status of command determined the designation of the vessel.[1] If commanded by a post captain the vessel was rated a frigate, if by a commander she was rated a sloop. Since the appointment of the commanding officer depended, as we have seen, principally upon the strength of his interest, that is, on patronage, we have here a system in which the rating of steam paddle vessels depended upon patronage rather that upon, within fine limits, their size, armament or power. There were paddle frigates first class commanded by a post captain with four lieutenants and between 300 and 400 ratings, paddle frigates second class with a post captain in command, three lieutenants and between 75 and 250 ratings. Vessels could be moved up or down between these two classes as their armament and complement might vary with modification and refits. There were three classes of sloop: the first had a commander, three lieutenants, and 145 ratings, the second had a commander, two lieutenants and 110 ratings, and the third had a commander, two lieutenants and 100 ratings. In total, under these classifications there were commissioned between 1836 and 1849 twenty first class paddle sloops, seven second class and ten of the third class.

1 See Timewell, 'Paddle Frigates in the Royal Navy', *The Mariner's Mirror*, Vol 67, No 1, pp 93–94.

These two classes of vessel, the paddle frigate and the paddle sloop, represented two distinct strands in naval thinking about steam vessels which become apparent in the early 1840s. One strand, that of the paddle frigate, represented a struggle towards the unachievable – the paddle steamer capable of carrying a full broadside on her main deck, a vessel which could take on a ship of the line. The nearest vessel to achieving this was *Terrible* (see below), but at enormous expense. The other strand, that of the sloop, was realistic and saw the paddle steamer as a very useful naval vessel if she had high speed and the power to tow large vessels; she could also be quite formidably armed on her upper deck. In fact, it was this strand which was followed in practice, and even the paddle frigates were used in a way which exploited these qualities, as this and the ensuing chapters will show.

But to many naval officers the older classifications based on armament and where it was carried remained the only proper basis for rating vessels. Thus Captain (later Admiral Sir) Henry Chads, a noted gunnery officer of his generation, giving evidence to the House of Commons Committee, declared [2]

Few of our steamers of war are equal to go alongside a French steamer. They have broadside armament, whereas many of ours are only armed at bow and stern. Our steam sloops carry two heavy guns; a 95 hundredweight 68 pounder, and an 86 hundredweight ten inch gun, and 4 broadside guns, 32 pounders of 40 or 42 hundredweight. We have only three real steam frigates (carrying guns on the main deck), namely, the *Odin*, the *Sidon* and *Terrible* – and the screw vessels.

The vessels to which Captain Chads referred were heavily armed with a full main deck battery of sixteen heavy guns and six more on the upper deck. In 1844, the design was approved of a vessel which was to become the first class paddle frigate *Retribution*, and which was planned to carry a main deck armament. This, however, was probably not mounted until 1850, after she had been re-engined and re-rigged from brig to barque. In the same year, Oliver Lang, the master shipwright at Woolwich Dockyard, was invited to prepare the design of an 800 horse power frigate to have powerful armament on both main and upper decks. But the construction of this paddle frigate, the largest ever built, which became *Terrible*, one of the navy's most successful paddle vessels, was not begun until 1843. She was commissioned in 1846. Larger than a contemporary 74 gun sailing vessel, she was equipped with a battery comprising eight 68 pounder 95 hundredweight guns and eight 56 pounder 98 hundredweight guns, a considerable armament. She also had the power to tow a big ship of the line at 8 knots. She served with distinction in the War with Russia. The most

2 Murray, *op cit*, p 158.

formidable of all the paddle frigates, she was very expensive to maintain and run and, though she showed that a really effective paddle fighting vessel could be built (at a cost), she was overtaken by the screw propelled auxiliary frigate for naval purposes before she was launched.

The distinction of being the first real first class paddle frigate is therefore usually given to *Penelope*, converted and commissioned in 1843.[3] Built as a 46 gun sailing frigate in 1828, the decision was taken in 1842 to convert *Penelope* to a paddle frigate on the recommendation of John Edye, Assistant to the Surveyor of the Navy and responsible for new design work. *Penelope* was already obsolete as a sailing vessel and by her conversion she escaped the fate of a number of her sisters which was to be 'razeed', that is cut down, to be corvettes. She was a sister ship to *Unicorn* which, never commissioned and preserved from the worst effects of rot by the permanent wooden structure built over her, still lies in Dundee in the 1990s.

A visit to *Unicorn*, which is open to public viewing, reveals a good deal about the early paddle frigates. Her massive construction, with frequent recourse to the use of fine ironwork in the place of compass timber, the restriction of some interiors and the limited space available for the accommodation of a full crew of 300 or so, all bring home the true nature of living conditions at the period, always bearing in mind that conditions ashore for many were even worse. Sixty-five feet longer than *Unicorn* and equipped with massive sponsons and paddle wheels, *Penelope* must have been a great lump of a vessel and very difficult to handle at low speeds.

It was originally intended to equip *Penelope* with steam power without substantial alteration to her hull, and in this connection there is an interesting letter from Captain Sir Edward Parry, Comptroller of Steam Machinery, to Sir William Symonds, Surveyor of the Navy at the time.[4]

5 April 1842.

My Dear Symonds,

As I now understand it to be Mr. Edye's wish to let Seaward & Capel construct the Engines for the *Penelope* I think the proposal should be made by him to Sir G. Cockburn. If the case were my own I should prefer at least 3 or 4 other Engines to Seaward's but their's though not in my opinion the best are *good* beyond doubt & if Mr. Edye prefers employing them I will not only not object but will give him my best assistance in carrying out his wishes. It shall not be for want of pulling together that his frigate does not make a good steamer.

---

3 Osbon, 'Paddle Wheel Fighting Ships of the Royal Navy', *The Mariner's Mirror*, Vol 68, No 4, p 431, and Brown, *Before the Ironclad*, p 67.
4 PRO ADM 92/4 485–6.

Will you be so good as to mention this to him that no time may be lost.

I think however that Seaward should not be given to understand that there is no competition.

I think you have given a very short engine room. Mr. Edye told me he expected 75 feet. I would strongly advise making it that if possible.

W. E. PARRY

Sir Wm. Symonds.

On the subject of Seaward's engines Parry minuted Sydney Herbert in May 1843[5] to say that experience had shown Seaward's engines more costly to operate than those of Napier and liable to breakages of component parts, but Seaward's were the first to develop direct acting engines. Increasing the available power by two-fifths, direct acting engines of 320 horse power could be installed in the same space and were of the same weight as side-levers of 220 horse power. Other manufacturers had been slow to adopt direct acting engines. Between June 1842 and March 1843, *Penelope* was lengthened by 65 feet at Chatham and then between April and June 1843, she was given engines of 650 horse power of the type installed in *Gorgon* by Seaward and Capel[6] at Limehouse. She was also, with the Admiralty yacht *Black Eagle*, one of the first two naval vessels to be equipped with tubular boilers, a development in which the navy was well ahead of the merchant shipping industry, but these boilers, originally expected to last until January 1849, gave a great deal of trouble and seem to have been replaced with a new set, also tubular.[7] These tubular boilers were both smaller and lighter than their predecessors. *Penelope* was equipped with a surface condensor, a development designed to save fuel which was, however, not very successful in its early years of development.[8] *Penelope*, like her exact contemporary, *The Great Britain*, had iron wire standing rigging which, according to her first commanding officer, Captain William Jones, worked well at first. She was rigged as a barque and equipped initially with ten 68 pounder guns on the main deck and twelve 42 pounders on the spar deck.

★   ★   ★   ★

Captain H W Giffard, when he had been posted, was too senior for his appointment in the China seas and so resigned his command of the brig *Cruizer* (see page 124). He recorded in his log that 'On 1st November [1841] having been promoted I left, Captain Blake giving myself and many others a

5 PRO ADM 92/4 534.
6 PRO ADM 53/2956.
7 PRO ADM 53/2956 and 106/2295, August–November 1848.
8 Smith, *Marine Engineering*, pp 133, 154.

passage to Madras'.[9] This was in *Larne*. In his usual laconic style, he recorded[10] that they arrived in Madras on Christmas Day and that he crossed India to see his brother[11] who was near Coimbatore, Madras Province, a hill station. Here he stayed in what must have been pleasant circumstances from 9 to 19 January 1842. He then travelled down the Cochin river to Cochin and, having crossed southern India by several different means of transport, embarked on 26 January at Cochin in the steamer *Seaforth* which took him to Bombay. From Bombay he sailed to Suez, arriving there on 19 February, and crossed to Alexandria in four days. He embarked in *Great Liverpool* (an East India Company paddle steamer which, with *Oriental*, maintained the UK/Alexandria service at that time[12]) on 24 February, arriving at Falmouth on 13 March 1842, less than seven weeks from Cochin.

Giffard returned home to find that a government under Sir Robert Peel's premiership had been in power since 1841. Not surprisingly, he spent the next four and a half years, the remainder of that government's period of office, on half pay. He visited family and friends; in August, jointly with his brother[13] and two friends, he hired a 'moor on the Isle of Skye' for the shooting. Next spring he made a Grand Tour, from February until the end of May, visiting France, Italy, Switzerland and 'up the Rhine'. Then 'in June, 1843, I went to Woolwich to study steam and took my certificate in August. Then went home and remained there and visited my friends and trying hard for employment'.[14] An example of how he 'tried hard for employment' is provided by his father's correspondence with the Earl of Ellenborough, the First Lord of the Admiralty. For instance, on 28 June 1846, at a time of transition to a Whig administration, the Admiral wrote[15]

Southampton

June 28th/46

My Lord

Had I not cause to feel the deepest mortification at Captain Giffard not getting employment afloat, I should not have presumed to have intruded upon your Lordship, nor would I do so now but that your Lordship states 'that had I adverted to the very small number of Captains commands which have fallen to your appointment and to the high character of the officers you have nominated to such commands I should

9   NMM JOD 30, personal notes.
10 NMM Log N/H/3.
11 James Combes Giffard, 1820–1884, Captain in the East India Company's Service.
12 Maber, *North Star to Southern Cross*, p 2.
13 Edward Carter Giffard, Major, 60th Rifles.
14 All the short quotations are from NMM JOD 30.
15 The Ellenborough Papers, 30/12/4/20 FF 91/2.

feel that the circumstance of Captain Giffard not being employed is one which cannot be a subject of reasonable dissatisfaction'. I know not how many Captains your Lordship has employed but I have yet to learn what have been the services of Captain Symonds, Elliot or Watson which has entitled them to such preference, those of the latter acknowledge to be good, but for them he was promoted to the rank of commander and Captain, to which was added the Companionship of the Bath, but he is sixteen months junior to Captain Giffard.

I regret your Lordship should consider me unreasonable and I beg to assure you that during my long life that has never been a trait in my character, and nothing but the conscious desire for a deserving son's welfare should have induced me to trouble your Lordship.
etc. etc.

Giffard had attended the steam factory, just completed at Woolwich (see Chapter 2, page 43), studied there and gained his Steam Certificate, which established that he had gained considerable familiarity with steam machinery. It is evident that the lessons of the China War had not been lost on him and it was clear to him, as to many other officers of his generation, that the future belonged to steam and that, whatever his interest when the Whigs returned to power, identification with steam was going to be advantageous.

On 17 October 1844, Giffard sought to broaden his qualifications still further by 'going to college at Portsmouth to study' and there he stayed until January 1846. This was the old Royal Naval College of which he had been a graduate in 1825 and of which his father had been Lieutenant Governor (see Chapter 5). From 1837, the college had ceased to be a training establishment for young gentlemen, who were now given theoretical instruction at the Gunnery School or by instructors in ships at sea, and became open to half pay officers of up to commander rank[16] and, it is apparent from Giffard's career, to half pay post captains as well, on occasion. Here steam was now among the subjects taught and there were naval engineers as instructors of marine engineering among the staff. A post captain gave a course of lectures followed by practical work in *Bee* (see page 147) and, according to Penn, who does not give his source,[17] it was laid down that 'a thorough knowledge of the steam engine, both in principle and in its application to sea purposes, is to form an essential part of the college education'. In 1847, a naval writer remarked that 'officers have devoted much time, while on half pay, and toiled hard, through dirt, smoke and oil to acquire a practical knowledge of the steam engine'.

Giffard's spell at the college was broken in a most interesting way. Between 14 July and 9 September 1845, he joined the wardroom of HMS

16 Lewis, *Transition*, p 107.
17 Penn, *Up Funnel, Down Screw!*, p 53.

Trafalgar, Captain W F Martin, a unit of the Experimental Squadron under Rear Admiral Sir Samuel Pym, which was to carry out sailing trials 'between the parallels of 47° and 49° north latitude and the meridians of 9° and 11° west longitude'.[18] These trials were exhaustive of their kind and period. Seven ships of the line were used in trials of sailing with the wind 7 points abaft the beam, 6 points abaft the beam, on the wind and with the wind abeam. At times, all seven vessels were tried against each other; at other times two or three vessels sailed in competition. Given the absence of any modern system of exact measurements, the results were necessarily very approximate and must have reflected the general state of maintenance of the vessels, the distribution of their ballast and the degree to which their crews had been worked up to be efficient teams, together with the competence of the officers and petty officers, at least as much as any qualities of design the vessels may have possessed. Nevertheless, sailings under these competitive conditions must have proved excellent experience for everybody concerned.

But there was more to it than that. These trials were part of a series which were at least partly political in origin. The object of some of the participant Tory captains was to discredit vessels designed by the Whig appointed Surveyor of the Navy, Sir William Symonds. Captain William Martin, eldest son of the former Comptroller of the Navy, Admiral Sir Thomas Byam Martin, was an extreme conservative from a deeply conservative family. How the Whig Henry Giffard came to be on board the Symonds designed *Trafalgar* (which came badly out of the trials) under Martin's command is not clear, but he must have been open to some suspicion as a Whig spy, sent to check that the poor performance of *Trafalgar* was not the result of deliberate mishandling in various subtle ways.

'On the 19th March, 1846, I married my dear wife Ella Emelia Stephenson' Giffard records. She was the daughter of Major General Sir Benjamin Charles Stephenson, and the couple were to have two sons born in 1849 and 1850. But their time together as newly-weds was short. In June 1846, the government of Sir Robert Peel fell and was replaced by a Whig administration under Lord John Russell which was to remain in power for six years. Giffard, with five years' seniority as a post captain, his Steam Certificate from Woolwich, his further study in steam at Portsmouth, and his excellent Whig connections, might be supposed to be assured of a satisfactory future, and this indeed proved to be the case. On 13 October 1846, he was appointed to be the commanding officer of *Penelope* and his career for the next eight years in command of three paddle frigates gives an excellent picture of the employment of these vessels during the short period in which they represented the navy's principal steam power.

18 Report in *The Times*, 2 September 1845, p 5.

Penelope, on completion of her conversion, went straight out to West Africa, under the command of Captain William Jones, on anti-slavery patrol as the flagship of a flotilla of six paddle steamers which included *Gorgon*. This was the first time the Commodore of the station had flown his flag in a steamer, although the first steamer to be sent to West Africa as early as 1826 had been *African* (see Chapter 2). Although named for the job and clearly a successful vessel, she had not stayed long on the coast. As might be expected with such an experimental vessel as *Penelope*, several difficulties developed including the corrosion of her paddle frames as a result of electrolitic action with her copper, and trouble with her tubular boilers. By early May 1846, she was already back in Portsmouth for a refit including re-coppering and engine repairs which cost £3691. Nevertheless, Captain Jones had reported favourably on her, especially on her sailing qualities, claiming that she could keep company with the fleet under sail and be a formidable opponent to a line of battleship when under steam[19] although she was inclined to make leeway under sail. While she was refitting, Captain Jones died in Haslar Hospital, in O'Byrne's words, 'from the effects of disease contracted on the coast of Africa',

Giffard then took command of *Penelope* during refit, commissioning her on 16 October 1846. Her crew were gradually assembled[20] and stores loaded. It is evident that much of the ship's company had already been made up (in 1852 her complement was to be 311) but Giffard entered seventy-five seamen, Lieutenant Hall and twenty-eight marines, petty officers and the master, Mr Edington. He also discharged Robert Larny, second engineer, with disgrace, offence not recorded. On 9 January 'steam up, weighed and left past Nab Light', she was bound towards Funchal where she took on 376 tons of coal. There was already trouble with the engines which required maintenance work on 18 and 19 January. On 20 January they weighed anchor under steam at 6.20 am, by 10.40 am 'banked down fires', and at 11.10 am 'stopped and disconnected engines, proceeded under sail'. Two days later, steam was again raised and the following day engines disconnected again as she continued under sail alone. The boilers were now leaking. Lime juice was issued at the surgeon's representation, and at noon on 25 January they reached the limit of the African Station[21] and passed under the command of Commodore Sir C. Hotham. At 3.45 pm the same day they 'buried Acting Master J.C. Cunningham'. In 1845, forty-eight men in every thousand in British naval vessels on the African Station died from disease. The loss of 5 per cent from this cause is considerably less than might

19 PRO ADM 95/88, 30 September 1843.

20 Giffard's career in *Penelope* is covered in his captain's log in PRO ADM 2956 and 2957.

21 In 1847, the limits of the 'African Station', by which Giffard presumably meant the West Coast Command, were from 23½° north to what is now called Cape Fria in 18° 28′ south, in Namibia.

be supposed from the popular idea of nineteenth century conditions in the Bight of Benin.[22] Thus Giffard began his brief career on anti-slavery patrol.

The political and diplomatic history of the slave trade is vastly complicated. In briefest summary, it could be an enormously profitable business and in the eighteenth century the running of slaves to the West Indies and later to a smaller extent to the United States, made the fortunes of a number of British merchants. Towards the end of the century, campaigns against the institution of slavery, and particularly against trade in slaves, began to develop, but it was not until 1808 that it became illegal for Britons to engage in the slave trade and not until 1833 that slavery was legally abolished within British territories, with due compensation for the slave owners. American participation in the trade became illegal in 1809 but not until 1865 was slavery abolished in the United States. French participation in the trade became illegal in 1815 and in Spain and Portugal in 1820.

Nevertheless, there remained a very profitable market for slaves smuggled into the United States and the business of transporting slave cargoes from Africa remained potentially extremely lucrative. There arose a complex situation in which there was little consistency in the various national laws against the trade and in which the slave traders could take advantage of numerous legal loopholes. Moreover, Venezuela did not finally end slavery until 1854, Puerta Rico in 1873 and Brazil in 1888. Slavers sometimes flew whatever colours seemed safest at the time. A further complication was that although the US Navy by the 1840s was joining in the campaign against the slavers, the United States reserved the right of search of vessels flying the American flag to themselves, which meant that a slaver flying American colours was often safe although British naval vessels were present[23].

Against this trade the British government, to the benefit of the British West Indian planters, who had to produce sugar without slaves more expensively than their competitors with slaves, and against much parliamentary opposition, waged war for nearly the whole of the nineteenth century both through diplomatic activity and through the navy. The difficulties were immense. As Professor Michael Lewis wrote [24].

The suppression of the slave trade by the Royal Navy was always an uphill fight against not only lawless (and often stateless) slave masters

22 Bryson, *Report on the Climate and Principal Diseases of the African Station*, 1847, p 177.

23 The literature on slavery and the slave trade is voluminous. For accounts of the British Navy and the trade see Lloyd, *The Navy and the Slave Trade,* London 1949; Ward, *The Royal Navy and the Slavers,* London 1969; and for a well researched and generally accurate picture of the trade in the form of an adventure story, see Fraser, *Flash for Freedom,* London 1971.

24 Lewis, in *The Mariner's Mirror*, 1969, Vol 55, No. 3, p 338.

but, even more, against reluctant governments – governments which, paying lip service to abolition, yet allowed themselves to be persuaded, or out-witted, by minority or monied interests among their own people.

Lloyd quotes a good example of the difficulties from an American source.[25]

> We have made ten captures, although they are evidently owned by Americans, they are so completely covered by Spanish papers that it is impossible to condemn them . . . The slave trade is carried out to a very great extent. There are probably no less than 300 vessels on the coast engaged in the traffic, each having two or three sets of papers.

It is no wonder that in 1844 a volume of *Instructions for the Guidance of Her Majesty's Naval Officers Employed in the Suppression of the Slave Trade* was widely issued. This book was intended to assist commanding officers and their subordinates to avoid the legal and diplomatttic pitfalls which could lie in the path of duty.

In the early days before 1840 the slave trade squadron on the African Station comprised only five to eight vessels mounting eight to ten guns each. The resources allocated were therefore strictly limited at this time. But in 1841 the total was increased, and by the time Giffard arrived on the coast in *Penelope* there were fourteen sailing vessels and seven steamers in the squadron.[26] On this assignment the paddle steamer came into her own. Independent of the baffling winds of the coasts and of the estuary currents, able to maintain a steady pursuit, highly mobile and affording better living conditions for crews in an unhealthy situation, the steam vessels made a major contribution to suppression of the trade. The main difficulties were the problems of fuel, which limited a steamer's range of operation, and, as the experiences of *Penelope* will show, that of maintaining the boilers and engines of these vessels in operation for months on end in adverse conditions far from any engineering facilities ashore.

At the time *Penelope* arrived on the coast, the Brazilian slave trade was booming as a result of the opening of the British sugar market by an Act of Parliament of 1846. Five years later, this great trade had been ended through the activities of British naval steamers on the coasts of Brazil and through political developments in that country itself. But during *Penelope*'s second commission on the West African Station under Giffard, British naval vessels were operating under a British Act of Parliament of 1845 which empowered them to 'capture Brazilian slavers, full or empty, north or south of the line, and bring them before British Admiralty courts'.[27]

25 Soulsby, *The Right of Search and the Slave Trade in Anglo-American Relations*, Johns Hopkins University, 1933, quoted by Lloyd, p 51.
   26 Lloyd, *op.cit*, pp 123/12
   27 Lloyd, *op cit*, p 141.

Commodore Sir Charles Hotham, formerly the commanding officer of *Gorgon* when she went aground (see page 65), under whose flag *Penelope* now passed, had assumed command of the squadron in 1847 at a time when parliamentary opposition to the continued and growing expenditure on the anti-slavery patrol was very active. His policy was to put the ships of the squadron on to offshore cruising, rather than close blockade of the coast. He maintained that the force at his disposal was too small to be effective, that the number of steam vessels was too small and the facilities for coaling and maintenance inadequate. These views brought him into sharp conflict with some of his fellow officers. Nevertheless, 161 slavers were captured during the time he was in command.[28]

A great deal can be read into the brief entries in Giffard's log. *Penelope* put into the Cape Verde Islands, where they stayed from 27 January until 7 February visiting each island, making extensive repairs to the engines, bolting new plates to leaking boilers and replacing four floats which carried away on the starboard paddle wheel. They also coaled ship with a mixture of north country and Welsh coal of bad quality 'being very light and foul'. On 10 February 1847, *Penelope* was anchored off Cape St Mary, in what is now the Gambia, and three days later she arrived in Sierra Leone harbour. Here she took on board coal and water, discharged nine seamen as 'unfit' and three more, with a marine, as 'invalided' and again there were engine repairs to do. She then steamed out to the Banana Islands, off Sierra Leone, where she embarked Commodore Hotham and his luggage and gave him an 11 gun salute, hoisting the pendant red at the main. Presumably because of further trouble with the engines, she was towed out by the paddle steamer *Devastation* and she remained in tow for the next five days. There followed a year of patrolling against the slave traders. On 7 March *Penelope* was lying in Accra Roads, still in company with *Devastation* with whom she exchanged masters. She then, despite frequent boiler leaks and component failures in the paddles, worked steadily down the coast and on 18 March chased a strange sail, capturing at 9.30 am the Brazilian felucca *Saron*, fully equipped with slave decks and irons for the trade in human beings and with a crew of thirty-one, who were landed at what appears from the not very clear log entry to have been Corbinda. She then had a further bout of trouble with the engines. They spent 27 March 'tightening connecting rods and parallel motion bearings', stopped and boarded an English merchant brig next day, and that afternoon anchored off the mouth of the Congo, taking in fresh water for all the boilers and then steaming to Luanda. There, in the next two days they performed major maintenance work on the engines, summed up in the log entries, using engineering terms now long obsolete, 'sent down spare piston from upper deck – disconnecting rods and unshipped platform – Got up Plumber block caps intermediate shaft cleaned

28 Lloyd, *op cit*, pp 121-122.

flue and tubes – placed spare piston'. They coaled with 75 tons of 'indifferent' quality and steamed out of Luanda with their prize, the felucca, in tow, but just before 1 am had to stop 'owing to port cam balanced weight screw being stripped 1.30 suspended temporary weight and proceeded'. On 30 March *Penelope* gave chase to a schooner, but did not cast off her prize. The schooner was *Felicidad*, without colours or papers with 315 slaves on board, some of whom were transferred to the felucca. The schooner was taken in tow also, so *Penelope* now proceeded trailing two prizes.

On 4 April a strange sail was sighted and in due course the schooner *Juanita* from Rio de Janeiro, fitted out for the slave trade, was detained and added to the tow. Next day there was a 'large leak in the after tube plates of the after port and starboard boilers' and *Penelope* anchored at St Helena in the afternoon. Here they lay for over a fortnight dismantling the prizes, coaling and provisioning, 'repairing port piston' and doing extensive work in the rigging while taking on board eighty sheep for Ascension, where they arrived five days later. *Penelope* lay for two months at Ascension 'changing wire rigging for rope, altering rig and upper works' and provisioning. A year earlier the iron wire standing rigging of *The Great Britain* had been replaced with traditional hemp[29]. Even allowing for the sailing ships' seamen's suspicion of new materials, it is evident that the great advantages of iron wire rigging must have been outweighed by defects in the material at this very early stage in its production.

In July, August and September, *Penelope* went back to close inshore patrol on the stretch of coast north and south of Corbinda. There was a good deal of gun drill, but no action, and both engines and boilers seem to have behaved themselves. Still on close inshore patrol in October, *Penelope* took a Brazilian brig, *Silfide*, fitted out for the slave trade and with a crew of thirty-nine. She was sent into St Helena in charge of one of *Penelope's* lieutenants. At the end of the month, *Penelope* was back at St Helena and here, Giffard records, he sent in his resignation from command. The vessel then sailed to Ascension where she coaled and they cleaned and caulked ship, lying there from 23 November until 12 December 1847. Back on close patrol in December, *Penelope* reached the Banana Islands again on 8 January and then worked slowly back east, anchoring off Monrovia on 8 February. Here President Roberts and his suite dined on board. Eight days later, they anchored off Accra and then on 25 February again off Fernando Po, now called Nacias Nguema, before working south again to Corbinda where she arrived on 9 March. Here Captain Lewis T Jones arrived in the steamer *Firefly* and, on 26 March 1848, read his commission replacing

29 Corlett, *The Iron Ship*: p 105. For a brief account of the history of iron wire rigging see Macgregor, *Merchant Sailing Ships 1815–1850*, London 1984, pp 150–151. See also Martin, *The Development of Wire Rope: An Innovation in Maritime Technology Reaches the Great Lakes* in Fischer, ed., *International Journal of Maritime History,* 1992, Vol. IV No. 1, pp 101–120

Captain Giffard. Next day, Giffard began his journey home in *Bonetta*, Lieutenant Forbes, which took him to Ascension from where he sailed in *Styx* on 27 April 1848, arriving at Spithead on 26 May.

The unsatisfactory performance of the boilers and engines led Commodore Hotham to write to Captain Giffard on 5 April 1847, to complain officially of the boilers, and again to the Admiralty on 22 April on the same subject. It may be that Giffard's resignation was precipitated by strained relations with his Commodore, who was a difficult character, for all that Cooper Key judged it wise to praise him after the salving of *Gorgon* (see page 65). A Tory, and therefore not likely to be sympathetic to Giffard, Hotham was later to become a controversial Governor of South Australia. The crew of *Penelope*, given the methods of recruitment of the crew of a warship for a commission on the African Station current at the time (see Chapter 3), may have been a scratch lot, but the number of offences recorded in the log suggests low morale on board. Most punishments, disrating to a lower rate as well as flogging, were for drunkenness.

As for *Penelope* herself, her commission under Captain Jones was a short one. By 18 August 1848, the Steam Department were minuting the Surveyor of the Navy.[30] 'I request you will furnish us with a tracing of the engine room of the *Penelope* with a view to providing new boilers which will be required to replace the present ones on the right of the vessel.' On 6 September 1848, drawings were sent to Mr Murray for a new set of tubular boilers 'bearing in mind that it is most desirable to keep the boilers below the water-line if practicable'. In 1849, she was back in Portsmouth for another major refit, which in fact lasted for two years and involved considerable expenditure, a large unit of which went on the new boiler. She saw service in the Baltic during the War with Russia of 1854–56 and went aground under the Russian guns at Bomarsund in the Åland Islands, a position from which she was released at the cost of two men killed, six wounded, and the loss of all her twenty-two guns thrown overboard. The graves of the two seamen who lost their lives are still to be found on lonely Fjälskär in the great inland sea of the Lumparfjärd in Åland.[31]

★ ★ ★ ★ ★

Lieutenant Gordon gives a good account of tubular boilers and what was wrong with *Penelope*.[32]

Over the furnace are numerous brass tubes of 2 inches in diameter, and about 5 feet 1 inch in length. They are fixed into plates similar to those of

30 PRO ADM 106/2295 135.
31 Greenhill and Giffard, *The British Assault*, pp 251, 266.
32 Gordon, *The Marine Steam Engine*, p 122.

a locomotive engine, and the smoke from the furnace passes through them to the uptake.

The dimensions and weight of boilers of this construction are reduced about one-fifth, and expose a greater heating surface. The quantity of water which they contain is reduced about one-half, thereby causing less radiation of heat, and the time occupied in getting the steam up is likewise reduced.

As at present constructed, the surface of the water in the boiler is reduced about one-half; consequently, when Hall's condensers are not applied, great attention is required to keep the water at a correct level in the boiler; and, owing to the want of a proper circulation, heavy firing will be apt to bring down the crowns of the furnaces, an accident which lately occurred in her Majesty's steam vessel *Penelope*.

John Edye, the Assistant to the Surveyor of the Navy, who furthered the idea of the conversion of *Penelope*, was a sound, dockyard trained professional naval architect who served the Admiralty for more than fifty years. At this perod, in the mid 1840s, when the screw was under trial, the situation was confused by the strongly held views of a number of senior officers. There were those who saw the future in the screw, those who like Captain Lord John Hay, the influential Third Naval Lord, who advocated steam but saw its future, as far as ships of the line were concerned, in the provision of efficient tugs, one paddle frigate per ship of the line, a system already applied in the Mediterranean fleet, and those who still did not believe in the future of steam at all. Fortunately for the navy, the situation changed with the appointment of the highly practical Sir Baldwin Walker as Surveyor in succession to Sir William Symonds in 1848, and from then on the movement was steadily to the establishment of an auxiliary steam screw battle fleet. There were no more conversions of sailing vessels into paddle frigates, but to the screw. The next frigate to be so treated was to be *Amphion*, and she was to be much more successful than *Penelope*. John Edye, who really believed in the paddle frigate, was faced with a situation in which hull design came from one office, still dominated by a Surveyor, Symonds, who although ready to accept and develop steam still thought in sailing ship terms, and engine design from another. To get *Penelope* commissioned at all was something of an achievement.

9

The Employment of the Paddle Frigate: 2 *Dragon* on Mediterranean Service

The steamer *Dragon* has been variously described as a paddle frigate of the first class or the second class.[1] By the rating of the time (see p 163) she exactly fitted the definition of neither since she had a post captain in command, four lieutenants, twenty-eight officers in total including six engineers, but only 172 ratings – forty-one petty officers, seventy-four men, twenty-eight boys and twenty-nine marines.[2] She was built at the naval dockyard at Pembroke in 1844–45 and equipped with her direct acting engines of 560 nominal horse power by Fairbairn in the East India Dock, London, in the summer of 1845. The company built only four naval engines and was to go bankrupt in 1847. She had tubular boilers built of iron, she stowed 342 tons of coal plus 40 more tons on the troop deck. She was armed in 1850 with six guns, on the quarterdeck one 68 pounder gun of 95 hundredweight and two 10 inch guns of 85 hundredweight, on the forecastle one 68 pounder and two 10 inch guns. She drew 17.7 feet aft and 16.5 feet forward. She carried no ballast.

Already by 1850, her boilers were giving trouble. She was refitted at Portsmouth between early June and late September of that year, and it was recommended[3] that it was doubtful whether the boilers were worth repair. The Admiralty determined, however, that only such repairs as could be made without the aid of the steam factory should be done. The consequences of this decision were to shorten *Dragon*'s next commission.

Captain Giffard, after leaving *Penelope*, arrived at Spithead on 26 May 1848 and, no doubt financially reinforced by the prize money from his slave trade

1 Brown, *Ironclad*, pp 64–65.
2 All particulars from PRO ADM 53/7874, NMM JOD 30.
3 PRO ADM 93/8 Steam Department, Submission Book, 387, 7 April 1852.

captures, passed what he recorded as 'a very happy life living with my father and mother at Southampton and visiting our friends'. But this period of domesticity ended when, on 3 August 1850, the Whig government of Lord John Russell still being in power, Giffard, now firmly established as a paddle frigate commander, was appointed to *Dragon* while she was under refit at Portsmouth.

In her company were the former master of *Penelope*, Mr. Edington. John Giffard, a relative, was carried as a naval cadet, Giffard exercising his right to look after members of his own family, while the first lieutenant was one Alfred Royer who was to play his role in the loss of *Tiger* four years later. He was the son of the port captain of Port Louis, Mauritius, where he was born in 1815. He was admitted to the naval college at Portsmouth in April 1828, at the age of thirteen. Here he did very well, not surprisingly revealing himself a competent French scholar and completing the course in 142 days less than the time allowed. He passed for lieutenant in 1834, was involved in the China War, and promoted in 1841. He had been almost continuously employed as a lieutenant, latterly on the African Station.

Dragon carried a number of service passengers to be landed at Plymouth, Lisbon, Malta and Tangier. After a brief stop in the Tagus she entered the limits of the Mediterranean Station and passed under the orders of Sir William Parker on 10 August 1850. On the 12th she was in Gibraltar where she took on board coal and water. The weather was bad and a Dutch galliot, the name of which Giffard records as *Peruse van Schiedam*, got into trouble, losing her fore topmast. *Dragon* went to her assistance and eventually, after a collision in which *Dragon*'s cutter and gig were destroyed by the galliot's jibboom, towed her to safety.[4] From Sir William Parker's correspondence[5] it is evident that *Dragon* also went to the assistance of another Dutch galliot, *De Beurs* 'at the back of Gibraltar', commandeering for the purpose a boat from the well known schooner yacht *Gondola*, RYS (see Greenhill and Giffard, *The British Assault*, pp 213–215) which was damaged and eventually repaired in the dockyard.

Dragon sailed for Malta where they arrived on 24 August, and here the 'back balance weight of the port engine fell into the condensor – sent weights ashore to use as patterns for new, stronger items'. *Dragon* lay in Valletta until 17 November when she steamed to Port Mahon and joined Sir William Parker's squadron comprising HM Ships *Queen* (the flagship), *Caledonia, Ganges, Superb* and *Powerful*, together with the steam frigate *Terrible* and the steam sloops *Firebrand* and *Scourge*, later to be joined by the steamers *Spiteful* and *Janus* and the hydrographic steamer *Spitfire*. Sir William Parker had recorded his attitude to the paddle steamers under his

4 Giffard's log is in PRO ADM 53/3874. The events recorded in the following pages are as in this log and in Giffard's personal notes in NMM JOD 30.
5 PRO ADM PAR 26 Nos 5, 6 and 9.

command in a letter to the First Lord, the Earl of Auckland, of 24 April 1849.[6]

> With regard to steamers I think there should at least be one for every line of battleship besides what will be necessary for detached service, for frigates will be useless if they have to contend with an enemy well provided for in the branch of steamers; but these steamers must be well looked-to, for, without alteration, owing to the flames emitted from the funnel they are not safe to tow alongside; and if an attack is made on a force at anchor, or on heavy ships in a *calm* when towing is necessary, they ought to be lashed *alongside*, or they may be sunk or disabled, in approaching the enemy.

The arrival of *Dragon* brought Parker's ratio of steamers to sailing vessels roughly into line with his theoretical ideal. Paddle steamers were in Parker's view, and this view reflected that of many of his contemporaries, now essential, if auxiliary, units of the fleet. But they were already obsolete. The Admiralty was by this date committed to the rapid development of the screw. Giffard had noted in his log during his brief stay in the Tagus the arrival of the vessel which, more than any other, had convinced the naval authorities that the screw was the answer to the 'riddle of the age'. He wrote 'October 9, 6 pm, steam frigate *Arrogant* arrived', but he made no comment.

'On 2 December fleet weighs, *Powerful* towed by *Scourge*'. They were bound towards Barcelona but the threatening weather forced them back to sea 'leaving many officers behind . . . On the 16th we arrived at Cagliari, Sardinia. On the 2nd we all sailed, at noon we parted company and arrived at Naples on the 23rd. An American squadron there.' This American squadron, the log records, comprised the United States 60 gun frigates *Independence, Cumberland*, and the steamer *Mississippi*. Giffard's personal notes continue 'We remained [at Naples] until 17th April, 1851, receiving and keeping various refugees'.

In the late 1840s, the long period of peace which followed the end of the Napoleonic wars and the Congress of Vienna of 1815 was coming to an end. Britain's massive lead in economic development created its own momentum for capital accumulation and expansion. Industrialisation was beginning in some regions of Germany, in Saxony and Silesia, and with it came a degree of political and social awareness among the workers and demands from the middle classes for a rôle in society. To a certain extent the same developments were occurring in France. The eastern half of Europe, Russia and the Austro-Hungarian Empire had not shared in these developments and was still dominated by the old systems of aristocracy, land ownership,

6 Quoted in Laing, 'The Introduction of Paddle Frigates into the Royal Navy', in *The Mariner's Mirror*, Vol 66, No 4, November 1980, p 342.

and autocracy. The difference between the two Europes was reflected in political attitudes. In 1848, the stresses in Western Europe burst out in revolution in France. The King was forced to abdicate and a Republic, based on universal suffrage, was proclaimed. The unrest rapidly spread throughout Western Europe, to Germany, Denmark, and even to Austria and Sweden. Italy, unified by the French under Napoleon, was again dismembered at the Congress of Vienna, and so was at this time still divided into a number of princely states, some big and relatively powerful, some small and poor. The dominant influence was exercised by Austria, very strongly in the north, indirectly, but still significantly, as far south as Naples. Divided as they were by wide differences of language, race, temperament and historical development the Italians were beginning to develop 'that principle of nationality which was the one great and novel feature of the international difficulties of the nineteenth century'.[7] The result was a period of great unrest through much of the century, of civil disturbance and local conflicts, with the inevitable refugees. This was the time of Giuseppe Mazzini and his *La Giovine Italia*, the Young Italy Society, which he founded and which was dedicated to revolt through guerrilla bands, a concept of political activity which spread far beyond Italy and led Metternich to describe Mazzini as the most dangerous man in Europe. It was the time of the first phase of Garibaldi's activities, of the siege of Rome by the French and of conflict with the Austrians at the end of the 1840s which failed for lack of organisation and unity of leadership. In this rising the King of Naples played a somewhat half-hearted role and took the first opportunity of joining the side of reaction. The result was disorder in Naples, which was suppressed, the withdrawal of a short-lived constitution, the dismissal of an equally short-lived parliament and the invasion of Sicily, which had declared itself an independent state with a constitutional government. The intervention of both French and English fleets stopped further military operations, but Naples and Sicily returned to the old regime of royal autocracy.

It was in the latter part of this period of political and social ferment that *Dragon* lay for three and a half months off Naples 'receiving and keeping various refugees'. Her presence encouraged some sort of stability and in devious ways a degree of protection for some who would suffer with the return of the old regime. For the whole of her time with the Mediterranean fleet, *Dragon* was to be involved in a series of operations in the protection of British interests, some of which involved work of a delicate diplomatic

7 Grant and Temperley, *Europe in the Nineteenth and Twentieth Centuries*, edited and revised by Penson, London 1953, p 224. For a modern study of nationalism in ninteenth century Europe, see Gellner, *Nations and Nationalism*, Oxford 1983. For an easily readable view of Garibaldi's activities at this period, see Hibbert, *Garibaldi and His Enemies*, London 1987. The most recent textbook is Gildea, *Barricades and Borders, Europe 1800–1814*, Oxford 1987.

nature. Employed in this way, she showed another important function of the steam frigate in the mid-nineteenth century. Despite Admiral Parker's ideas on the proper use of these vessels, *Dragon*'s log shows only limited towing duties. She is constantly employed as a presence to discourage what would nowadays probably be considered acts of terrorism or intimidation and to keep the local political temperature off the boil. This may not have been an economical use of a steam vessel, but her speed and ability to transfer herself without delay to any potential scene of trouble made her uniquely suited to this kind of service which may, however, have been performed at the cost of attention to those drills and exercises which should have kept her in a constant state of readiness as a fighting ship. Giffard appears to have done what he could. On 16 May 1851, the log records steaming out to sea for gunnery practice, firing twelve rounds, and back at anchor after fourteen hours at sea. On 26 July there was another duty to perform and the log notes 'Ermengildo Giortte of Morono and Luez Voller of Shere in Surrey married aboard ship by William Whitmarsh Chaplain'.

The affair of the refugees is covered fully in Sir William Parker's correspondence.[8] It has a very modern flavour. It would appear that several groups were received on board at different times.

> *Queen* at Malta
> 17th January, 1851

Sir,

I have received your letter No. 4 of the 13th instant acquainting me that four Refugees had been received on board HM steam Frigate *Dragon*, under your command at the desire of His Excellency the Hon. Wm. Temple HM Minister at Naples.

In the reception of Refugees, you are doubtless guided by my Instructions of the 18th July and 1st September 1849 addressed to Captain W.F. Martin of the *Prince Regent* the Senior Officer at Naples who I concluded furnished his successor with copies, which have been duly transferred to yourself. But as the admission and continuance of Refugees on board HM Ships at Naples is attended with much inconvenience to the Service which is greatly increased by the difficulty of their being afterwards removed it is expedient that you should point out these objections for the consideration of HE, to prevent any parties being recommended for refuge except their cases are of a pressing nature and such as may entitle them to the humane protection which they seek.

Such applications must of course be made to you by HM Minister in writing except under circumstances adverted to by Lord Palmerston in his communication to the Admiralty of the 4th August 1849.

I may add that HE the Governor of Malta has reason for viewing with a

8 PRO ADM PAR 26 1, 2, 3 and 4.

scrupulous eye the disembarkation of Refugees here, from the information of which he is possessed, that many of those who have before arrived
have endeavoured to hatch mischief with discontented and unprincipled
individuals of the Island.

W.P.

Captain H.W. Giffard,
HMS Frigate *Dragon*

The affair of the refugees appears to have given rise to a document found
among the papers of Admiral John Giffard. Addressed 'Al Illustre Capitano
Signore Henry Giffard' and headed 'Sonetto', it gives some indication of the
relationship of some of the refugees to one another. Written with dialect
variations it has, with some difficulty, been translated by the late Hugh A
Warren to read

> Signore,
> From whom I have come to expect with confidence manifestations of a
> magnanimous, kindly and generous heart, please receive this with my
> respect and love. What happy dreams in such sad circumstances; and yet
> I can only give him the clasp of a new burden. You are rescuing a father,
> a son, and a dear wife. And solely to follow justice and honour I would
> perjure myself, Signore, [to see] such woes 'rose tinted.' And the little
> girls – what comforts they are indeed. You, exiling yourself from
> homeland and hearth, only find such, I feel sure, additonal links in the
> chains of your bitter burden.
>
> For us you are an angel, and that is a true saying in parity with those of
> Milton, and thus I say: to God be the glory, with your name, and that of
> England.
>
> With the highest respect and gratitude.

This expression of heartfelt thanks is, perhaps wisely, not signed.
On 17 April 1851, *Dragon* sailed north under steam, via Civitavecchia
and Genoa, arriving at Leghorn on the morning of 26 April. The purpose of
the passage is made clear by a letter of 25 April from Sir W Parker to the
Admiralty.[9]

Queen at Malta
25 April, 1851

Sir,
I transmit for the information of the Lords Commissioners of
Admiralty the copy of a letter which I have received from Captain
Giffard of HM steam frigate *Dragon* reporting, that in pursuance of
Instructions which I had sent him, previous to the establishment of the

9 PRO ADM PAR 20 No 66.

Quarantine at Naples, of which my letter No. 64 of this date informed their Lordships, he had quitted that Port to visit HM Legations and Consulates in the North of Italy.

I shall direct Captain Giffard in the event of long quarantine being imposed on the *Dragon* on her return to Naples, to repair to my flag at Malta, provided his Excellency Sir William Temple is of opinion that her presence is not essentially necessary at the former place.

Their Lordships will observe that at the request of Sir William Temple five Political Refugees have been received in the *Dragon* for conveyance to Genoa.

W.P.

The Secretary of the Admiralty.

Dragon returned to Naples Bay on 5 May and lay there until 24 June when she steamed north again for Leghorn. Again, the reason for the move was apparent from Sir William Parker's correspondence.[10]

Queen at Malta
22nd June, 1851

I yesterday received a private communication, of which I enclose a copy, from the Honourable R. Campbell Scarlett, in charge of HM Legation at Florence, in consequence of which I have directed Captain Giffard to proceed without delay in the *Dragon* to Leghorn, for the object adverted to by Mr. Scarlett, and to support British Interests.
A copy of my orders to this effect are also enclosed for their Lordships information.

The news Mr Scarlett had conveyed to the admiral is apparent from Giffard's private journal where he records

We proceeded to Leghorn on the 24th June, arriving on the 26th, in consequence of the imprisonment of the Stratfords by the Austrians. Here we remained until relieved by the *Scourge*, left on October 28 with the body of Mr. Shiel on board: called in at Naples on the 1st [November] and left next day arriving at Malta on the 4th November and deposited the body.

Mr Shiel was a prominent Whig politician who had died while making the Grand Tour. He was of sufficient importance to warrant his body being brought home at government expense.

The case of the Stratfords was reported fully in *The Times* on Saturday 28

10 PRO ADM PAR 20 No 117.

June 1851. The opening paragraph of the account summarises the circumstances of the affair.

TUSCANY
(From our own correspondent.)

FLORENCE, June 21.

I have a very unpleasant duty to perform to-day, in bringing before your notice the facts of a case which no doubt has already been more or less made public. I allude to the arrest of three young Englishmen, sons of the late Lord Aldborough, and claiming to be his legitimate heirs, who were detected on the evening of the 10th, at the villa of their mother near Leghorn, in the very act of destroying incendiary and treasonable papers, with concealed firearms in their possession, a printing press, the third number of a Republican journal, and the new-fashioned infernal machine of walking canes, containing a reservoir from which vitriolic acid may be ejected on the dresses of ladies seen with Austrian officers, or wearing Austrian colours. I am aware that the question involving the legitimacy or illegitimacy of these young men is still before the courts, and that a son of the late lord by a previous marriage enjoys one of the family titles, but I do not affect to determine with whom is the legal right, and I only mention the fact as giving more importance to the case, and of showing the delusions into which Englishmen of aristocratic pretensions may be betrayed. Of their guilt, I am sorry to say, there is no doubt, as the officers of police who effected a forcible entry caught them *in flagrante delicto* and not only found evidence of the most valid nature, but papers which, it is said, show that they were members of that conspiracy, which, under the pretext of regenerating the peninsula, seeks to plant the Red Republic in the centre of Italy.

. . .

A correspondence was further laid hold of implicating 14 persons in the vicinity, who were at once arrested, and bringing the whole party into immediate contact with the party of 'La Jeune Italie'. Much of the correspondence was in English, and coming from London, and, if what I hear to be true, these young men were not only the dupes but the agents of the central committee. Had the so-called Lord Aldborough and his brothers, or, as they are better known, Messrs. Stratford, been Tuscan or Austrian subjects, they would have been tried at the drumhead and shot within an hour. But the interference of Mr. Macbean [the British Consul] induced the Commander in Chief to give them every fair chance, and they are now in prison waiting until 'the instruction', as it is called, be finished, when they will be brought before a court-martial and allowed the fullest privilege of defence. I may add that, from private information, the Austrian officer is determined to spare their lives, if possible, and to exact banishment from the Tuscan States as a too lenient punishment:

Dragon appears to have carried not only a body but also some living passengers. Sir William Parker wrote to Giffard on 14 July 1851.[11]

> *Queen* off Malta
> 14 July 1851
>
> Sir,
>
>   I have received your letter No. 20 of the 3rd Ult. reporting that at the request of HM Minister at Naples, you had received two Refugees on board the *Dragon*.
>
>   I approve of your compliance with His Excellency's Wishes, and desire that you will land the Parties referred to at the first place where they can be disembarked without endangering their Persons, or Liberty.
>
> W.P.

   The whole incident would appear to be a classic case of 'send a gunboat'. Further light is cast on *Dragon*'s operations and the fate of the Stratfords by a letter from Parker to Giffard.[12]

> Private   Rosas
>   Queen Rosas Bay
>   6 Oct 1851
>
> My dear Captain Giffard,
>
>   I hope you have received an official letter which I forwarded to you from Barcelona on the 19th Sept directing you to proceed as soon as circumstances admitted to Naples, where Sir Wm Temple in a letter of the 3rd ult. expressed a strong desire to have a steamer placed in consequence of the excitement caused by Mr. Gladstone's Pamphlets.
>
> I therefore know not where this will find you, but cannot let the *Scourge* depart without a few lines of thanks for your letters of the 21 and 23rd Aug & 6 Sept all I believe since I last wrote to you.
>
>   The *Scourge* is intended to relieve you at Naples eventually if you are gone there and if you have Messrs. Stratfords on board a steamer shall call to relieve you of them, if anything goes to Malta before the *Dragon*,
>
> I conclude the terms of their banishment apply only to their removal from Tuscany & not compulsory that they are to be immediately conveyed to Malta, however they should not be landed anywhere without permission of the authorities, or regular passports.
>
>   Rear Admiral Dundas who has been making a holiday tour of recreation passed 2 days with me at this anchorage & assured me that there never has been any idea of sending home the remains of Mr. Shiel in the *Dragon* – whenever a small steamer is ordered home she will call to convey them, but none will be sent for this special purpose.

11 PRO ADM PAR 26 10.
12 PRO ADM PAR 97 Private of 6 October and 10 October 1851.

In case this should follow you to Naples, I will merely say that the *Firebrand* is to accompany the *Albion* to Malta from hence as her rudder head is found partially defective, she has besides carried away her lower yards in a hard gale on 27th ult.

The *Phaeton* is now on her way to us from Malta. *Vengeance* and *Encounter* are to join after visiting Alexandria, & *Bellerophon* is shortly expected from England. She is to bring out *Hercules* to replace the *Ceylon* which is to be broken up. The *Superb* and *Ganges* will return home in the Winter.

The Squadron will probably steer for Malta about the end of the present or early in next month, by which time or before I shall hope to see you.

I have only to address my good wishes & remain etc.

W.P.

Sir William Temple, British Minister and head of the Legation in Naples, was a brother of Lord Palmerston and his request for a steamer consequently carried great weight. 'Mr. Gladstone's Pamphlets'[13] were evidently seen as a possible source of action hostile to British interests. The pamphlets were not generally available in Naples,[14] though they were, presumably, available to the Neapolitan authorities. It may be from this cause that *Dragon* was, in fact, not required in Naples but sent off post haste on another quasi-diplomatic mission in the western Mediterranean.

Giffard laconically records

Admiral and Squadron arrived [at Malta] on the 20th [of November 1851] and on the 29th we were suddenly started off at 9.30 pm. Anchored Gibraltar at 11.30 am on the 4th December, *Hogue* coaling'.

These episodes in the employment of *Dragon* are explained in the commander-in-chief's correspondence.[15]

> *Queen* at Malta
> 2 December 1851

Sir,

I transmit for the information of the Lords Commissioners of the Admiralty the copy of a letter which I received on the 29th ult. from HM Consul at Cadiz, relative to the departure from that Port of a French

13 *Two letters to the Earl of Aberdeen on the State Prosecutions of the Neapolitan Government*, by the Rt Hon W E Gladstone, MP, for the University of Oxford, 4 editions, London 1851.
14 We are indebted to Professor John Vincent of the University of Bristol for this information.
15 PAR 21 203.

Squadron, for the supposed purpose of operations against the Dominions of the Emperor of Morocco.

As in the event of hostilities occurring, or the French taking possession of any part of the Morocco territory, the British Consular Functionaries would probably strike their Flags and take their departure; and the *Janus* being the only steam vessel stationed in the vicinity, I despatched the *Dragon* without delay on the 29th Gibraltar, to communicate with His Excellency the Governor, as also with HM Charge d'Affairs at Tangier, with a view to rendering any assistance for the embarkation of Mr. Drummond Hay or the English Consular functionaries on the Morocco coast, should it be necessary.

I enclose a copy of my orders to Captain Giffard, as also of a secret memorandum on which he is to act in the contingency therein specified.

sailing orders 29.11.51
secret memo 29.11.51   W.P.

The secret memorandum, unfortunately, has not survived in the record.

Admiral Parker had already written to the Governor of Gibraltar, Sir Robert Gardiner,[16] in a letter in which the first rumblings of the coming War with Russia can be heard.

Malta 29 Nov. 1851

My dear Sir Robert,

I have only 5 minutes to thank you for your letter of the 25 inst just received and in consequence of the Intelligence it contains & a further communication from our Consul at Cadiz relative to the supposed movements of the French Squadron I have deemed it expedient to detach the *Dragon* to Gibraltar, where Captain Giffard, whom you will find a most amiable & excellent officer, is directed to take Commr. Powell under his orders & act as may be most beneficial for British Interests in protecting the Consular Functionaries and English Subjects; after conferring with yourself & Mr. Drummond Hay on the best course to be adopted, taking care to observe due courtesy in his communication with the French Admiral or whoever may have command of their forces.

Captain Giffard will also place the *Dragon* at the disposal of Commodore Martin to assist in any chastisement of the Riff Pirates should any Squadron come for that purpose, which for the moment is of course to be considered as a confidential communication.

The *Dragon* will remain at Gibraltar for the present unless the angry feeling of the French induces them (as their Ambassador at Constantinople threatens) to send a strong squadron to blockade the Dardanelles, in

16 PAR 97 Private.

which case it may be necessary to concentrate our ships in readiness for any orders which our Government may think necessary.

This quarrel about Jerusalem seems very absurd but I suppose both French & Russian have other policy in view than the Ecclesiastical Government of the Holy land.

Both are offended with the Sublime Porte & the latter are not pleased at the visit of the *Vengeance & Encounter* at Alexandria.

I am glad Commr. Powell is sufficiently recovered to render assistance about the Riff Coast if wanted.

I am, in great haste etc. etc.

Dragon's move to Gibraltar comprised an important and delicate mission. Ever since a French punitive expedition (stemming, originally, from the activities of Algerian pirates) to Algiers in 1830 had (despite French assurances to the contrary) ended with the permanent occupation of the country and the construction of a naval base of considerable strategic importance, successive British governments had been concerned at any further French activity in North Africa and particularly in Morocco. From time to time this concern was enhanced by French activity as when, for instance, the French fleet bombarded Tangier in 1848 as punitive action against a Moroccan administration which was supporting Algerian rebels. The incident of 1851 involved further punitive action by the French in consequence of the activities of pirates from the Riff Coast, east of Tangier, and culminated in a further bombardment. According to Giffard's notes, the French squadron comprised the 16 gun steamers *Gomer* and *Sané* and the iron steamers *Caton* and *Narval*.

Giffard himself records

went to Tangier on the 6th, French Squadron of steamers there and on the 10th we left for Sallee anchoring off the bar the next day; taking Mr. Elton the Consul with us: we landed on the Rabat side, examined the effects of the French wanton bombardment and procured two of their shell. Returned to Tangier on the 16th [of December 1851.] On the 17th heard of the death of my dearest mother. On the 22nd proceeded to and anchored at Gibraltar.

The correspondence about this episode is rounded off by what would in a later generation have been described as a semi-official letter to Giffard from the Admiral, couched in personally familiar terms.[17]

17 PAR 97 210.

Malta 11 December 1851

My dear Captain Giffard,

Accept my thanks for your interesting letter by the *Euxine* & I am glad you had a good passage to Gibraltar to enable the *Dragon* to be very useful in assisting Mr. Hay, tho' not in the nick of time that you would have preferred.

Commander Powell seems to have acted very judiciously in his intercourse with the French Squadron, as well as inspiring confidence at the different points which he visited on the Coast of Morocco.

The events in France will very probably call the attention of the French Squadron to their own shores.

I trust you will have received all your absentees by the *Ganges*.

Accept our united good wishes.

W.P.

The incident was one episode in the long history of piracy by the inhabitants of the Riff Coast, the area immediately east of Tangier. The Riff were a non-Arab tribe, possibly related to the Berbers. They were a very poor people who inhabited the coast, an area not properly subordinated to the Sultan of Morocco who invariably shrugged off complaints, claiming lack of authority. For the Riff, the capture and looting of the occasional foreign merchant vessel was almost an economic necessity. For centuries there had been attacks on merchant vessels in the narrows of the Strait of Gibraltar and they continued until the end of the 1800s.[18]

The particular incident which occasioned *Dragon*'s hasty journey across the Mediterranean appears to have been triggered by the capture by pirates in 1851 of a Spanish vessel, *Joven Emilia*, followed on 5 October by the capture, and apparently the murder of some of the crew, of the brigantine *Violet*. This led to the despatch of the British steam paddle sloop *Janus*, whose people discovered the remains of the pillaged *Violet* on the beach. They attempted reprisals against the pirates who were, however, present in great numbers and drove off the naval party with eight wounded including the commanding officer, Lieutenant Powell, who was promoted commander as a result of the action.[19]

The incident led to much talk of mounting a major British punitive expedition against the pirates, but in the event no such action was taken. Admiral Parker wrote semi-officially to Giffard on 9 January 1852, a letter which referred again to the possibility of punitive action and also revealed that Giffard, despite his evident success in operations requiring discretion and diplomatic skill while in command of *Dragon*, was nevertheless seeking a home appointment.[20]

18 See, for instance, Slocum, *Sailing Alone Around the World*, London, no date, pp 37–39.

19 Laird Clowes, *The Royal Navy*, p 362.

20 PAR 97 unnumbered, 9 January 1852.

Malta, 9 Jan 1852

My dear Giffard,

I condole with you most sincerely on the loss of your Mother & the heavy affliction which your aged Father has to sustain entering most fully into your sentiments of filial attentions which you feel called upon to render to him in consequence of this lamented bereavement.

I am free to confess I am not surprised at the unfavourable reply which your Father has received to his application for your appointment as a Comptroller of the Packet Service because I believe these duties have hitherto been reserved (& very properly) for *Senior* Officers & I honestly think that those in the vigour of life & health like yourself should be kept in practice afloat to perfect themselves in their Professional experience which they can never acquire in a comparative sinecure of the nature you allude to, nor could Sir E. Baring easily refute the charge of lending himself to a considerable job if he consented to your Father's request tho' I as frankly admit that your actual claims may be as great as those of any other officer of your Rank or much your senior.

With these expressions I do not feel myself at liberty to touch on the subject of the Packets or any other appointment out of the direct line of service but I will with pleasure take an opportunity of assuring Sir Francis how truly I have appreciated your abilities & character as an officer ever since I have known you & I heartily wish that some arrangement may be made satisfactory to your Father as well as to yourself . . .

When you write to your Father which *I* cannot do by this Packet pray offer to him the assurance of my sincere condolence & kindest regard & Believe me etc.

W.P.

I have found your account of your visits to Sallee & Rabat most interesting & thank you for them.

The Riff Coast incident had a sequel. Giffard recorded it with his usual brevity.

On the 5th January, 1852, I went to Tangier and returned on the 14th, bringing back some captives [the log shows that there were four of them] delivered up by the Reef Pirates. I then made a reconnoitering visit to the Reef Coast in the *Janus*.

This laconic account evidently covered some very useful intelligence work and negotiation which led to the ransoming of the survivors of the crew of *Violet* as recorded in an official letter from Sir W Parker of 1 February 1852.[21]

21 PAR 26 1852, 3.

Queen at Malta
1 Feb 1852

Sir,

I learn with great satisfaction by your letter of the 23rd ulto. that the few survivors of the crew of the late English Brig '*Violet*' who were captives in the hands of the Reef Pirates, have been recovered, and highly approve of the measures you adopted to avail yourself of all the information they were able to afford in connexion with the haunts and predatory habits of the Marauders on the Reef Coast, as detailed in your enclosed statements also of your having afforded clothing to the Ransomed Prisoners as suggested by Mr. Drummond-Hay.

The information thus acquired and the judicious consideration with which you obtained two of the newly invented French shells which had been discharged against Sallee during the late bombardment will I have no doubt be satisfactorily appreciated by the Lords Commissioners of the Admiralty.

W.P.

Dragon was now ordered to the Tagus. During these operations in the Mediterranean the log shows that although the severity of individual punishments was actually less than on board *Penelope*, floggings were just as numerous. Fifteen men of the crew of 131 who could be punished in this way were flogged in the twenty-two and a half months of the commission, a rather high percentage for the times. For all his apparent charm and diplomatic skill and readiness to master and exploit technical innovation, Giffard appears to have been among the more conservative of naval officers of his generation in matters of the enforcement of discipline. But the Italian insurrections in which he was so much involved were conducted in an atmosphere of violence and cruelty. While *Dragon* was protecting British interests in the Italian ports, Italian actresses were publicly flogged by the Austrian authorities for singing patriotic songs.[22]

Dragon was in the Tagus from 7 February 1852 to 27 May. Giffard was senior officer in the Tagus for much of this period and carried out the administrative duties that went with the frequent comings and goings of units of the British fleet. *Dragon* was employed from time to time as a tug to get windbound vessels out of the Tagus. These duties were varied. On 27 April a waterlogged hulk was reported off Cape Roca. The story is best told in the words of Giffard's declaration before the British Consul at Lisbon on 25 May 1852.[23]

22 Crankshaw, *The Fall of the House of Hapsburg*, London 1987, pp 138–139.
23 Loose Paper attached to NMM JOD 30.

We the undersigned Captain and Officers of Her Majesty's Steam Frigate *Dragon* do hereby solemnly and sincerely declare that in consequence of information received on the 27th April last that a water logged vessel was reported to be floating about off Cape Roca, Her Majesty's aid ship *Dragon* immediately proceeded out under steam in search of the wreck; on arriving off Cape Roca nothing was seen of her – after running off shore about ten miles the wreck was discovered at 5.45 pm.

The wind blowing very fresh from N.E. and the sea making a clean sweep over her rendered it dangerous to attempt taking her in tow – fires were therefore banked up and HM ship laid by her for the night. On the morning of the 28th the wind and the sea having abated the wreck was taken in tow by HM ship with stream hemp and stream chain cables, then being distant about 40 miles SW of Cape Roca.

From the vessel being completely waterlogged and the rudder-head bent off, considerable difficulty was experienced in taking her in tow as she was not under any command. By means of Capstan Bars lashed across the rudder they succeeded in getting her head the right way; Though now rendered more manageable there was still great difficulty as they could not steer her perfectly and when with good way on the broad sheer of the vessel on either quarter carried away the lashings on the end of towing chain cable and on the evening of the 28th at 5 pm it parted; That they sent a sheet cable on board which sustained the great strain and enabled them to bring her in safely on the 29th but not without considerable difficulty in crossing the Bar where HM Ship was often rendered unmanageable from the causes before mentioned.

That no living creature was found on board the vessel and she had evidently been many months floating about – The cabin accommodation was all gone – apparently destroyed by fire as also the Fore and Main masts – the raked bowsprit only remained with two anchors and one cable.

Giffard goes on to record the vessel's dimensions and that the cargo was 'American pine' in various baulks marked with initials. On board were a few fragmentary relics, part of the bottom of a bottle with a Bristol maker's name, part of a thermometer marked 'King & Coombes, Bristol', on one side and on the other 'J.D. King, Optician, Bristol'.[24] The vessel's cargo was

24 A number of Bristol vessels were employed in this business. J D King was a well known and well established supplier of navigational and optical equipment with a shop in Clare Street near the Broad Quay in Bristol. A possible longshot identification of the derelict is *Superb*, built at New Bideford, Prince Edward Island, Canada, in 1826 by William Ellis and owned in Bristol from 1828 to 1835 when the register bears the notation 'Vessel sold to aliens and registry closed'. Her registered dimensions were within reasonable range of those recorded by Giffard and her eventual fate is not known. At this date (before the 1855 Merchant Shipping Act) there was no official number carved into the vessel's main beam.

discharged in Lisbon and presumably the officers and men of *Dragon* shared some sort of salvage award.

For an operation of this kind, *Dragon*'s paddle box boats would have been used. The idea that the upper parts of the paddle boxes of steamers might comprise usable boats was put forward in 1838 by Captain George Smith. After trials in 1839, the idea was adopted for paddle frigates, although it met with some opposition on the grounds that the boats were too large and unhandy and difficult to launch. These big boats were stowed upside-down on top of the paddle boxes. Indeed, they themselves comprised the top of the box. There was a large square hole in the top of the paddle box through which spray was ejected into the boat, thereby keeping her constantly wet. This was a great advantage, for it meant that the planks of these wooden boats never dried out and shrank as did the planks of boats stowed on deck or slung from davits, which had to be kept constantly wetted to ensure that they would be watertight when required for use. Over 30 feet long, very burdensome and massively built, the righting and launching of paddle box boats, given that the frigates had no steam deck machinery, required special devices. James Peake's *Rudiments of Naval Architecture*, published in London in 1851, on pages 145–148 describes and illustrates in detail one of the several methods by which this job was done and one method is illustrated very clearly in Plate 23. Paddle box boats can also be seen in several other illustrations in this book.

One paddle box boat survives. She was captured by the Finns during a raid by the paddle frigate *Vulture* on the town of Kokkola on the Gulf of Bothnia coast of Finland in 1854, and she is displayed in the English Park at Kokkola today.[25] She is diagonally built, has eight thwarts and eight positions for oar crutches on either side, four mast positions and two large holes where the boat was hit by gunfire during the raid in which she was captured. She is 9.7 metres long, 3.3 metres in the beam and the tops of the stem and sternpost (the boat is double-ended) are 1.4 metres above the lowest part of the rockered keel.

On 27 May 1852, *Dragon* steamed out of the Tagus bound towards Spithead. She had been, it appears, unexpectedly recalled. It is evident, although there is little about it in the log, that her boilers had been giving trouble and that Giffard had reported accordingly. His report was commented on by Captain W H Henderson.[26]

7 April 1852.

In forwarding for their Lordships information the enclosed report on the state of the boilers of the *Dragon* I beg to call their attention to the circumstances under which she was commissioned.

25 Greenhill and Giffard, *The British Assault*, pp 185–190.
26 PRO ADM 93/8 Steam Department, 387, 7 April 1852.

It will be seen by my minute of the 10th June, 1850, a copy of which is herewith enclosed, that I was apprehensive that little dependence could be placed on these Boilers, they having been shipped in 1845, unless they were repaired to a considerable extent, and I recommended that before the repair was commenced, considering it doubtful whether the Boilers were worth it, that an Estimate of the probable expense should be forwarded.

Their Lordships however informed me on the following day that 'as it was intended to recommission the *Dragon* without delay, they had ordered the Engineers defects to be taken in hand immediately by the engineers under the Captain of the Steam Reserve without the aid of the factory.'

Although the Boilers of this vessel have lasted as long as was anticipated, yet it appears from Captain Giffard's Report that for some time past her efficiency has been very questionable and I fear this must always be the case to a greater or lesser extent whenever a steamer is paid off before her Boilers are worn out unless a large amount is expended for repairs.

If such repairs are not made and a vessel is employed on Foreign Service, she probably may not prove fit for active duty when her services are urgently required, and if she is laid up and considered available only for temporary service on the Home Station, the evil is incurred of adding to the number of vessels in Harbour, whose services can be depended on for only a comparatively short time, continually becoming shorter, it being impossible entirely to prevent the deterioration of Boilers, even in Harbour.

The only remedy I can suggest effectually to meet these evils and to obviate the necessity of incurring the expense of heavy repairs when under ordinary circumstances they would not be necessary, is to make arrangements for not paying off steam vessels until their Boilers are worn out, when new Boilers would be fitted, the engine, and if necessary the ship thoroughly repaired and refitted, and everything made efficient for active service with a reasonable prospect of remaining so for 4 to 5 years.

Should their Lordships be pleased to adopt this system not only would the efficiency of the Steam Branch of the Service be greatly increased, but a saving would be effected in the expenditure of rigging, sails, stores, & etc., and in the repairs to the Hull, Boilers and Machinery, amounting in the whole to a sum which although difficult to estimate would most certainly be no inconsiderable fraction of the entire expenditure on this Branch of the Service.

Submitted that Captain Giffard be directed to reduce the pressure on the safety valves of the Boilers of the *Dragon* from 8 lbs to 5 lbs on the Square Inch.

As a result of these comments Thomas Lloyd, in effect the head of naval steam engineering, and John Dinnen, formerly of *Lightning* and now one of the two Inspectors of Machinery Afloat, visited Portsmouth on 10 June and reported on the state of *Dragon*'s boilers.[27] They recommended that although the visible parts of the boilers were in relatively good condition and the vessel could run another year at reduced steam pressure, the bottom of the boilers were, on the evidence, probably in such a state that they must be lifted for examination and, once lifted,

> We beg further to state that from our own knowledge of the general condition of Boilers which have been so long in place as those of the *Dragon*, that when these Boilers have been removed they will be found not worth repair.

The result of this report was, in Giffard's own words, that

> We arrived at Spithead on 1st June and after various surveys of our Boilers by the people at the Dockyard, and by people from Admiralty, we were finally turned over to the *Tiger* on 19th June 1852.

Dragon's Mediterranean commission was conducted at a time when the paddle frigate was already obsolete. No more were to be built and no more large sailing warships were to be built either. The Admiralty had been increasingly committed to the screw since the mid 1840s. *Dragon*'s commission demonstrated both the strengths and weaknesses of the fully powered paddle steamer at the current stage of development of marine steam engines and boilers. Until small, fully powered screw steamships were developed during the coming War with Russia there was still a special role for her to play. No sailing vessel had the mobility of *Dragon*, able to move rapidly around the western Mediterranean in response to the emergencies produced by the shifting political scene. As a vehicle for the rapid transmission of orders the paddle steamer was ideal, as she was in hostilities, against less technically advanced foes such as the Riff pirates.

On the other hand, all marine steam engines were still far from reliable mechanically at this period. Some years later, Sir Baldwin Walker who, as Surveyor of the Navy was responsible more than anyone else for the rapid introduction of steam screw propulsion, gave evidence to the Parliamentary Committee on marine engines[28] to the effect that the engines of *Dragon* and *Odin* were badly planned and built. But at the time of their collapse

---

27 ADM 93/8 Steam Department 473, 11 June 1852.
28 P.P. 1859 Vol XV, p 39.

Dragon's boilers were seven years old and had not had a full dockyard overhaul. This is not a bad record at this period. Captain Henderson's recommendation that a steamer's commission should equal the likely length of life of her boilers and likely high reliability of her engines after overhaul (four to five years) was a very sensible one. It called for greater serviceability than most merchant ships provided at the time, although these ships were making much shorter passages and usually running between good maintenance facilities. Many merchant paddle steamers at this period spent a month or two each year undergoing maintenance in a shipyard. The Cunard Company stuck to the wooden hulled paddle steamer with side-lever engines for the transatlantic service until 1862 because of the reliability of such engines, for all their disadvantages in what was financially a very high risk business.[29]

29 Hyde, *Cunard*, pp 28–29.

10

The Employment of the Paddle Frigate: 3 *Tiger* in the Preliminaries to War

During the second half of the 1840s it became clear that the future of the navy rested with steam propulsion and that steam propulsion must be combined with the line of battleships. Battleships in the principal fleets each had their own paddle steamer in attendance to give them mobility under tow, either ahead or, in action, lashed to the disengaged side of the battleship. The attendant paddle steamer also gave the battleship more rapid communication with the shore and with the rest of the fleet when such was called for. Although *Dragon* in the course of the commission described in the last chapter had, by chance, few if any occasions to tow, *Tiger*, as this chapter will show, was more typical of the paddle frigates in that she was frequently employed to give greater mobility to the sailing battleships, and her captain and crew had to acquire all the complex expertise which was beginning to evolve around towing.

But in this crucial decade of the 1840s not only was the screw propeller, installed under Smith's patent between the sternpost and the rudder, demonstrated as more efficient than the paddle but the post of Comptroller of Steam Machinery was abolished, thus stressing that all new ships would be steam-and-sail propelled. It was now the navy's policy to cease the building both of purely sailing vessels and of paddle steamers, and to concentrate on the line of battleship and the frigate equipped with an auxiliary steam engine driving a screw as the normal ship of war. At the same time, as a result of market forces during this crucial decade, machinery became lighter and smaller, boilers were improved and steam pressures increased. The result was an engine which could be stowed away below the water line and which did not occupy so much space that the vessels, even though screw propelled, could not carry an effective armament. The engine could now be aboard the battleship instead of in the vessel towing her, and give her a mobility and power which made the steam screw battle fleet which was to go to war with Russia in 1854 the most formidable weapon of war which had ever existed at sea. This battle fleet was to have a decisive effect on the outcome of the war.

The paddle frigate, of course, also benefited from the technical advances of the 1840s, and those built at the end of the decade were mechanically considerably more efficient than the vessels of the early and mid 1840s. They had better boilers and condensors and were much better able to perform their limited range of duties, and during this transitional period from sailing vessel to screw propelled steamer, they were to play a very important role in the coming war. The War with Russia was to prove to be both their apogee and their end.

Tiger was one of these efficient new vessels but her completion was a long, slow process. Designed by John Edye, she was, as the draught reproduced here Plate 21 shows, a flat floored vessel, breaking away from the sharp floors which had characterised Sir William Symonds's steamers, built in the sailing vessel tradition. Her draught was submitted on 27 July 1847, and her construction begun at Chatham in November of that year. Her building fell behind schedule and she was not floated out of her dock until 1 December 1849 when she was taken up the Thames to the East India Dock to have her propelling units installed. These were oscillating engines of 399 horse power by John Penn of Greenwich[1] which gave her a speed of 9 knots under ideal conditions, and they took from 9 December 1849 to 14 March 1850 to build into the vessel. She had two funnels, side by side. She then lay for five months fitting out at Deptford and then another three months back at Chatham where she was completed and coppered.[2]

The oscillating engine was the third type of marine steam engine which was installed in the paddle frigates and was perhaps the most efficient in terms of weight, bulk and, in its developed form, of reliability. It was the speciality of two London engineering firms, Penn, and Miller and Ravenhill, and by 1852 had been installed in a number of frigates including *Retribution* and *Magicienne*. It was also much favoured for fast Post Office packets. Murray describes its working.[3]

Of all the direct kinds, however, the oscillating engine, which has derived from Mr. Penn so much of its elegant simplicity and present perfection of workmanship and arrangement, is generally preferred. It need hardly be explained that this engine derives its name from the fact of the cylinders 'oscillating' upon hollow axes or 'trunnions', through which steam is admitted to, and withdrawn from, the valves, the piston rod by this means accommodating itself to the motion of the crank without any parallel motion being required. This construction has now been proved

1 Murray, *Marine Engines*, p 204.
2 PRO ADM 180/14.
3 Murray, *op cit*, p 15.

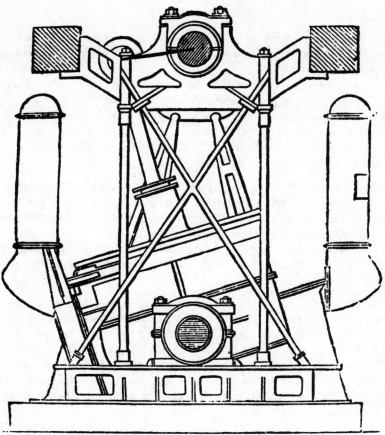

An oscillating engine. (From Murray, *Marine Engines*, 1852)

as applicable to ocean steamers as to the small boats on the Thames where it has long been a favourite . . .

The action of the oscillating engine can be seen in almost any toy stationary steam engine. A working set of these simple (not compound) oscillating engines dating from 1857 built, as were *Tiger's*, by John Penn of Greenwich, can be seen in the paddle steamer *Diesbar* preserved at Dresden in Germany.

It had originally been intended that although equal to carrying a heavier main-deck battery, *Tiger* should be lightly armed with only four 32 pound guns of 56 hundredweight each on a regular basis.[4] It was, however, decided in September 1850 to equip her with a much more formidable armament.[5]

4 PRO ADM 95/13 518 2 July 1849.
5 PRO ADM AO 7782 26 September 1850.

Surveyor to Admiralty, 26 September 1850.

By their Lordships' order of the 24th May last the armament of the *Magicienne* was increased from ten to sixteen guns and the ship has been fitted for that number.

I therefore see no objection to the *Tiger* and the *Valorous* being in all respects as to guns, pivots, and slides, as *Magicienne* and the space intended for a shell room being adapted to an After Magazine, and a new Shell Room built in the After Hold.

If approved by their Lordships, I would submit that the necessary orders be given.

Tiger was therefore duly equipped with 16 guns, ten 32 pounder, 50 hundredweight, 9 foot guns on the main deck, four of the same on the quarterdeck and two 10 inch, 85 hundredweight, 9 foot guns, one on the quarterdeck and one on the forecastle.

She sailed from Portsmouth on 9 December 1850 on trials. Here, within two months the Surveyor of the Navy was recommending major modifications.[6]

As the stability of the *Tiger* appears to be insufficient for carrying the additional Armament on the Main Deck now given to ships of this class, with the increased masts and yards and the coals stored up to the Upper Deck, I submit that the Main Deck of this vessel be made a continuous deck as in the *Furious* and the *Valorous* by which the body of coal would be stowed wholly below this deck, and the weights, generally, kept sufficiently down to give her the necessary stability for her present sail and armament.

As a result of her trials which, with the modification to the main deck, appear to have lasted most of the summer of 1851, *Tiger* was further modified, notably by having her lower masts shortened by 4 feet without taking them out of the vessel.[7]

She was 215 feet long, 36 feet of maximum beam and of 1221 tons by the current naval measurement. Her hull had cost £32,984, her machinery £24,385, her masts and spars £835 and her rigging £2079. The modifications and fitting out for sea cost another £4502, so her total cost was £64,785, ready for sea less stores, armament and ammunition.[8]

Captain Giffard was the first commanding officer of the new paddle frigate and it would appear likely that his appointment was determined before the Whig government of Lord John Russell, which had been in power since 1846, fell on 20 February 1852 to be followed for a few months

6 PRO ADM AO 8168 449 8 February 1851.
7 PRO AO 1874 564 30 July 1851.
8 PRO ADM 180/14.

by the minority Tory administration of Lord Derby, and later in the year by Lord Aberdeen's coalition of Whigs and Peelites (the Tories had broken with Peel) which was to take Britain into the War with Russia. His crew was largely that of *Dragon* and, according to the master's log which is confirmed by the Master Roll for 1854,[9] comprised twenty-seven officers, 134 petty officers and seamen, thirty boys and twenty-seven marines. There were three lieutenants with Lieutenant Alfred Royer as the senior lieutenant; the master was Frank Edington with J C Solfleet as the second master. There were four midshipmen, including John Giffard, now promoted from cadet, and one cadet, H E C Robinson. There were also the surgeon, Henry Domville, the purser, the lieutenant in charge of marines, five engineers, one of whom was later 'sent home for drinking', four warrant officers, the bosun and his assistant, the carpenter and the gunner, a 'fifer' and a musician, a cooper with his crew and a caulker with his, ten stokers, a painter, a steward, cooks, sick berth attendant, clerks and a blacksmith. On the basis of her crew, *Tiger* was therefore, technically, a second class steam paddle frigate.

The crew were well treated, being given all the pay due to them from *Dragon* and a fortnight's leave, presumably fully paid, to the officers and to the men, who were, it would appear, on three year or continuous agreements. Thus the great majority of the men of *Dragon* appear on *Tiger*'s muster role, and it is perhaps an interesting commentary on the psychology of the times that, although the stay in Portsmouth gave them an opportunity to desert, twelve of the fifteen men who had been flogged for various misdemeanours on board *Dragon* joined *Tiger*. This was a floating world, balanced both socially and technically between the 'old barbarism' of the eighteenth century and the less inhumane society which was developing in the 1840s.

As *Tiger* was lost in the dramatic circumstances described in Chapter 1, the captain's log was burned. For a detailed account of her activities prior to the outbreak of the War with Russia in 1854, we are dependent largely on Giffard's personal notes in his summary of his naval life and on the master's log, which survived because the master, Francis Edington, brought it ashore with him to use as evidence for his defence at the inevitable court martial.[10] *Tiger* steamed from Spithead on 21 August 1852, 'disconnected and made sail off Cape Finisterre at 5 pm on the 25th'. Mr Edington's log goes into detail. During the fitting out period, which lasted from 20 June to 21 August, among other incidents the machinery for raising the starboard funnel broke down and the funnel had to be raised with a sling tackle. They did the measured mile in Stokes Bay on 14 August, achieving 8.6 miles per hour. On the sailing day, 21 August, they unmoored and lay to a single

9 PRO ADM 38/5136 0992 Muster Book of Her Majesty's Ship *Tiger*.
10 NMM JOD 30 and PRO ADM 54/293.

anchor at 4.20 am, at 10.15 lit fires, and at 12.10 began to raise the anchor. At 12.20 they proceeded under steam. On 22 August they had to stop engines for seven minutes 'to ease bearings of starboard piston rod'.

On 28 August *Tiger* passed Cape St Vincent and was now on the Mediterranean Station under the orders of Rear Admiral James Dundas. On 30 August 1852, they spent four hours in Gibraltar, steaming in and out, but they did not coal. The next day they exercised the guns, firing at a mark. They arrived at Malta on 5 September. Here they coaled and watered and then steamed on 8 September to find and join the admiral and his squadron. This conjuncture was achieved the following day and from 14 September until they arrived at Vourla Bay, an anchorage just outside the entrance to the Dardanelles, to water on 17 September, *Tiger* towed both *Trafalgar*, 120 guns, and *Bellerophon*, 80 guns, astern.

★ ★ ★ ★

From now on *Tiger* for the rest of her short life was deeply involved first in the complex naval movements which preceded the outbreak of the War with Russia in 1854, and then in the earlier stages of that war itself. This war has been the subject of much misunderstanding, both in the popular conception of it and in the accounts of many historians.

The immediate occasion for the events which led to the war was the matter of access to the Holy places of the Christian faith in and around Jerusalem. These had long been places of Christian pilgrimage. Protestants, Roman Catholics and members of the Greek and Russian Orthodox churches visited them every year, spending money and enjoying convenience and privileges in a Muslim society under Turkish administration which were graded according to the influence the government of their country of origin could bring to bear upon the Turkish administration in Constantinople. This system worked well, with the Russian Orthodox church sending the greatest number of pilgrims and enjoying the greatest privileges, until Louis Napoléon Bonaparte, then president of the French Second Republic, in 1850 saw advantage in putting pressure on the Turks to improve the position of Catholic pilgrims in order to increase his popularity with his own population of Catholic persuasion, at the same time adding strength to French influence in the eastern Mediterranean and, in consequence, to French prestige generally. This brought the French into sharp conflict with the interests of Russia under Tsar Nicholas I. The strengthening of French influence with the corrupt and decaying Turkish administration was seen as a threat to a Russia whose territories adjoined those of the Turks on the Danube frontier of what is now Romania, and which had built up a vast trade in grain out of Odessa and through the Bosphorus and the Dardanelles into the Mediterranean and so to the outside world – through a narrow sea route controlled entirely by Turkey.

In recent years there has been considerable reassessment of the nature, the strategy and the reality of the war. The very term Crimean War has been shown to be a misnomer and there is a move to return to the original title 'Russian War' for a conflict far wider in its geographical scope, its scale and its importance in European history than conventional scholarship has allowed. As far as Britain was concerned it was, perforce, largely a naval war, in the sense that it was the navy, the fighting arm with which Britain was totally dominant, which, without a major engagement played the vital role. It was the threat to St Petersburg mounted by the navy which ended the war in 1856, and the Baltic was throughout the war a more important theatre than was the Black Sea. As will become apparent, the shifting political scene in Britain never gave birth to an agreed strategy – the perception constantly changed with the varying ascendency of different personalities in the cabinet, and there was no co-ordinating unity, as there would have been later, in a structured cabinet with a career civil service.[11]

It was these events which precipitated the very complex diplomatic and political manoeuvres together with the attendant pattern of naval move-ments – since the navies of Britain and France were those countries' expressions of physical power in the eastern Mediterranean area – in which the steam paddle frigate *Tiger* now became involved, and which led in the next two years to the outbreak of hostilities, first between Turkey and Russia after Turkey's declaration of war and then, inevitably, between Russia and the Western maritime powers, Britain and France, for the time being uneasily allied.

But, of course, the real causes of the tensions which led to the two years of war lay much deeper than the squabbles of Christian priests in Muslim Jerusalem, even though the priests were supported by the great powers. Great Britain and Russia were the only superpowers of that age. A burgeoning manufacturing Britain had become, partly through her develop-ment and ready adoption of the steamship, the world's great maritime power. Russia had all the resources necessary for industrialisation on a vast scale, but the wrong social system to exploit the opportunities. Tensions were almost bound to break out into war sooner or later. Moreover, in the public eye (and in Britain the public eye was at last beginning to enter a little

---

11 For the best modern general studies of the war, see Lambert, *The Crimean War*, and his papers 'Preparing for the Russian War: British Strategic Planning, March 1853–1854', in *War and Society*, Vol 7, No 2, pp 15–39 and *Anglo-French Rivalry: 1854–1856*, Vincennes, *Service Historique de la Marine*, 1990. For the complex political background see Vincent, 'The Parliamentary Dimension of the Crimean War' in *Transactions of the Royal Historical Society*, Vol 31, London 1981. For the Russian point of view, see Curtiss, *Russia's Crimean War*, Durham, NC 1979, and *The Russian Army Under Nicholas I, 1825–1855*, Durham, NC, 1965. For the first modern study of the conduct of the Baltic campaign of the Royal Navy and of its fundamental significance to the outcome of the war, drawing partly on Finnish sources, see Greenhill and Giffard, *The British Assault*. For a very readable classic account of the complex preliminaries to the war, see Temperley, *England and the Near East, The Crimea*, London 1936, reprinted unaltered and unabridged, London 1964.

into political calculations, a part of the social changes of the time to which we referred in Chapter 3), Russia was a reactionary and at the same time an expansionist power. The events of 1848, to which we referred in the last chapter, and the social, political and economic changes which had been taking place in the preceding decades in Britain, had had no parallel in Russia, and the Tsar's autocracy was seen as the embodiment of the older order. Furthermore, Russian society was rightly seen as something completely alien, with different ideas of government, of the nature of political ideas and human relations, and with a completely different history from that of Western Europe. The parallel with the period between 1945 and the mid 1980s is not altogether without foundation. The British feared that the steady Russian expansion east of the Caspian Sea which was taking place (and which was actively accelerated after the war was over) represented a potential threat to India, and more especially to the land route to India across Turkey from Trebizond on the Black Sea through Tabriz and Tehran into the Persian Gulf, which ran close to the Russian border.[12] It will be remembered that this was still fifteen years before the opening of the Suez Canal. A feared extension of Russian influence in Turkey could again be a threat to communication with India via Damascus and Bagdad. Thus the coming war can be seen, among many other things, as an episode in the 'Great Game', as it has been called,[13] the contest for political influence in central Asia which was played out, on and off, for much of the nineteenth century.

There were deeper reasons still for the coming war, which was only eighteen months away as *Tiger* towed the sailing battleships, *Trafalgar* and *Bellerophon* into Greek waters in August 1852. Since the Congress of Vienna in 1815, the major powers had played their roles in what has been called the 'Concert of Europe', an uneasy system of international control, to mutual advantage after the destruction of the wars of the early part of the century. It was inevitable that, sooner or later, the long era of balance, more or less, would break down as great changes in economic and social conditions took place. Again, it is possible to see some degree of qualified parallel with the last years of the twentieth century. The war between Britain, France and Turkey on the one hand and Russia on the other marks the point of that breakdown.

There had been a long period of unease. The Russian administration had been determined for years to maintain effective control of the, to Russia, vital waterway between the Black Sea and the Aegean, and to allow no power but a Turkey susceptible to their influence to hold this passage between Europe and Asia. The movement of Russian troops and ships into Turkey in the early 1830s to assist a Turkish government faced with internal

12 Curtiss, *op cit*, p 23.
13 See, for instance, Edwardes, *Playing the Great Game*, London 1975.

stresses led to a treaty, that of Unkiar Skelessi in 1833, under which Turkey undertook to close the Straits to all warships in time of peace. The relevant and ostensibly secret clause of the treaty was directed principally at Britain and led to the beginning of a period of strong British and French interest in events in the region, expressed initially by the movement of the British and French ships into Besika Bay, an anchorage immediately south of the entrance to the Kanakkale Bogazi (still usually known in Britain as the Dardanelles) off the settlement now called Kumkale. The mound which marks the site of classical Troy is visible from this anchorage, which was to feature many times in the naval movements of the next twenty-five years.

Suspicion and tension developed between Britain and Russia. Each believed that the other had territorial ambitions in Turkey. Further internal crisis in the Turkish Empire in 1840 led to the Straits Convention of 1841, which confirmed the closure of the Mediterranean–Black Sea seaway to warships in peacetime but allowed the 'passage for light vessels under Flag of War, which shall be employed as is usual in the service of Missions of Foreign Powers'.[14] There followed a relaxation of tension, and a (mistaken) Russian understanding that Britain and Russia, with Austria, would seek to preserve the integrity of Turkey. Meanwhile, the great Russian grain trade out of Odessa (conducted quite largely as far as the trade to Britain and northern Europe was concerned in ships of the Russian Grand Duchy of Finland) was developing. The merchant vessels took forest products to Britain, sailed to Odessa in ballast, and there loaded grain for Britain or a north European port. Russian grain from Odessa formed a significant part of Britain's grain imports.[15] The free passage of the seaway from the Black Sea to the Mediterranean was therefore of great importance to both Russia and Britain, but at the same time the British trade with Turkey was growing to proportions which led the British Chargé d'Affairs at the Embassy in Constantinople in 1853 to comment that the safety of Britain's vast commercial interests was more important than European policy and the maintenance of peace.[16] There was plenty of room, therefore, for suspicion and tension on both sides and suspicion and tension there was. The public feeling in Britain against Russia as a potential menace grew at the end of the 1840s, especially when the Russians intervened in Hungary after the disturbances of 1848, and again when Russia demanded the surrender of political refugees who had fled into Turkey from Poland and Hungary. This crisis developed to the point at which British warships actually violated the Straits Convention and forced the passage into the sea of Marmora. The

14 'Convention between Great Britain, Austria, France, Prussia, Russia and Turkey, respecting the Straits of the Dardanelles and of the Bosphorus signed at London, 13th July, 1841, Article 2'.

15 Ahlström, 'The port of Odessa and Finland's Shipowners', *Nautica Fennica* 2, Helsinki, p 62.

16 Curtiss, *op cit*, p 23, and Rose to Clarendon, 25 March 1853; FO 78/930 F 365/9, quoted in Lambert, *The Crimean War*, Manchester 1990, p 4.

situation had a kind of inevitability about it. As Curtiss wrote,[17]

> A few wise Britons saw that its [Russia's] relations with Circassia, Georgia, Persia, are the same as ours with Rangoon, Scinde, the Sikhs and Oudh. This expansion was not based on a master plan, for 'they encroach as we encroach in India, Africa and everywhere – because we can't help it.' The objectivity here displayed by Sidney Herbert, Secretary for War, was rare, however, and most Englishmen wanted to check the Russian expansion.

It has to be remembered that Sidney Herbert was the second son of the Earl of Pembroke by his second wife, Countess Catherine, only daughter of Count Woronzoff, formerly Russian Ambassador to Britain. He was, therefore, of half-Russian descent, which exposed him to criticism during the war so perhaps he was not as objective as Curtiss gave him credit for.

The crisis over the Holy places in 1850–51 led the French to break the Straits Convention, sending a steam screw battleship, *Charlemagne*, to Constantinople in a show of force designed to boost the position, internationally and nationally, of Louis Napoléon. This incident nearly led to a Russian invasion of Turkey, ostensibly to protect the community of the Orthodox church. However, diplomatic means were resorted to and this crisis was avoided. But during the course of complex negotiations in 1853, British policy, under the uneasy coalition government led by Lord Aberdeen, swung against Russia. Meanwhile, the Russians, anxious to regain lost prestige and influence, backed up their major diplomatic offensive against Turkey with large scale military plans and preparations which led the Turks to request the sending of British and French squadrons to Vourla in March 1853, a move early in the season from winter quarters in Malta which would have been seen as a positive political gesture. But Admiral Dundas did not take action to meet this request, transmitted through the British Ambassador in Constantinople, and his decision not to do so was endorsed by the Admiralty.[18]

★ ★ ★ ★

In the intervening months from September 1852 to March 1853, *Tiger* had been employed on the general duties of a paddle frigate in a Mediterranean fleet, the fleet which, in the nineteenth century, in Lambert's words[19] 'occupied the central position in the defence of Empire. While it varied in strength, depending on the level of tension, it remained a premier sea-going command in the Royal Navy'. *Tiger* was one of ten paddle frigates and sloops in the squadron attending upon the sailing battleships and frigates and constantly employed in towing duties.

17 Curtiss, *op cit*, p 33.
18 Lambert, *The Crimean War*, p 14.
19 Lambert, *The Crimean War*, p 14.

She shifted around the eastern Mediterranean the 84 gun *Vengeance*, the 90 gun *Albion* with the 120 gun *Britannia* astern of her, while *Trafalgar*, 120 guns, and *Bellerophon*, 80 guns, were her regular customers. She coaled at Piraeus, at Smyrna, in Malta and Gibraltar. 'Coaling soap' was issued to her company on 19 October 1852. It was possibly a less inefficient medium for getting clean after the filthy job of coaling than such ordinary soap as was then available. She carried passengers 'Admiral Elliot and the Bishop' from Gibraltar to Malta, and then 'the Bishop Doctor Vogel (African Traveller) and Mr. Baynes' to Tripoli. She had her adventures: '7th December, 1852, 8.0 ship on fire from deck under galley, through to troop deck, 8.05 fire extinguished remove galley, repair deck, and raise higher off deck'. Then, in January 1853, she went to the aid of the 'Russian barque' *Pandora* (probably a Finnish vessel) which had sprung a leak and had been run ashore in Tunis Bay, but *Pandora*'s mate, left in charge of the vessel while the captain was in Tunis, refused all assistance and the vessel 'went to pieces' afterwards. *Tiger* also had to have minor repairs from time to time. Part of the starboard sponson was washed overboard in a hard gale but was repaired in Gibraltar a week later. Her funnels had to be 'repaired' in Malta. On passage from Malta to Gibraltar, 'port wheel fouled guard iron, stopped, cleared wheel and proceeded'. But at no stage is there any record in Giffard's own notes or in the master's log of the kind of mechanical and boiler difficulties which had dogged *Penelope* and *Dragon*. *Tiger* was an efficient steamship, well suited to the duties for which she was designed. The technology of the paddle frigate had, in the ten years since the building of *Gorgon*, reached maturity, but only when she was already obsolete.

She arrived in Malta from Benghazi on 12 February 1853 to join the main body of the fleet, the 120 gun *Britannia* and *Trafalgar*, the 90 gun *Albion* and *Rodney*, the 80 gun *Bellerophon* and the 50 gun *Arethusa*, which sailing vessels together with the paddle steamers *Retribution, Wasp, Sampson, Vulture, Fury* and *Triton*, the survey steamer *Spitfire*, the screw *Niger*, and the tender *Oberon*, comprised the Mediterranean squadron. The sailing vessels and large steamers had wintered at Gibraltar and assembled in Malta in early February. On 14 February *Tiger* was 'sent off in a hurry', as Giffard noted the event, after a hurried coaling, anchoring in Besika Bay on 17 February, and the next day steaming up to the Dardanelles. She lay off the entrance for five days awaiting the completion of the necessary formalities with the Turkish authorities. She then went up to Constantinople, anchoring in the Golden Horn on 24 February. Here she lay until 27 April 1853.

This movement was in response to a request from the British Ambassador-designate for a faster steamer to be stationed in the Bosphorus. At this time, as has already been said, under the Straits Convention of 1841 there was always a small warship or a large but lightly armed vessel, always a steamer, lying in the Golden Horn to be a British presence, to look after

British interests, and to assist the British Ambassador to the Sublime Porte, as the Turkish court was called, if and when necessary.

The British Ambassador was then Stratford Canning, Lord Stratford de Redcliffe, who since 1812 had already been four times Ambassador in Constantinople, which gave him unrivalled expertise and influence. Because of this, and because the government of Lord Aberdeen wanted this man of strong and overbearing character out of the opposition in the House of Lords, he was appointed again in early 1853 and, as Giffard records, he 'arrived in the [paddle vessel] *Fury* on the 5th April'. The master's log of *Tiger* records a salute of nineteen guns and that the Russian steamers *Bessarabia* and *Thunderer* and the French *Chaptal* were also in the Golden Horn, soon to be joined by the French paddle steamer *Caton*, which brought the French Ambassador, and the Russian 'War brig' *Percie*. Given the undertone of suspicion and rivalry which constantly existed between the French and British fleets, an incident recorded in the master's log must have given Giffard some satisfaction. It reads 'April 28, French *Caton* ashore off Castle Asia. Stopped to render assistance. 11.15 sent cable. Towed off 3.15'.

On 4 May 1853, *Tiger*, having been relieved in the Golden Horn by the 14 gun paddle steamer *Wasp*, was back in Malta, but not for long. Events were building up towards war. On 16 March the Russians had presented a memorandum to the Turks calling for an alliance against France, and followed this up with the demand which would have given them the right to interfere in Turkish affairs, as far as the 12 million members of the Orthodox churches who were Turkish subjects were concerned. The Russian long term objective at this stage appears to have been to force upon the Turks an alliance which would have closed the vital Black Sea seaway to the British and French. To encourage Turkish agreement, with the coming of the summer four Russian divisions were prepared for action. The complex events which followed have been well summarised by Lambert.[20] The coalition under Lord Aberdeen which comprised the British government at this time was unable for some weeks to come to an agreement as to the significance of the Russian moves and the Turkish reactions to them. There was little confidence in the fighting powers of the French fleet following a disastrous exhibition of incompetent ship-handling in Greek waters which resulted in a series of collisions. After great debate in the cabinet a vital meeting took place on 2 June 1853, at which it was decided to send the fleet to Besika Bay to join the French. This was an event of the greatest significance in the run up to war, since it committed British support for Turkey in her difficulties with Russia. In Lambert's words, 'Admiral Dundas' ships were the guarantors of good faith, they could not be

---

20 Lambert, *The Crimean War*, pp 19–23.

withdrawn without a tremendous loss of prestige. This marked the shift from interested observer to participant'.[21]

The events which followed, insofar as the captain of a paddle frigate was concerned, were summarised by Giffard in his notes.

> On the 8th June we all left in a hurry for Besika Bay, towed out the Admiral. 10th took the *Britannia* in tow and arrived Besika Bay on the 13th, I went to Dardanelles and back [this was to arrange a supply of coal through the British Consul and this is confirmed by the Master's log which records that Admiral Dundas boarded the Tiger for the brief passage into the Dardanelles and that the Consul also came on board.] On the 14th French squadron arrived from Salamis [and anchored at sunset, the Master's log records.] I took Captain Carter down to meet them.

The French squadron comprised seven line of battleships, three with some sort of steam screw assistance, and five 16 gun paddle steamers. The presence of the British and French squadrons off the entrance to the Dardanelles committed the two governments to resist Russian pressure on Turkey. In a further gesture Admiral Dundas sent two of his best steamers, the paddle frigate *Retribution* and the screw frigate *Niger*, into the Golden Horn to relieve *Wasp*, which had been there since taking over from *Tiger* in late April, in the duty of supporting the Ambassador and British interests. To have two large steam frigates on this station could be regarded as an act in breach of the Straits Convention of 1841, as they were scarcely 'light vessels', but they were lightly armed. The move of the French line of battleship *Friedland* into Constantinople, on the other hand, did not constitute a breach of the Straits Convention of 1841 since she was in distress. Giffard records '*Friedland* aground off Rabbit Island, she laid there four days and then got off and went to Constantinople to repair'. This incident once again demonstrated the low standards of ship-handling of the French navy. *Friedland* ran aground through poor handling while attempting to shift berth. The French navy, although constantly thought of by British politicians as representing a serious threat, lacked both competent seamen and officers, trained engineers, and the vital industrial base from which to operate in the steam age.

★ ★ ★ ★

Reference has already been made in this book to the various scares which developed in Britain as a result of imagined French threats to Britain's naval supremacy. Paixhan's conception of fast steamers armed with guns firing exploding shells had caused consternation in the early 1820s, but French industry and technology were nowhere near making the threat a reality.

21 Lambert, *The Crimean War*, p 22.

French progress was slow and Roberts has recorded[22] that even in the late 1830s, when Britain was producing side-lever engines of 450 horse power, there were very few engineering works in France capable of providing marine engines of any size. After the success of *Great Western* in 1838, there was something of an explosion of entrepreneurial interest in steam propulsion at sea which led, after much political manoeuvring, to the establishment in France of steamship lines dependent largely on government support, the public rather than the private sector taking the initiatives and retaining detailed control of the management. This policy emerged in the circumstances of France's relative industrial weakness as a means of providing a reserve of steamers for the French navy in time of war, and it was given added urgency by the Syrian crisis of 1839–40, which is itself part of the long saga of Russian, French and British rivalry for control, through influence on Turkey, of the Mediterranean–Black Sea waterway.

Mohamed Ali, Pasha of Egypt, a province of the Turkish Empire, was, nominally at least, subject to the Sublime Porte. But he had constituted himself an independent warlord and defeated the Turks in a bid to take over much of the territory of Syria at the eastern end of the Mediterranean. The British government backed Turkey as likely to hold the Straits against the Russians. The French saw their interests in the support of Mohamed Ali. The British Foreign Secretary, then Lord Palmerston, achieved a diplomatic triumph in facing the French government with a *fait accompli* in which Britain, Austria, Prussia and Russia dictated terms under which Mohamed Ali was forced back from northern Syria. French political opinion was outraged, and one of the many consequences was to be an acceleration of the French steam packet building programme and the enforced and rapid development of French marine engine building capacity, with a massive government subsidy on the grounds that it was no longer safe to depend on the purchase of machinery from Britain, even though that machinery was both cheaper and of much greater reliability than its French equivalent. The French packet lines failed commercially, and eighteen of the packet ships were transferred to the navy. These paddle vessels were already obsolete, but the apparent strengthening of the French navy caused another invasion scare in Britain, which was in due course followed by yet another in 1851, when the steam battleship *Le Napoléon* was launched and at the same time an intensive programme of building sailing battleships and converting existing ships to auxiliary screw propulsion was begun.

It was this invasion scare which played a large part in the British decision to go over entirely to a battle fleet comprising auxiliary screw steamers. The French followed in 1853 and, in Lambert's words,[23]

22 Roberts, 'The French Trans-Atlantic Steam Packet Programme of 1840', *The Mariner's Mirror*, Vol 73, 1987, pp 273–286.
23 Lambert, *Anglo-French Rivalry*.

By the end of the year every available slipway in both countries was occupied by steam battleships or large frigates, in addition to those converting in dry dock. Throughout the Russian war both states continued their efforts, despite the irrelevance of any further battleships to the conflict in hand . . . Both governments were aware of the situation, neither made any effort to decrease tension, the alliance was too fragile for the full and frank discussions needed to improve relations . . . the rivalry that underpinned the naval race was unaffected by alliance. If anything two years as allies worsened relations.

British and French motives and objectives, while they were in alliance, were in fact quite different and mutually incompatible.

In fact, *Le Napoléon* was a fully powered steamship with a reduced square rig which offered considerable windage when she was under power alone. She was built principally to protect the trans-Mediterranean sea route between Toulon and Algiers, and she was not capable of long range operation. Moreover, her first set of engines was unreliable and under-powered, and she was at first more of a liability to the French navy than an asset, requiring virtually complete rebuild when she should have been playing an active part in the Russian war. During the period when events were building up towards war, the real situation was that the French navy had available in the entire Mediterranean only one effective paddle frigate and one of the packet boats taken on for naval purposes.

Britain's power in the developing crisis rested on the sea. She had no large standing army with which to exert political pressure on the continent, but her navy was by far the largest, most effective, and technically the most advanced the world had ever known. The First Lord of the Aberdeen Coalition was Sir James Graham, who had been responsible for Admiralty reforms and the abolition of the Navy Board in 1832 (see Chapter 2). He was a man whose apparent coldness and self-sufficiency made him enemies. He is considered nowadays to have been, again in the words of Lambert,[24]

. . . the most independent First Lord of the 19th, or perhaps any century, and he dominated British strategy, the key element in allied planning until late 1854 . . . Throughout the period under review he was prepared to adopt major strategic initiatives without professional guidance or cabinet sanction . . . However he was arrogant, mistrustful and essentially cold, and unable to excite the loyalty of colleagues or subordinates . . .

Strategically, he considered that the experience of the Napoleonic wars would provide all the background required for planning. He was faced with

24 Lambert, *Preparing for the Russian War*.

a period when the defence estimates were at a peacetime low, and his main preoccupations throughout were to keep within the estimates and to arm the navy, not in preparation for the coming War with Russia, but against the long term enemy, although temporary ally, the French. The steam navy which was being built in the years immediately before and during the War with Russia was designed, not for that war, but for hostilities with France[25] and there was no money to spare to prepare properly for the Russian War which called for equipment of a different kind, notably to attack land fortification from the sea, and this situation led to many of the difficulties in the conflict which was to come. Politically, the situation was not improved by tension between Graham and Palmerston, latterly the Home Secretary.

As far as Russia was concerned, Graham's plan, to reduce it to its simplest terms, was twofold, a naval campaign in the Black Sea essentially to protect Constantinople and the seaway through the Bosphorus, and a campaign in the Baltic where the long coastline of the Russian Grand Duchy of Finland, with its ports which provided by far the greatest part of the Russian merchant fleet, lay exposed. Exposed also was the great Russian naval base and fortress of Kronstadt and, sheltering behind it, the capital of St Petersburg, the seat of government and of the political and international prestige of Russia. But at this early stage, in 1853, a combination of over-reliance on the experience of the French wars and limited intelligence as to the present state of the fortifications in the Baltic and of the Russian Baltic fleet led to the conclusion, which was later to prove erroneous when the right equipment became available, that Kronstadt was impregnable. Moreover, the nature of the Finnish relationship with Russia and of the Finnish people themselves, with their entirely separate culture, language, social structure, system of government and, largely, economy, was never understood, either by the British government or the naval administration, or by individual naval officers.[26]

For the next four months the British and French fleets lay in Besika Bay. This was an unhealthy part of the world. *Tiger* was lucky in that the master's log shows that they were able to break the monotony with trips to the Greek islands in search of water for the fleet. During these trips they were able to exercise the guns. Captain Giffard at this stage in his life may well have been suffering from the long term consequences of malarial and other infections acquired during his earlier service, particularly after Navarino (see Chapter 5). He records

---

25 Lambert, *The Crimean War*, p 20.
26 For an account of the relations between Finland and Russia and its relevance to the war, see Greenhill and Giffard, *op cit*.

I had two attacks of fever and ague, which was raging in the fleet. Mr. Ozzard [the purser] and Pool [the chief engineer] invalided. [They were sent home from Besika] . . . All this time Captain Drummond was at Constantinople in the [paddle frigate] *Retribution*. In our salutes on our birthdays we hoisted no French flags and on their days they hoisted no English colours but we did French and they did vice versa. We were reinforced by the *San Pareil* [HMS *Sanspareil*, an auxiliary screw steamer of seventy-one guns and 350 horse power] and *Furious* [a paddle sloop of six guns and 400 horse power]. 12 Sept., some steamers went to Constantinople the Authorities being fearful of a row at the feast of the Courbom Bairam. Captain Wardle of the *Inflexible* [a paddle sloop of six guns and 378 horse power] died of fever. By the 8th Oct. the steam squadron had returned.

Thus events appeared to the captain of a crack steam paddle frigate on the spot. Giffard accurately records events as he saw them and indicates the dangers of the anchorage to health as, no doubt, to the morale of the ships. But behind these events were complex moves. The Russian divisions which had been readied at the beginning of the summer had occupied Moldavia and Wallachia, two principalities under Turkish suzerainty, areas now part of Romania and the adjacent territory of the former Soviet Union. The presence of the British and French fleets at Besika Bay was a diplomatic counter to this Russian move. Together with significant improvements by the Turks in the defences of the Bosphorus, under the advice of Captain Slade RN, seconded to the Turkish Navy, it had the desired effect in that the Russians decided that an amphibious attack on Constantinople was no longer a practical possibility. In these circumstances, a conference was called in Vienna in July 1853 in an attempt to bring about a peaceful resolution to the period of tension, but its conclusions were rejected by the Turks. So the stalemate continued. There was dispute inside Lord Aberdeen's cabinet as to how the situation should be handled, but the Prime Minister had a majority in support of his policy, which was not to declare war when Turkey had not done so, and that only a Russian attack on Constantinople itself would justify the major breach of the 1841 Straits Convention encompassed by moving the fleet up to the Golden Horn.

The situation was not helped by Sir James Graham's continued suspicion that the French would at any time act independently, without consultation, where they saw it their advantage to do so. There was an argument as to whether the climatic conditions would justify entering the Dardanelles for shelter in the winter, and the French, less sure than the British of the ability of their ships to survive winter conditions, supported the proposed move. But war fever was rising in Turkey and the 'row' or 'disturbance' of Giffard's notes (p 213) was engineered by the Turkish Minister for War. It was ended by the arrival of the steamers to which he referred, the 6 gun

Furious and the 14 gun *Niger*, together with two French steam vessels, but the event was used, partly as a result of some French duplicity and partly because Aberdeen gave way to internal pressures in the government, as the occasion to order the movement of the fleet from Besika Bay to Constantinople. This aggressive move was presented to the Russians as made in protection of British life and property. The Turks had indeed formally requested the presence of the British and French fleets in the Golden Horn. The British Ambassador, Lord Stratford, who had been working to avoid such a situation, was obliged to transmit the message 'at the Sultan's request'.[27] The instruction to the fleets was conveyed from Constantinople to Besika Bay by the duty paddle frigate *Retribution*. The fleets began to enter the Dardanelles on 21 and 22 October 1853. The Turks declared war on Russia on 23 October.

Tiger was, of course, deeply involved in the problem of moving the British fleet through the Dardanelles and up the Bosphorus with its strong adverse current (the great Russian rivers flowing into the Black Sea ensure a constant movement of water through the seaway from east to west), and both Giffard's notes and the master's log contribute to the picture of a major fleet operation in which the paddle frigates played a vital part. This was an historic event which perhaps might be taken to mark the coming of age of steam in the navy. Never before had a fleet attempted to move under such adverse conditions at such speed. The screw steamers could look after themselves. The paddle frigates looked after the sailing vessels which comprised the bulk of the fleet. As Giffard's notes and Admiral Dundas's reports to the Admiralty show,[28] this first attempt at the rapid movement of a large number of vessels with the aid of steam in narrow waters had somewhat chaotic results. The operation was in fact a first class mess. Certainly, if the coasts of the seaway had been in hostile hands the results would have been disastrous and there could have been no question of a rapid movement to the Bosphorus to reinforce the Turks against an actual Russian attack. Giffard recorded (the place names are as he spelt them)

Retribution came down about 2 am in the night *Albion* [90 guns, sail] *Vengeance* [84 guns, sail] *Sampson* [paddle frigate, 6 guns, 467 horse power] and the 28 gun, 400 horsepower *Retribution* [these two presumably towing the sailing vessels] and a like number of French started for the Bospherous. At daylight the remainder of French & at 7 am the remainder of our squadron started, we towing *Trafalgar*. Coming on to blow a gale & the current running very strong we were all obliged to anchor, some inside, some outside the Dardanelles. On the 29th we

27 *Russian War, 1854*, Navy Records Society, London 1943, p 205, footnote.
28 Admiral Dundas's Reports are to be found in, for instance, Dundas to Admiralty, 22 October 1853, No 340 ADM 1/5617.

made another start the wind having lasted one week. The *Napoleon* towed the *Ville de Paris* beautifully, passing all the others as if they had been at anchor & against the breeze and current. The French got to Point Nagara & we to the Bay above Barber's point except ourselves with *Trafalgar* & a few others. *Arethusa* got ashore as did *Rodney* during night, both got off without damage.[29] On the 30th we got *Trafalgar* up, current running very strong in the Bay. On the 31st Adml. started for Stamboul in the *Furious*, [paddle frigate, 6 guns, 400 horse power] we & the *Niger* following. At 4 *Furious* grounded some 12 miles outside Gallipoli we anchored in 3 fathoms & gave her our best bower. Admiral came on board, and we proceeded, leaving *Niger* to assist. On the 1st Nov. passed *Vengeance, Albion* & steamers & the French liners at anchor off St. Stephano. The French had been waiting 40 hours for *Albion* as they had agreed to go up together, notwithstanding Capt. Lushington passed right on, merely saluting Adml. Tinion. We arrived with the Admiral at Therapia giving various salutes as we passed up. On the 3rd we went to Constantinople to coal. *Furious* arrived on the 2nd, on the 7th returned to the Dardanelles for the fleet. On the 8th arrived. I fouled *Inflexible* & did us both some damage. [The master's log records 'in endeavouring to cross H.M.S. *Inflexible*'s bow found current stronger than expected and ship not answering her helm we fouled her – carrying away her jibboom and damaging her bowsprit cap and our starboard quarter destroying our gig. Let go starboard anchor to allow *Inflexible* to slip clear of us, which she did with our 7½ inch hawser fast to her cable and which carried away. 1.20 cleared *Inflexible* weighed and proceeded to anchor inshore of *Rodney*. Lost 26 feet gig, 6 oars, 2 boathooks and all boat gear'.] On the 9th we towed *Trafalgar, Retribution* assisting thro' the Dardanelles, her hawser parting took off William's (Ropemaker's) leg. On the 10th we both anchored in Beicos Bay. On the 14th we went to Constantinople & back as market boat; *Leander* [a 50 gun sailing frigate] arrived to join the fleet. On the 17th we discharged Mr. Parker Eng. for drunkenness & proceeded to the Golden Horn. On the 24th *Terrible* arrived with Sir E. Lyons to join squadron. 26th *Napoleon* returned to Toulon for repairs, having damaged herself while towing. On the 3rd December we heard of the destruction of Sinope by the Russians.

---

29 The grounding of *Arethusa* is described in detail obtained from the captain's log in Thompson, *A Portscatho Mariner, Edward Peters,* Roseland, Cornwall 1990, p 18.
On 10 November on setting sail for Gallipoli, *Arethusa* again ran aground. At 3.30 pm. sounding found no bottom but 20 minutes later, two miles offshore, and in 7 fathoms sounded 'the ship took the ground quietly'. She lay quietly during the night. A cable was streamed out to the neighbouring vessel *Firebrand* and a cutter despatched to *Rodney* at Gallipoli. At 9.00 *Retribution* joined in the rescue. Finally HMS *Fury* was lashed alongside, *Arethusa*'s upper deck guns and 500 shot transferred to her and 43 tons of water pumped out. Now 'with *Retribution* . . . and *Fury* alongside the ship came off without damage' . . .

11

The Employment of the Paddle
Frigate: 4   War

What happened at Sinope, a small town with a roadstead and a harbour, on the south shore of the Black Sea, roughly half way between the Bosphorus and the Turkish–Russian frontier at Batum, is still a matter of some controversy amongst historians. But there is no doubt as to the immense significance of the incident in the rapid progress towards war which was now taking place. After the combined squadrons of Britain, France, Turkey and Egypt had assembled in the Bosphorus and, at the same time, from the lateness of the season, fighting between the Russians and the Turks on the Danube frontier had been reduced to the holding of mutually defensive positions, the question was what to do next? Constantinople was now immune from Russian attack by sea, the Black Sea–Mediterranean seaway was held. The underlying suspicion of France in the British government, and especially in the mind of Sir James Graham as First Lord of the Admiralty, was as great as ever. It was expressed in a communication from Lord Clarendon, the Foreign Secretary, to the British Ambassador in Constantinople, Lord Stratford.[1]

> The naval preparations of France are prodigious, there has been nothing like the present activity in their dockyards for a long time past. Eighty gun screw steamers are the ships they are chiefly occupied with.

The War with Russia was a distraction from the real rivalry. The memory of the long, long wars of 1793 to 1815, and especially of the role of the navy, Britain's principal contributor to France's eventual defeat, had bitten very deep indeed into British thinking, and this consciousness of the navy's role extended far down in the levels of British society.

In London, the cabinet was divided as to the next move. It was rendered indecisive by rivalries and stresses between ministers and especially between Graham, Lord Palmerston, who was Home Secretary, and Lord Aberdeen's

1 Clarendon to Stratford, 8 December 1853, quoted in Lambert, *Crimean War*, p 59.

The Black Sea region, (From Wilmot. *The Life of Vice Admiral Lord Lyons)*

predecessor but one as Prime Minister, Lord John Russell. These men of power and ambition worked in an uneasy coalition, and the process of decision taking was further confused by rivalry between Palmerston and Russell over a new reform bill. Palmerston, with rising popular feeling against Russia on his side, used his aggressively anti-Russian policy to strengthen his opposition to this bill. In so far as there was agreement, it was that the presence of the naval squadrons at Constantinople should be used to put pressure on the Turks to bring about an end to the tension by diplomatic means. But the Turks had declared war on Russia and a state of war existed. Batum was bombarded in November 1853 by a Russian squadron, and two Turkish paddle steamers were captured. The Turks had launched a series of raids on land across their frontier with Russia at the eastern end of the Black Sea. Against the strongest advice from Lord Stratford the Turks despatched a squadron of sailing frigates and corvettes accompanied by two paddle steamers into the Black Sea (they had already been running supplies to their forces around Batum in paddle steamers) with instructions to attack Russian vessels. The Turkish ships put into Sinope for shelter – the British trained commander of the squadron, Osman Pasha, had little confidence in its ability to meet bad weather. The Turkish vessels were detected by a Russian squadron of three 84 gun ships. The Turks remained at anchor, despite the fact that they were only the width of the Black Sea (180 miles) from the great Russian naval base of Sebastopol on the Crimean peninsula, from their arrival at Sinope on 13 November until they were destroyed by a Russian fleet, including three 121 gun ships of the line, on 30 November.

For several reasons this was a historic encounter. British and other nations' naval vessels had been carrying General Paixhan's exploding shell guns for twenty years or more, but they had rarely been fired in anger. The Russian ships at Sinope had them in limited numbers and used them. The Turkish squadron was annihilated in only two hours. Although the extent to which the exploding shell guns of the Russians contributed to the Turkish defeat is a matter of debate, and although it can be argued that such a superior force should have destroyed them even more quickly, the battle of Sinope has been seen as an historic encounter marking the end of the long, long era of the wooden fighting warship.[2] The War with Russia as a whole certainly marked the end of that era. Sinope perhaps began the process, rather than itself being the turning point. Nevertheless, it was an encounter of immense contemporary significance.

Immediately, it led to the first penetration of the Black Sea by British warships since the Treaty of Unkiar Skelessi of 1833.[3] The paddle frigate *Retribution* and the only serviceable French paddle steamer, *Mogador*, were despatched to Sinope to find out what had happened – Constantinople was full of rumour after the only Turkish vessel to survive the battle, the paddle steamer *Taif*, had arrived there with news of the disaster on 2 December 1853. At more or less the same time, the paddle frigate *Fury* [6 guns, 515 horse power] and a French despatch vessel were sent to Varna in Bulgaria to bring back the British Consul. On 4 January 1854, units of the British, French and Turkish fleets entered the Black Sea in force and lay at Sinope. Giffard, supporting the fleet in *Tiger*, records the circumstances.

> *Sidon* [paddle frigate, 22 guns, 500 horse power] and *Vesuvius* [paddle sloop, 6 guns, 280 horse power] had arrived to join the squadron. On the 23rd *Highflier* [paddle frigate, 21 guns, 250 horse power] arrived, 30th *Banshee* [paddle sloop, 2 guns, 350 horse power] arrived.

The steam navy was being assembled for war and, for all the weaknesses of the paddlers, until a large screw propelled fleet had been built up, warfare at sea could not now be conducted without them. On 4 January 1854, eighteen battleships, a frigate and no less than twelve paddle steamers entered the Black Sea.

At the same time Admiral Menshikov, the Russian naval commander at Sebastopol, was notified that the allied navies would protect the Turkish

---

2 Notably by Baxter in *The Introduction of the Ironclad Warship*, Harvard 1933.

3 The fact that the Black Sea was completely closed to warships other than Russian and Turkish after this Treaty has not always been understood. For instance, the National Maritime Museum's publication *Masters of the Sea*, Oxford, Greenwich and Newhaven 1987, p 87, has the 44 gun frigate *Meander*, Captain the Hon Henry Keppel, as cruising in the Black Sea in 1850. In fact *Meander* spent the whole of 1850 in the Pacific, see Keppel, *A Sailor's Life*, Vol 2, pp 151–189.

fleet, and that all Russian warships encountered in the Black Sea would be compelled to return to a Russian port. The Russian Ambassadors in Paris and London were instructed to ask the governments to which they were accredited whether they would protect both Russia and Turkey equally. Lord Aberdeen admitted to the Russian Ambassador that the fleet had instructions 'to favour the Turkish flag'. The news of Sinope had a great effect on British public opinion, nurtured in the belief that the British navy, supported by Britain's infant but rapidly growing industrial power, had saved Western Europe from domination by Britain's natural enemies, the French. Part of the navy of an ally had been destroyed. The idea of the invincible navy, increasingly the policeman of the world, the symbol of all that made the explosive growth of Britain's prosperity in the mid-nineteenth century possible, and which would continue to keep the acquisitive French in their place, was enormously strong.

So Sinope became in popular estimation an affront which must be avenged. The cabinet's indecision was overtaken by events and the next stage in the relentless progress towards war was a letter from the Emperor Napoléon to the Tsar, Nicholas I, in which the French emperor asserted that attempts to bring about peace had failed because of the Russian occupation of Moldavia and Wallachia and because of Sinope, which had been an outrage and an affront to the military honour of France and Britain. Sebastopol, the base from which the Russian fleet which attacked the Turkish fleet at Sinope had sailed, became in Britain the symbol of Russian sea power with its challenge to the navy. Public opinion demanded the destruction of Sebastopol and of the Black Sea fleet, while Sir James Graham and his principal adviser, Sir Baldwin Walker, the Surveyor of the Navy, saw the war develop to a rapid conclusion with a very early attack on Sebastopol, to be followed by a switching of resources to the northern sea and to Russia's capital, St Petersburg, with its protecting fortress of Kronstadt when the ice of the Baltic broke up. Shortage of resources, of proper equipment, lack of information as to the defences of Sebastopol, misinformation about the defences of Kronstadt, all combined to make this strategy for rapid defeat of the Russians an impossibility.[4] Nevertheless, war was now inevitable. As Schmitt put it[5]

> the truth is, the French and British governments in February, 1854, did not desire peace . . . it is clear that she [Russia] was not given a last opportunity to accept the terms of peace acceptable alike to Turkey and to the Powers.

4 Lambert, *The Crimean War*, pp 64–65.
5 Schmitt, 'The Diplomatic Preliminaries to the Crimean War' in *The American Historical Review*, Vol XXV, No 1, October 1919, p 61, quoted in Curtiss, *Russia's Crimean War*, p 236. Temperley, p 380, comes to the same conclusion.

Britain and France declared war on Russia on 27 and 28 March 1854, respectively. Russia responded on 11 April. On 10 April a Treaty of Alliance had been signed between Britain and France. Turkey acceded to it five days later. Thus the Russian war, later to be misnamed the Crimean War, began. The occasion for its outbreak was a naval defeat for a British ally. Throughout the war to its conclusion, despite much that has been written of the land conflict in the Crimea, it was the wider naval strategy, and particularly the British fleets in the Baltic, so often subsequently ignored by historians, which determined its course and eventual end.

In the period between the beginning of the year 1854 and the outbreak of hostilities, at a time of growing tension between the commander in chief, Dundas, and the Ambassador in Constantinople, Stratford, the steamers of the British fleet effectively controlled the areas of the Black Sea which were free of ice. They reconnoitred Varna and Sebastopol, where the Russian fleet was wintering. In February they convoyed sixteen Turkish ships carrying 7000 troops to Batum and then reconnoitred the east coast of the Black Sea. They were in constant movement in February and March on the west coast and maintained communication with the Turkish armies on the Danube. They took part in suppressing trouble in Greece. As Giffard in *Tiger* saw these events,

> February 7th proceeded to Golden Horn. Sir E. Lyons and Admiral de Tinian took a Turkish convoy to Batum. 10th *Vesuvius* sailed for Malta to have a thorough repair of her boilers. On the 16th of March Admiral de Tinian and some of our vessels proceeded to Greece on account of their piratical attack on the Turkish position. 17th we went to Buyukdere and back on the 18th, on account of a silly report of the Russian fleet being at sea. On the 24th both fleets proceeded to sea, *Sampson* remained. On the 25th my wife arrived. 28th towed *Arethusa* out, she had arrived with provisions. 30th arrived Kavarna Bay and joined the fleet; proceeded to Varna and finding despatches and an Aide de Camp of Omer Pasha's, I was sent back by the Admiral to Constantinople. Arrived on the 31st and found my wife still at Hanson's who had kindly put us up.
>
> April 5th proceeded to join the fleet, my wife leaving same evening by *Emeu*. 6th joined the fleet at Batjik, Kavarna Bay. 9th *Niger* arrived bringing news 'War Declared' ships cheered. At this anchorage we had sudden and heavy squalls off the land proceeded by a falling glass and shortly before coming, dust was raised onshore in clouds. 14th French received their declaration of war. 15th being requested by French we hoisted French and English and Turkish colours at the mast heads, manned yards and cheered ship.

On 6 April an incident occurred which led to the paddle frigates being used for the first time for the purpose of sustained bombardment of a position on land. HMS *Furious* (paddle sloop, 6 guns, 400 horse power) was sent into Odessa at the request of Ambassador Stratford to take off the British Consul there. She returned to the fleet on 9 April 1854 with the news that one of her boats had been fired on, despite the fact that she was flying a flag of truce. Giffard wrote to his father, the Admiral, in what appears to be almost his only surviving personal letter.[6]

After a line about a family wedding, he began

HMS *Tiger* blockading Sebastopol, 2nd May, 1854.

My Dearest Pater,

. . . On the 15th the French, having received their declaration of war made a grand theatrical display by hoisting English, French and Turkish colours at their mast heads, manning yards and cheering, we doing the same at their request, a snow squall rather spoilt the spectacle. On the 17th both fleets put to sea en route for Odessa to demand satisfaction for their firing on a flag of truce, in the boat of the *Furious* a short time before. We were preceded by the *Retribution* and *Niger*. We arrived off Odessa and anchored in line of battle the afternoon of 20th some three or four miles off the town. The French and English Chiefs had a long meeting that evening.

Giffard's notes at this stage take up the story rather more fully. He wrote[7]

. . . a letter was signed to be sent at daylight [evidently by the *Retribution* paddle frigate] but the arrival of the *Retribution* (21st) and the Governor [of Odessa] Osten-Sachen had volunteered a letter to Captain Drummond containing a very lame account and excuse for having fired on the flag of truce . . .

Osten-Sachen's reply was, in fact, in all respects reasonable. It read[8]

Aide de Camp General Baron Osten-Sachen thinks it right to express to Admiral Dundas his surprise at hearing that shots were fired from the port of Odessa upon the frigate *Furious*, bearing a flag of truce.

At the arrival of the *Furious* two guns were fired without ball, in consequence of which the vessel hoisted its national flag, and stopped her course beyond the reach of cannon shot. Immediately a boat was sent out with a white flag in the direction of the mole, and the officer on duty, in answer to the question of the English officer, said that the English

6 NMM, BGY/9/4.
7 NMM JOD 30.
8 Nolan's *Illustrated History of the War against Russia*, Vol 1, p 66.

Consul had already left Odessa. Without further question, the boat took the direction of the ship, when the frigate, without waiting for it, advanced towards the mole, leaving the boat at its left, and approached the batteries within cannon shot. It was then that the Commander of the battery of the mole, faithful to his order to prevent any vessel from coming within reach of the guns, thought it his duty to fire, not upon the flag of truce, which had been respected to the end of the mission, but upon a vessel of the enemy which had approached the land too nearly after having been twice fired upon without ball – the signal to stop.

This simple explanation of facts, as they have been related to the Emperor, ought of itself to destroy the supposition, otherwise inadmissable, that in the ports of Russia there is no respect paid to the flag of truce, the inviability of which is guaranteed by the laws common to all civilised nations.

Baron Osten-Sachen Aide de Camp General to His Majesty the Emperor.

But in the city 60,000 troops were reinforcing the defences. Odessa was a great supply base for the Russian forces, and from time to time it sheltered units of the Russian navy. It was, therefore, a prime military target and its governor must have expected an attack of some kind on the pretext of the flag of truce incident, or on no pretext at all. Giffard continued in his notes

this occasioned another long conference between our Chiefs and it was late in the afternoon, when they sent in by the *Caton* [a French paddle steamer] a demand for the French and English vessels to be allowed to start; and for all Russian vessels to be given up. This letter the Admiral read to us, his assembled Captains. I will now give a very slight description of Odessa. It is a handsome city built of stone with the greatest regularity, on a plane elevated some 100 feet above the level of the sea, you ascend to it from the beach by a broad flight of stone steps. It has two moles, the one to the north being the Imperial, and to the south the merchant mole over which is the citadel, and the hillside and summit was here lined with batteries. Each mole had circular batteries at their head along their southern sides and there were batteries between the moles and furnaces for heating shots. They had a boat moored off the Imperial mole showing the range of their guns. On the morning of the 22nd no answer having been received from the governor, the Admirals determined to destroy the shipping inside the Imperial mole but to spare the town and the merchant mole which contained our vessels and many neutrals. The masters of our vessels however deserved all that might happen to them for they had been well warned to be away in time.

Giffard's letter to his father gives a brief and clear account of the bombardment which followed and the subsequent events.

At daylight on the 22nd *Sans Pareil* and *Highflier* moved rather nearer the shore as supports but out of gunshot. The merchant mole was full of neutral vessels, we were to destroy the Imperial mole and shipping within, which was all, or chiefly, Russian. Jones in *Sampson* led in, followed by *Vauban*, a French steamer, *Tiger* and *Descartes*, a French steamer. We took two turns round the boat placed there by the Russians to show range etc. At 6.35 am *Sampson* opened fire we taking it up in close succession. The first tour a red hot shot took effect in *Vauban* and dropping down the lining of the ship it lodged under the magazine. She hauled out and had to clear her powder away. She returned again as soon as all was right. We also towed in some rocket boats under Commander Dickson who took up a position inshore of us. After our two round turns we took an inshore berth as much as possible the Russians having most unaccountably neglected to throw up a battery on the low beach; at 9.50 the *Retribution*, *Terrible,* and *Furious* and the French *Mogador* and *Caique*, all steamers, joined and opened fire. At 12.44 the magazine on the mole head blew up, the fort and several of the vessels were on fire. At 2.00 we ceased firing, because there was no return and we all moved out a little but Jones' *Sampson*; when at 2.40 pm some field pieces came down under cover of the houses on the low beach and opened on the rocket boats and *Sampson* which she most promptly returned with good effect, the shot fell around the boats, knocked some oars away, but hurt no-one. We then all returned and opened fire, some of the houses were burned and we saw no more of our friends. *Sampson* had silenced them before any of us got up. At 6.00 we returned to the fleet all the vessels but one in the mole being burned or sunk and several explosions occurred in the evening. Two French and many English came out of the merchant mole during the fire and the *Arethusa* engaged the batteries on that side for some time as they had opened on us. Eight English vessels were still left, no material damage was done to the town which we had most carefully avoided. The Russians kept up a capital fire from two or three guns on the mole until the magazine blew up. *Terrible* had one man killed and there were some wounded in several of the vessels. We only had two shots strike doing no material damage; this is a pretty full account of the first skirmish. South winds detained us at Odessa until 26th when we made a start; in the night *Fury* and ourselves returned and got back by daylight, they were repairing damages, we then took a turn by the Sendra peninsula and the north part of the Crimea but had no luck in making prizes. On 29th we joined the fleet off Sebastopol and I am afraid we shall have some monotonous cruising. They will not come out and we shall not go in, I am perfectly ignorant as to what we are to do, but when the army arrives if more active measures are not pursued the war may last for many a year; and now, selfishly speaking, that my time is served, I wish it was over – I am now ready with a letter for you the first opportunity that occurs.

10th May the *Emeu* arrived with provisions yesterday so I will conclude. On 5th Sir E. Lyons in the *Agamemnon* with *Sampson*, *Retribution, Highflier, Firebrand* and *Niger* English, and *Charlemagne*, screw liner and two steamers French, left us to proceed first to Kaffa Bay near the entrance to the Sea of Azov and then to the coast of Circassia. They will have some fighting I suppose but I do not know what their orders were, and the Russians have given up many of their forts there. I fancy their chief place, Anapa, would require a stronger force to attack it successfully; they have taken some Circassians with them whom they got at Constantinople and will I suppose open a communication with the inhabitants, but those on the coast are not the brave race under Schamyl and are divided into clans which are continuously fighting with one another. We appear to have no chance of firing another shot at present, as the Russians will not come out and we shall not go in. We are not keeping a close blockade and just now the season of fog has begun and we are a whole day without getting a glimpse of one another, Cape Aia is what we sight every day when clear and the lighthouse on Kherson Point. Monotonous and tedious it will be, however I hope our steamers will have an occasional trip for coal etc.

The bombardment of Odessa as a prime military target was a somewhat half-hearted operation in which the admirals were inhibited by political disunity in the British cabinet, by stresses between the Ambassador in Constantinople and the British commander in chief and between the British and French commanders, and lack of adequate resources to mount a really sustained and damaging assault. The limited objectives, the destruction of Russian vessels and temporary silencing of the defences were achieved, but as Curtiss[9] says, this was 'no positive result'. There was also, inevitably, damage done to the civilian parts of the town. Captain Giffard was quite correct in his statement in his letter to his father that the Russians had given up many of the forts on the Circassian coast. These were isolated forts containing small military units whose function was a policing one, the control of the civil population, rather than coastal defence. The orders to the squadron detached from the blockading fleet to cruise to the eastward, the coast of Circassia, which Captain Giffard did not know, were to

---

9 Curtiss, *Russia's Crimean War*, p 293.

endeavour to establish communications with 'Schamyl'[10] and to reconnoitre the coast.

As Lambert narrated the events which followed,[11]

> The squadron left the fleet off Sebastopol on 5th May, steering along the southern coast of the Crimea and examining Kaffa Bay. *Highflier* [paddle frigate, 21 guns, 250 horse power], *Firebrand* [paddle frigate, 6 guns, 410 horse power] and *Niger* [screw frigate, 14 guns, 400 horse power] entered the Straits of Kertch, *Niger* ran aground, though she was not damaged. Lyons went on to Anapa, which, [as Giffard rightly presumed] was too strong for an attack . . . the Black Sea theatre was already suffering from the tunnel vision of a Crimean dominated strategy. The Russian coast was open from the Danube to Poti, but the opportunities were ignored.

Ten days after he wrote his account of the bombardment of Odessa to his father, Giffard with *Niger* (Commander Leopold Heath) and the paddle sloop *Vesuvius* (Commander Richard Powell) were ordered to the bay of Odessa.

The events which followed have been narrated in Chapter 1.

So it was that in the War with Russia the paddle frigate came of age when she was already obsolete. The 'riddle of the age' had been solved by industrial and engineering advances which had given the navy the screw and the compact, reliable, auxiliary steam engine, the overwhelming advantages of which had been demonstrated from the screw frigate *Arrogant* onwards. But it would not have been possible to conduct the naval campaigns of the Russian war, nor to support the land forces, without the paddlers, although

9 Curtiss, *Russia's Crimean War*, p 293.

10 Imam Schamil (1797–1871). In 1827 Kazi Mulla, a holy man, began to preach in Daghestan, in the area between the eastern coast of the Black Sea and the Caspian Sea, in what is now Georgia in the former Soviet Union, against the Russian administration, then occupying that area. He proclaimed a Holy war against foreigners, with considerable success. He was killed by Russian forces in 1832 and was succeeded two years later by Schamil, who combined burning religious conviction, a powerful personality and brilliant military ability. He inflicted a series of defeats on the Russian forces and considerable parts of the area remained outside Russian control at the time of the war. It is evident that there were communications between Schamil and the British forces as early as April and May 1854. At the end of June a delegation from Schamil visited the French commander, Marshal St Arnaud, and proposed a joint attack on Anapa. A landing on the Circassian coast, combined with risings in the Caucasus and a Turkish offensive on land, might have achieved results as an alternative to the raid on Sebastopol, but the political forces at work both in London and Paris led to the decision to attack the Russian naval base. No major action was taken at the east end of the Black Sea – see Seton-Watson, *The Russian Empire 1801–1917*, Oxford 1967, pp 292–293 and 324.

11 Lambert, *The Crimean War*, pp 104–105.

by the end of the war many of their functions had been taken over by the great fleet of small steam gunboats, schooner rigged and screw driven, which were constructed to meet the requirements of the campaigns. The paddlers, in the generation before the Russian war, had introduced steam to the Royal Navy, indeed into the navies of the world. They had bred a corps of lieutenants, commanders and post captains, with great knowledge of steam, and they had bred a body of engineers to drive and maintain the machinery. They had been the test bed for the development of reliable boilers and engines, developed to meet exacting naval requirements. They had carried out many functions, within their limitations, patrols against the slave trade, service as fast despatch boats, as a highly mobile presence to reinforce diplomacy at times of tension. Above all, they gave a degree of mobility which no ship of war had ever had before to the great sailing squadrons which survived from an earlier era. Although this was a transient function, overtakenn, as far as the Baltic campaign of the Russian war was concerned, even during the war, by the employment of the new steam screw battle fleet, it was vital to the Black Sea campaign. Vital also was the role of the steam frigate in amphibious warfare, troop landing and reconnaissance.

The Russian war dragged on for two years. Lord Aberdeen's government fell to be replaced by a largely Whig administration under Lord Palmerston. It was an exceedingly complex world-wide conflict of great long term significance in the modern history of Europe, and its convolutions, and the involvement of the paddle frigates and the new screw steamers, can be followed in considerable detail in Lambert's *The Crimean War* and, partly from the Finnish point of view, in our own *The British Assault on Finland*. The brutal facts are that the great raid on Sebastopol, home of the fleet which destroyed the Turks at Sinope, was a largely pointless operation, 'scratching at the giant's toe', as King Oscar I of Sweden put it. As we have already pointed out, and as Lambert's work has massively endorsed, the War with Russia was in the end won in the Baltic, by the tireless and highly professional hydrographic work of Captain (later Admiral Sir) B J Sulivan who, in the navy's first steamer, the historic little *Lightning* in 1854, and in the paddle sloops *Driver* (which had first used steam to circumnavigate the globe) and *Merlin*, found the way into Kronstadt. With the development during the war of the armoured floating battery, the progenitor of the ironclads which were to follow only five years later, it was believed that the forts could be reduced and St Petersburg laid open to the great fleet which was assembled in the spring of 1856. This threat to the capital city and the total humiliation which would follow its success could not be accepted by the Russians, who had no effective steamers and whose sailing fleets had remained in harbour throughout the war. To come out against the screw steamers of the British fleet would have meant annihilation. The British plans, conceived by Sulivan, to attack Kronstadt from the north, where it was most vulnerable, caused the Russians to bring to the Baltic General

Franz Totleben, the hero of the defence of Sebastopol, and to begin moves towards peace.

The Russians accepted the peace terms of the Treaty of Paris and then greatly accelerated their expansion to the eastward. Thus it is one of the ironies of modern European history that the Russian war was won by the Royal Navy's steam fleets without one major naval engagement. It is ironic also, but typical, that Captain Sulivan, a man with little interest to work in his favour, was never employed again by the Royal Navy, although he went on to have a second career of great distinction in civilian life.

The great steam propelled fleet which would have attacked Kronstadt in the early Baltic summer of 1856 was partly represented at a Fleet Review by the Queen on 23 April. Two hundred and forty ships of the line, frigates, sloops, armoured floating batteries and gunboats were present in a demonstration of overwhelming industrial, technical and professional superiority. Steam had taken the navy to the zenith of its powers. On that day in 1856, it was without rival in the world.

12

Prisoners

At the end of Chapter 1 we asked several questions. We have, we hope the reader will agree, provided an adequate, if by no means complete, answer to all the questions except the last, 'how did *Tiger* come to be aground outside Odessa within fatally easy artillery range of the shore in May 1854?' Now we propose to make some attempt to answer this, the most difficult question. As a Finnish merchant seaman friend has recently said of another marine casualty which one of the authors recently investigated,[1] 'things go wrong at sea', and the causes of things going wrong can be complex and hard to determine. Somewhere down the line there is almost always a human failing, especially when errors of navigation and pilotage, of the type which clearly must have occurred on board *Tiger*, are concerned. Consciously, or perhaps only partly consciously, a web of mutually protective deceit can begin to be spun which leaves obscure the results of the Court of Enquiry, or the court martial. This is all the more so when interested parties, a government in wartime or, anxious to limit its liabilities to possible claimants for compensation, a merchant ship owner with a reputation and with insurance premia to pay, do not see it as advantageous for too clear an explanation of events involving human error or faulty policies to become public knowledge. Nevertheless, the court martial following the loss of *Tiger* produced evidence which is in some ways revealing.

But first, what was the fate of *Tiger*'s men? We left them in Chapter 1 on their way to quarantine. Here they remained for one month, by all accounts very well treated although the officers found the workings of the Russian bureaucracy very tedious and the absence of reading matter trying. Captain Giffard, meanwhile, sickened. The stump never healed properly, and on 1 June 1854 he died, undoubtedly of gangrene, probably the first British commissioned officer to die as a result of action in the so-called Crimean War. Among the several surviving accounts of his death perhaps that of

---

1 See Greenhill and Hackman, *Herzogin Cecilie*, London 1990, especially Chapters 7 and 8.

Tiger's second master, J C Solfleet, is a proper tribute. Writing to a cousin in Edinburgh from his home in Devonport, after his repatriation he said,[2]

> He [Captain Giffard] suffered a great deal in mental health. He died on the glorious 1st of June after being wounded nineteen days, and buried on the 3rd with great pomp and ceremony. I would have preferred to have seen him placed near the others [the other fatal casualties, including John Giffard the midshipman, who had been buried in the vicinity of the quarantine station. Captain Giffard was buried in the old town cemetery, four miles away. This cemetery could not be identified by a Russian guide in 1985. In 1992 Mr and Mrs Tony Willis were told in Odessa that it had been destroyed by the former Soviet authorities.] His wounds never cleansed which I judge he must have suffered a great deal in his mind, the loss of his ship and his officers and crew made prisoners his wife and two small boys, the shock was too great although he kept his memory until the last. His loss was greatly felt with us, being a good, straightforward and religious person an excellent officer which the service has to regret. I am afraid I shall never find his equal again in any ship that I may serve. In consequence of having served with Russia in the battle of Navarino against the Turks . . . the Emperor ordered him to be released from a prisoner of war and return his sword. The satisfactory news never reached him in this world . . . Mrs. Osten-Sacken, the Governor's wife, was exceedingly kind and attentive to all the sick, she sent every little delicacy from her table which is essentially necessary for the recovery of the sick, her kindness will never be forgotten by any of us. When she heard of the midshipman's death she requested a lock of his hair and enclosed it to his distracted mother in a gold locket and also ordered her gardeners to place a ring of trees over their graves.

The anonymous writer in the *United Services Magazine*[3] is more specific about the funeral and realistic about its true significance. He wrote

> The officials were frequent in their visits, and exceedingly busy making inquiry as to our custom in these cases of death, and offering to give the Captain's remains a public military funeral – an offer which the Senior Lieutenant thought best to accept; though, from the quiet, unostentatious habits of the deceased, many thought the graveyard in the quarantine ground, where the others were laid, would have been more in unison with the event.
>
> Some of the Russian customs were observed; the body was dressed in uniform, and laid for the inspection of visitors. The likeness was taken by

---

2 Scottish Record Office GD 1/135.
3 In Colburn's *United Services Magazine*, November 1854, pp 350–351.

photography, and kept by many as a souvenir . . . At the grave the Senior Lieutenant [Royer] read our burial service, and the Lutheran clergymen also performed service, interrupted by the discharge of five rounds of musketry . . . thus terminated this grand military spectacle, which served two purposes – honouring the Captain and honouring the captors, by displaying their prisoners to the people.

Tiger's surgeon Dr Henry Domville, recorded a more professional account of Captain Giffard's end.[4]

There was nothing in the character or gravity of Captain Giffard's wounds to lead me to anticipate any other than a favourable result, had his health at the time had not been impaired by an attack of Ague as recent as two days previous to their infliction. To this was added the extreme depression of spirits that no efforts to cheer on the part of myself or his friends could arouse, aided as we were by the assurances of a generous enemy that he had nobly performed his part under the most trying circumstances having manfully exerted himself to defend his ship in a position where nothing short of a miracle could have extricated her. His wounds progressed favourably til suppurative fever set in attended with increased mental and bodily debility.

Some days after Captain Giffard's death, an extraordinary incident occurred. His wife, Ella, had for some time been living in Malta with her two sons and her unmarried sister, Isabella Stephenson. She had paid at least one visit to Constantinople, in March 1854, to see her husband.[5] She was, it appears, back in Constantinople in May. On 9 June Commander Powell was off Odessa in his paddle sloop *Vesuvius* and, under a flag of truce, sent ashore the following communication to Governor Osten-Sacken.[6]

Mrs. Giffard on board *Vesuvius* earnestly desires that she may be permitted to share the captivity of her husband, freely accepting the restrictions that her position will render her liable to.

The following day, Commander Powell reported to his commander in chief, Admiral Dundas,

I was permitted to accompany Mrs. Giffard to the spot [her husband's grave] although in quarantine and throughout nothing could exceed the

4 PRO ADM 101/123/5, 132735.
5 Stephenson, *At Home and on the Battlefield*, London 1915, pp 70, 160.
6 PRO ADM 1/5627, 366.

courteous sympathy displayed by the Russian authorities. I saw several of the officers and visited the place where the men were confined, they all joined in praising the treatment they had received at Odessa.

On 1 July 1854, *The Illustrated London News* reported

Captain Giffard's widow – The widow of the lamented Captain Giffard visited Odessa, in the *Vesuvius*, under the safeguard of a flag of truce. She was permitted to land, accompanied by Captain Powell, and remained there twenty-four hours collecting particulars of her husband's dying moments, which were those of a hero meeting his death in his country's cause. The crew of the *Tiger*, on seeing a British naval uniform pass their place of confinement, were about hailing the wearer with a British cheer, thinking their moment of deliverance from captivity had arrived, but were very judiciously silenced in time by a sign from Captain Powell. The junior officers such as midshipmen and cadets have been placed in a college to improve them in their profession: the seniors are said to have removed to Moscow, the Emperor having refused to listen to any exchange.

The journal *Journale de St. Petersbourg* reported on 2 July[7]

Thursday 27th May, the British war steamship *Vesuvius*, carrying a flag of truce, appeared in our roadstead coming from Constantinople. This steamer had on board the wife of the defunct Captain Giffard, Commander of the steamer *Tiger*, destroyed on our shores. Madame Giffard applied to Monsieur the A.D.C. General Baron de Osten-Sacken requesting to be authorised to remain close to her prisoner of war husband. His Excellency was under the painful obligation of informing her of his death. Madame Giffard in a boat with the flag of truce then expressed to the A.D.C. General Baron de Osten-Sacken her desire to visit the tomb of her husband. On obtaining permission she descended on shore, surrendered herself, with all the sanitary precautions, to the town cemetery, and after praying at the tomb she returned on board the steamer. In these sad circumstances, Madame Giffard has inspired the most touching interest by the dignity and firmness of her deportment. The same day the English steamer returned to sea.

Mrs Giffard certainly impressed Governor Osten-Sacken. On 13 June he wrote to her

7 4, m Série, No 435.

Odessa, 13 June 1854

Madam,

His Excellency the Minister of War, from his office on 23 May/4 June informs me, that His Majesty the Emperor, my Royal Master, in recognition of the personal courage and serious wounds of your worthy husband, Captain Giffard, has asked me to return his sword to him immediately and not to include him amongst the prisoners of war.

His Majesty the Emperor has also instructed me to express to Captain Giffard the pain which he felt upon hearing of the death of Midshipman Jean Giffard, whom he supposes to be the brother or close relation of Captain Giffard.

Fate, having decided to recall your worthy husband from this base world, has deprived me of the sweet duty of fulfilling His Majesty's wish towards him, who had the honour of taking part in the battle of Navarin.

I am giving Captain Giffard's sword to Mr. Domville with the request that he should hand it to you.

I would like to express the feelings of deep respect and most sincere interest which you have inspired in me.

> B Dmitry Osten Sacken
> Aide de Camp General to His
> Majesty the Emperor of All the Russias

J C Solfleet told his cousin

I saw Mrs. Giffard, the Captain's widow, at Southampton. She was greatly distressed at seeing me again. She has got an income of £200 a year and £25 each for the two sons.

He need not have worried. Ella Giffard was the daughter of Major General Sir Benjamin Stephenson (1766–1839), formerly Master of the Household at Windsor Castle and Surveyor General of the Board of Works, and she was the sister of Sir William Stephenson, who became a Deputy Head of the Treasury, and of General Sir Frederick Stephenson. The Stephensons looked after their own. Captain Giffard's eldest son, George, entered the navy, played a distinguished part in the Arctic expedition in *Alert* and *Discovery* in 1875–76,[8] and became a rear admiral. His younger brother, Henry Rycroft, was sent to Eton. Little is known of his youth except that he may have been on board *Great Eastern* when she laid the second, the first successful, transatlantic cable in 1865.[9] He married a

8 Nares, *Narrative of a Voyage to the Polar Sea*, 2 vols, London 1878, numerous references.

9 See Russell, *The Atlantic Telegraph*, London, no date. W H Stephenson was an honorary director of the Atlantic Telegraph Company, and Captain A T Hamilton, a probable connection of his wife, a director. There is a family tradition that H R Giffard was involved in early cable-laying.

wealthy cousin, Cecilia Hamilton, and settled at Lockeridge House in Wiltshire, where he is remembered by one of the authors, his grand-daughter, as a rather forbidding old man. He died in 1934. Ella Giffard lived on until 1906 in her house in Hanover Square, London, and was remembered by those who knew her in their youth as a woman with a particular gift with children and a considerable wit.

When their quarantine was finished, the prisoners of *Tiger* were allowed wide liberty in Odessa. J C Solfleet gives an impression of the way in which the officers were treated.

A latter part of our stay at Odessa a private house was given for our use with a guard of soldiers attached. We were then allowed to visit in company of a Russian officer any private family we were invited to. Our treatment was very good and living the same. I visited the opera. It was rather small but the music I thought very good. The Prima Donna had a very sweet voice but not strong. The most of the ladies had retired to their country houses. What I did see they appeared to be very pleasing and amiable, but generally speaking not pretty. Their teeth was very bad. With all my experience I have not seen any that pleases me so much as my own country girls. . . . Their education consists in languages and music. About history or drawing they are mostly deficient. I met with two very pleasing girls and out of self defence was obliged to devote my hours to study [of French, the means of communication with his new friends] with the assistance of a Master. I found I improved a great deal more with their conversation. If I had remained about three months longer I should have been a master of the French language.[10]

The ratings had other compensations. The faithful *Vesuvius* went back and forth conducting negotiations for their exchange, and brought an advance of two months' pay for each man in order to enable him to buy the necessities of life should the imprisonment prove prolonged. Dr Domville in his journal tells what happened.

But one circumstance that must have exercised a baneful influence over their physical strength and materially impaired their constitutions had it continued in operation any length of time, was repeated general intoxication. Every man had received two months' pay shortly after we landed for the purpose of procuring necessaries and comforts for the journey to Riazan but when they heard that they were to be exchanged they made use of the time and opportunity that was afforded them and quickly got rid of their money by the purchase of intoxicating liquors in which they most freely indulged and the life of drunkenness and listless

10 J C Solfleet, *op cit.*

idleness succeeded to a system of order and sobriety that had hitherto elicited the admiration of the Russian authorities. James Howell a seaman was attacked with erysipelas of the foot from a small wound, congestion of the brain supervened and he was removed to the hospital where he died two days afterwards, the disease in this case I have no doubt was aggravated, if not induced by excessive drinking. The timely arrival of HMS *Fury* with the Russian prisoners in exchange, completely checked these irregularities, which had already commenced working their own cure by the general diminution of the means of supply and on the 10th July, myself, nine other officers and one hundred and eighty men were released from captivity.

The Russian policy of liberality towards the prisoners expressed itself in several ways. Lieutenant Royer, as senior surviving officer, was summoned to St Petersburg to have audience with Tsar Nicholas I. On his return to Britain he produced an early example of instant journalism, his book *The English Prisoners in Russia*, in reading which a late twentieth century psychologist specialising in the experiences of hostages might well recognise the symptoms of that peculiar condition in which a prisoner identifies with his or her captors.[11] After being treated with the utmost courtesy by the Osten-Sackens and others in Odessa, Royer was taken under the escort of a 'Mr. F. Sharman of the Corps of the Feldjäger' to St Petersburg, via Moscow. Sharman, whose full identity is never revealed, was probably a Swedish speaking Finnlander in the employ of an ancestor department of the KGB. The two men travelled in a small carriage.

Mr. Sharman and myself occupied the interior of the carriage, whilst my servant sat outside with the coachman. This vehicle, called a 'tarantas', had been purchased by the government expressly for the purpose of taking us to Moscow, from which place it has only just arrived. It consisted of a coupé, to hold two people, and a box in front for the driver and servant. These vehicles are strongly built, and not hung on springs,

---

11 Royer's book, for all that the Russians appear to have conditioned him to give the most favourable reports of his treatment, is a valuable account of travelling conditions and of the court at St Petersburg. He was much criticised for his rosy view of Russia in, for instance, *The Illustrated London News* for 22 October 1854, p 398, where the reviewer wrote 'The book, doubtless, will be well laughed at, and then forgotten'. For accounts of the state of Russia in the 1840s and '50s see, among many other works, Haxthausen, *The Russian Empire*, 2 vols, London 1856; Kohl, *Russia and the Russians*, 2 vols, London 1842; Rigby, *Letters From the Shores of the Baltic*, 2 vols, London 1842; Scott, *The Baltic, The Black Sea and the Crimea*, London 1854; and Custine, *The Empire of the Czar* (a translation of *La Russie*, published 1839) New York 1989. For a well researched adventure story of imprisonment and escape in Russia during the war, see Fraser, *Flashman at the Charge*, London 1973.

this being considered to render them less liable to accidents. Unfortunately, ours was much worn; and, as will be seen, broke down more than once before we reached our destination.

This springless barouche is drawn by three horses abreast, which are changed on the road, the length of the stages varying from ten to eighteen miles. The poor creatures are small, and, as the French would say, 'ne paient pas de mine', but we found them, as John Bull would say, 'good ones to go'.

The journey which followed, of over 800 miles across the muddy plains of southern Russia, on rough tracks, by river ferries, sometimes travelling overnight or sleeping in post houses that did not provide beds, in a small vehicle without springs, with mud flying up from the wheels into the carriage and covering its occupants, was taken by Royer with very little comment as to its hardships. He made a great deal of very favourable comment about Russian customs and practices and the people he met, although, latterly, he too was subject to periodic bouts of the recurring 'ague' Although the going was often very hard – on one occasion it took them twelve hours to cover 55 miles – they reached Moscow in seven days, and here Royer was for the first time able to take off his clothes, enjoy the luxury of a bath, shave, and sleep in a bed. His description of his first view of Moscow is worth quoting.

About noon on the 15th June I obtained my first view of the city of Moscow, from an eminence over which the road passed. It rivals the far famed view of Constantinople in the number of its towers, spires, and cupolas, some green, some of varigated colours, some gilt or covered with sheets of brass. These, shining in the sun and reflecting a variety of tints, look like bright spots of fire over the dark edifices, which they seem to crown with glory. As we drew near, the view expanded before us, and the beauty of the scene bore a closer inspection, without suffering from the scrutiny of the traveller. This is more than can be said for bright and gorgeous Stamboul, the position of which is so favourable, and the merits of which are enhanced by its political importance.

From Moscow he travelled to the capital, St Petersburg, by Russia's only main line railway, on which ran one train per day so there was, as he put it, no danger of collisions. He travelled in conditions apparently more comfortable than in a contemporary British train, although on this part of the journey Royer suffered from bad attacks of the ague. In St Petersburg, he appears to have been treated with the utmost courtesy and entertained by officers of rank greatly senior to his, which treatment appears to have somewhat coloured his accounts of his adventures. For instance, he was received by the Minister for War, 'Prince Dolgorouki',[12] with great civility and accommodated in a suite of rooms of his own choosing in a very good hotel. Here he was detained on very liberal terms, his only embarrassments being a further violent attack of ague and the fact that most of those with whom he had contact spoke either German or Russian. He had previously been able to communicate in French (it will be remembered that he, brought up in Mauritius, was bilingual) or English. He was also expressly forbidden to communicate with any members of the extensive British community resident (the war notwithstanding) in St Petersburg, except Dr Edward Law. This British community was large enough to support its own Anglican church of St Mary and All Saints, patronised by the staff of the Embassy and by prosperous British mill owners and others. It had its own chaplain, Dr Law, who was also chaplain to the British Embassy. He had been in St Petersburg since 1820[13] and evidently had the confidence of the Russian authorities.

On 23 June, Royer was taken by river steamer to the Peterhof from where he enjoyed the classic view of the great fortress and naval base of Kronstadt, and he could see the masts of the Russian Baltic fleet. On 24 June, Royer was immensely flattered to be given a long interview by the Grand Duke Constantine, commander in chief of the Baltic fleet and a second son of the Tsar who was, for part of the time during the conversation, accompanied by his wife. The Grand Duke, who revealed a great deal of professional knowledge of naval matters (and showed particular interest in the details of the bombardment of Odessa) had just returned from Kronstadt where he had been delayed, so that the interview took place late in the evening. What he did not tell Royer was that the reason for the delay was that on that very day, Saturday 24 June 1854, the steamers of the British Baltic fleet were reconnoitring the approaches to Kronstadt in the first of those sallies which were, in fact, to prove to be the most decisive factor in the war, and their masts and spars were visible from the Peterhof. In the words of Commodore Byam Martin, writing in his journal on 23 June, giving what must be the first eye-witness description ever written of the appearance of a steam battle fleet at sea,[14]

It is a very grand and remarkable sight, to look on this great fleet, steaming rapidly along in a calm, through a sea quite deserted – forty columns of smoke rising high in the air and then settling down on the northern horizon in a long dense black mass – making known the

12 Royer here appears to confuse Prince V A Dolgorukov, Minister of War, with Prince Iurii Dolgoruki, Chief of the Province of Voronezh, where significant serf revolts took place towards the end of the war. See Curtiss, *Russia's Crimean War*, pp 340–341 and 543–544.

13 See Pitcher, *When Miss Emmie was in Russia*, London 1977, pp 9, 25.

14 Greenhill and Giffard, *The British Assault on Finland*, pp 213–215.

approach of the hostile fleet towards the Russian capital by means of a cloud of Durham soil.

Captain Paget of the steam screw ship of the line *Princess Royal* (91 guns, 400 horse power) wrote

This enormous fleet, with its wreaths of smoke, must have looked like three black serpents wending their way through the air to encircle the devoted city, and the commotion among the small coasters was ludicrous. At night our way was illuminated by alarm fires on the coasts, to warn the people of our approach; and on Saturday, the 24th, we got sight of the golden cupola of Isaac's Cathedral, as well as the spires of Kronstadt. What must have been the feelings of the thousands of helpless beings when they saw this mass of enemies approaching! I speak only of those who were as ignorant of the real means of offence it possessed as the good people of England, who had been gulled by the press into the belief that we had only to walk over Kronstadt into St. Petersburg. Of course the Emperor, and indeed all military men, must have been quite at their ease as to the possibility of our capturing Kronstadt without a large land force, but it must have been to him even a very exciting sight.

Two years later the Russians, faced with the reality of a similar threat supported by armoured floating batteries capable of penetrating the fortress system as well as by a land force, gave in and accepted the terms of the Treaty of Paris which ended the war.

It was not until the next day that Royer learned what was going on when an ADC to the Grand Duke Constantine told him 'Your countrymen are determined to pay us a visit; they are only five miles off'. On 25 June Royer was summoned to the Tsar's presence and given a very brief audience while the Emperor was about to take a church parade. The conversation was, in fact, limited to an enquiry as to why *Tiger* had not been anchored before she struck, and the information, new to Royer, that Mrs Giffard had gone to Odessa to join her husband, not having heard of his death.[15] Royer, much to the Tsar's amusement, was very taken aback to be told he was to be released immediately and could choose his own route home.

Royer then attended church and was placed in a conspicuous position of honour in which he could be displayed to the assembled congregation of

15 Considering the difficulties of transport by road and the absence of an electric telegraph link, the speed and efficiency of communication between St Petersburg and Odessa seems to have been good. A remarkable example of the rapid transmission of information was provided when the captain of the paddle frigate *Leopard* of the British Baltic fleet went ashore at Oulu in the north of the Finnish coast of the Gulf of Bothnia on 3 June 1854, to be told of the loss of *Tiger* on 12 May and of the death of Captain Giffard. Since Giffard had died only two days before, the latter piece of information must have been based on rumour – see Greenhill and Giffard, *op cit*, p 179.

courtiers, household and officers, after which, accompanied by the ever present Sharman, he walked in the gardens of the Peterhof. These gardens were long closed for reconstruction after the destruction of the Second World War but in the 1990s have become familiar to many British visitors on package tours to St Petersburg. Many of them will have become embarrassingly familiar with the booby-trapped fountains.

> There are also many ingenious contrivances with the water, to amuse and astonish beholders; one of these struck me as quite novel: small pipes are laid along the trunk and branches of a tree, and coloured so as not to be observable; and from the ends of these innumerable tubes water is suddenly emitted, so that the tree appears to weep over the fountain below, shedding tears from every leaf. By another contrivance a globe of water is suddenly formed over a seat occupied by a chance passenger, who looks as if under a glass shade. The third is so arranged, that on a person taking a seat in a tempting spot, his weight presses on a spring, by which water is made to flow upon him in all directions, and he thus gets a shower bath *nolens volens*. Such practical jokes amuse the visitors; the ideas were borrowed from the Italians, in whose gardens are seen contrivances of the same kind.

Royer, delayed by further attacks of ague, returned to Britain, having given his parole to play no further part in the war, via Warsaw by horse drawn carriage and then by train via Berlin, Hanover, Cologne and Calais. He arrived in Britain on 9 July to face a court martial. The release of the rest of *Tiger*'s crew took place in stages as Russian prisoners of like rank became available for exchange. As Dr Domville had already said, the paddle sloop *Fury*, Commander Edward Tatham, six guns, 515 horse power, on 10 July took from Odessa some 185 officers and men including J C Solfleet and three engineers. The master, Francis Edington, and twenty-four junior officers and senior ratings remained at Odessa for lack of like ranks to exchange. At Riazan in central Russia were Lieutenants Hamilton and Stone, looked after by Carlo Bich, the captain's steward, and Anton Schembri, the gun-room cook. At Moscow University, where they were sent on the Tsar's personal orders to continue their education, were the three surviving midshipmen, together with Robinson, the naval cadet, and with William Beard, a gunner, Royal Marines, presumably there as servant.[16]

The 185 prisoners, who were returned in July, were immediately distributed among the ships of the Black Sea fleet, most of them to *Britannia*, which was short-handed after an epidemic off Varna, and some of them, it would appear, possibly on promotion. No court martial was yet

16 NMM BGY/9/4.

possible as the master and the lieutenants had not yet been freed.[17] It was not until another month or two had elapsed that the remaining officers and men returned via Stettin and Berlin, also on parole to take no further part in the war. On 12 April the following year, the inevitable court martial was convened at Portsmouth.

Meanwhile, the Russians were doing what they could with the remains of *Tiger*. Hundreds of snuff boxes appeared on the market in Odessa, allegedly made from her timber. A barometer from the vessel was hanging in late 1992 in the local naval museum. At least parts of the engines were probably salved. Certainly some of the guns were. One of them still stands today at the top of the great flight of steps from the harbour of Odessa to the heights above, the steps made famous by the brilliant sequence in Eisenstein's great film, *Battleship Potemkin*, of the disturbances of 1905, disturbances which some historians have seen as a long term consequence of the war of half a century before.

17 PRO ADM 1/5627, 473, 14 July.

13

Court Martial

The court martial of the officers and crew of HMS *Tiger* was held at Portsmouth on board HMS *Victory* on Thursday, Friday and Saturday, 12, 13 and 14 April 1855. The court comprised the Rear Admiral Superintendent of Portsmouth Dockyard, William Fanshawe Martin, as President supported by no less than eleven captains and the Deputy Judge Advocate. The captains included a number with extensive steam experience and among them was W Crispin of HM Royal Yacht *Victoria and Albert*, who had reported on the trials of *The Great Britain* (p 157).

The first act of the court was to acquit all the officers and crew except Lieutenant Royer and Francis Edington, the master. All the rest were to consider themselves witnesses in the investigation into the conduct of these two officers.[1] The court then proceeded to take evidence from a number of selected officers and crew members. These were, in the order in which they were called, J C Solfleet, the second master; John Butler, quarter master, a continuous service man with three badges (it is apparent that by 1849 a system of good conduct badges had been introduced); Lieutenants Hamilton and Stone – Lieutenant Hamilton was officer of the watch from midnight to 4 am on the morning of 12 May; James Saunders, quarter master with three badges; Richard Mallett, captain of the maintop, with two badges; Thomas Maxwell, boatswain's mate, with one badge; John Smith, captain of the forecastle, with two badges; Joseph Weaver, marine, third class, who was sentry with the deep sea lead under his charge; Frederick Hammond, midshipman; Percival Hinde, midshipman; Charles Wilkinson, mate, who was mate of the watch when *Tiger* went aground and whose evidence was therefore particularly important; several seamen who had acted as leadsmen on the fatal passage; James Baker, able seaman, who was leadsman on the starboard side of *Tiger* from 4 to 5 am on the morning of the stranding; Samuel McConel, able seaman, one badge, who was leadsman on the port side at the same time; and George Taylor, able seaman, who relieved Baker. The evidence taken from these witnesses

1 A complete record of the proceedings of the court martial in a form convenient to consult is to be found on p 4 of the *Portsmouth Times and Naval Gazette* of 14 April 1855. The official record is at PRO ADM 1/5671.

concerned the handling of *Tiger*, up to the time of stranding. Further evidence was taken as to the events after the stranding, the efforts made to get the vessel off, and the circumstances of the Russian attack and the subsequent surrender.

The evidence of the witnesses listed above was, of course, complex and inevitably had its inconsistencies. As always in such cases there will have been those witnesses who sought to avoid any statement which might be taken to reflect upon themselves, and others on whom pressure was perhaps brought by their seniors to avoid statements which might be embarrassing or incriminating. A pattern of mishandling of the vessel and of poor communication between officers and men does, however, appear to emerge from the evidence. There was no mention of dead reckoning – courses steered and distance run from the last known position, which was at noon on 11 May approximately 10 miles off Sebastopol – although the poor visibility throughout the passage meant that there was no other way of determining the vessel's position at any time. The vessel appears to have averaged 8½ knots through the night, at which speed she inevitably was approaching the coast at 5 am but, although land was reported to the master by two lookout men between 5 and 5.15 am the vessel appears to have been steamed generally too fast for the conditions of visibility.

Captain Giffard was reported as having gone below to his cabin at about 8.45 pm on the night of 11 May and not to have come on deck again until the vessel ran aground. But Lieutenant Stone (who was not on duty after midnight on 11 May and therefore could not be in any way responsible for subsequent events) in evidence said that the captain 'had never been so particular about giving orders concerning the lookouts and the steerage before, I concluded that there must be some great reason for his doing so'. The evidence generally shows that, although in his cabin, the captain was constantly consulted during the night. The evidence of the mate of the watch at the time of stranding, Charles Wilkinson, was of particular importance since it appears to establish that at the critical period immediately before the stranding the vessel was being steamed too fast. Wilkinson's evidence is worth quoting in full. He said

Charles Wilkinson being sworn, said: I was mate of the watch on the morning that the *Tiger* was wrecked. A few minutes after five I came on deck, and whilst I was there they were continually heaving the lead; 12 fathoms were called when I went up, the ship was then going 4½ knots; when I went on deck I found Lieutenant Royer, and Mr. Edington on the bridge; I received orders from Lieutenant Royer to steer N. by W., nothing northward; the leadsmen were in the chains and the leads were kept constantly going: he told me the captain was to be called when we got 8 fathoms, and also that I should be particular in keeping a good look out for vessels, and anything that might be reported; he staid on the bridge for about five or six minutes, and then he and the master left it and went on the quarter-deck. I continued taking soundings regular until we got 8 fathoms, when I gave the order to go as slow as possible without stopping, at the same time going down to call the captain; I called him and told him we had got 8 fathoms. He asked what rate she was going, and I said she was going as slowly as possible at present, but that she was going 4½ or 5 knots before I had eased her; he then asked what kind of weather it was; I told him it was very thick indeed; he said keep on about the same speed as before until you get five fathoms, keep her west, if you then shoal your water stop her immediately. I then went on deck and found Lieutenant Royer and Mr. Edington on the quarter-deck; I told Lieutenant Royer the captain's orders, and then went on the bridge, and gave orders for the engines to go at the same speed as before.

By the President: The captain did not come on deck until after she struck.

Mr. Wilkinson continued: We then went on for about six or eight minutes until we got about 7 fathoms; we were then going 4½ knots; no ships were in company or in sight since I went on deck, and no land was seen; we continued at 7 fathoms for about 6 or 8 minutes; then shoaled to 6, ¼ less 5, and the ship struck; I should say it was about 2 or 3 minutes from 6 fathoms being called until the time of the ship striking; there was no time to give any orders in that interval.

It would appear that once the water shoaled to 7 fathoms the vessel should not have continued to be steamed for another seven or so minutes at 4½ knots. It was clear that the water was shoaling rapidly and good seamanship required that the vessel should have been stopped. It is to be borne in mind that the only source of information as to the captain's specific orders came through Charles Wilkinson, who had his own position to protect if he wished to enjoy further employment in the navy, as also did Lieutenant Royer, Mr Edington and a number of others. Lieutenant Royer in his evidence in his own defence stated

knowing the orders which the captain had given to the officer of the watch, I was not alarmed to find the water still shoaler, which it continued to do rapidly from 5 to 2¾ fathoms.

He then went on to claim that she went aground before any order could be given. Both Royer and Edington did their best to clear themselves of responsibility and to impute blame to the captain's orders. Edington stated

I fear much that this honourable court may be under the impression that I showed a want of judgement in running the ship at such a speed through so dense a fog, but as I was not at all acquainted with the object of her service on that occasion, further than that the captain was anxious to be off Odessa as early in the morning as possible, I was induced to retard her course but little consistent with the safety of the ship, and trusting much to my previous knowledge of the locality.

The court found[2] subsequent to the court martial,

The COURT, pursuant to an order from the Commissioners for executing the office of Lord High Admiral of the United Kingdom of Great Britain and Ireland, dated the 5th day of April, 1855, and addressed to the President, proceeded to enquire into the circumstances under which Her Majesty's late ship *Tiger* was run on shore, on or about the morning of the 12th May, 1854, and subsequently surrendered to the enemy, and to try Lt. Alfred Royer and Mr. Francis Edington, the master, two of the surviving officers of the said ship, for their conduct on that occasion (the other surviving officers and ships' company of the said ship having been acquitted by a previous sentence by this Court); and having heard the evidence produced, and completed the inquiry, and having maturely and deliberately weighed and considered the whole, the Court is of the opinion that the ship *Tiger* was run on shore in consequence of her having been rashly conducted as she approached the coast of Odessa, and that after the ship had been run on shore the measures reported to get her afloat were injudicious; but in respect to the surrender of the *Tiger* to the enemy, that, as the ship was aground without any hope being entertained of floating her off, and as she was exposed to the enemy's guns, which had set her on fire, and upon which the guns of the ship could not be brought to bear, no blame can be imputed in consequence of such surrender. The Court is further of opinion that no blame is imputable to the said Lt. Alfred Royer, since he acted under the immediate directions of his captain, and the Court doth adjudge him to be acquitted. The Court is further of opinion that Mr. Francis Edington is blamable for the want of caution that was exhibited by him in approaching the shore near Odessa; but in consideration of his previous good character and long services, doth adjudge him to be only severely reprimanded; and the said Lt. Alfred Royer is hereby acquitted, and the said Mr. Francis Edington is hereby severely reprimanded accordingly.'
The court was then dissolved.

These findings were such as to reflect the least possible discredit upon the Royal Navy in time of war. Nevertheless, Colburn's *United Services Magazine* for May 1855[3] commented

---

2 As reported in *The Times*, London, Monday 16 April 1855.
3 On pp 121 and 122.

For our part, we must acknowledge ourselves to have been wholly unprepared for such an amount of incompetence, willfullness, and folly as seem to have been displayed by the authorities of the ship, throughout the untoward affair; and we are not less concerned that some of the witnesses should manifest a desire to throw all the blame on the poor captain, the only one who has atoned, by the sacrifice of his life, for his share in the disaster. The captain was not on deck when the vessel grounded; and both the first lieutenant and the master, who were at the moment in charge, were warned by the diminished soundings of the proximity of danger. Why was the vessel still permitted to approach at half speed nearer and nearer to the shore?

Lieutenant Royer's acquittal carried its own penalty. He was never employed again by the navy, but retired as a commander on 'reserve half pay' on 4 July 1857. His death was reported in the navy list for March 1875. Francis Edington suffered a similar fate. There is no evidence that he was ever again given a naval appointment, although he would have continued to draw his half pay and may well have been employed as master of merchant vessels. In 1859–60 he was employed as Admiralty Agent on board a contract mail steam vessel, and in June 1863 he was promoted to the rank of staff commander. This promotion was part of the general elevation of officers of his status which took place (regardless of whether they were employed or not) at this time. He was 'retired' in 1865 and died three years later.

★ ★ ★ ★

Further evidence of the unsatisfactory situation with regard to morale and communication between those on deck at the crucial period is given in an extraordinary letter received by Admiral (then Captain) George Giffard, Captain H W Giffard's elder son, forty-five years after the loss of *Tiger*. It reads

> 72 Park Rd.
> Freemantle
> Southampton.

Capt. Giffard   May 16th 1899.

Sir,

On the 12th was the 45th anniversary of the Loss of HMS *Tiger*, & as there are but a very few of us that formed the crew, left, & I doubt if one but your humble servant, heard the orders given by our much beloved Capt. before He left the Bridge, I was waiting my relief at the wheel at midnight when I heard them, & you Sir will see at a glance, *if* those orders had been carried out, the ship & all would not have suffered as all did.

The Capt. was suffering from a weakness of the chest, & the Fog was very thick. He could not speak or breath properly, but as he stood by me looking in the Compass, he told the Officers of the watch he must go below it was Mr. Hamilton who had just come on the Bridge to keep a exteria good look out, to keep the Lead a going, & if they got Bottom, to stop her, & call Him at once, & Sir none of that was obeyed, I may say the Navigating officer was present also, at 6 a.m. I was washing clothes, the clothes was pined up, whilst on the paddal box, hanging up my clothes, the man at the Lead S McConnall by name, called out by the mark 13, the 1st Leaut. Mr. Rawyer, & the master as they were then called, came over & ask him what he was calling out for as there was no bottom there, at 13, & said you dont know when you have bottom, & called out to Adams, the Bas un's Mate [The muster role shows him as Henry Adams, boatswain's mate, aged thirty-seven], to send a man to reliave him, the man went on hauling in the line, they standing by, the next cast, deep 11, they still doubting, & Mr. Rawyer called him an ignorant fool, the man was Irish, & he replied that he know his duty as a Seaman &c. (& he did Sir, he was a good & very intelligent man) [The muster role shows him as an AB born Belfast, aged twenty-eight, one badge]. Mr. Rawyer was good at sarcasm & commenced on him, the ship going at the same speed all the time, the next cast, they were paying greater attention to the line, & saw he was right, it was mark 5, Mr. Rawyer did not then stop the ship, but rushed off to call the Capt., I was just then sent to wash down the after part of the main deck, as he Mr. Rawyer came out of the Capt Cabin down she struck, going at the same speed, on Cape Fauntainia, throwing him & I on the deck.

As no opportunity was given to anyone to bring out those facts, at the Court Martial. I think it but right, some member of your family aught to know the Truth before all of us that know the facts, are gone, to our Eternal Rest.

You can use this as you chuse later on, but at the present, my chief support is a paterotic fund Pension of £13,12 per Annum, renewed every two years, I would not like it used to my hurt in that respect,

I have the Honour Dear Sir
to remain yrs

Respectfully,
JOHN HARFIELD

Capt. Giffard RN

John Harfield appears on the muster roll of *Tiger* as an able seamen, born at Bognor in Sussex, twenty-three years of age at the time of the loss of *Tiger* and therefore sixty-eight at the time he wrote the letter. It is not perhaps surprising that there are one or two small discrepancies between his statements and the evidence given at the court martial, but he can have had no possible motive in writing the letter other than to clear his conscience, to the best of his ability, of something which had worried him for over forty years.

★ ★ ★ ★

It might seem extraordinary that the court appears at no stage to have commented on the absence of Captain Giffard from the deck from 8.45 pm or, at the latest, from midnight on 11 May until after *Tiger* had gone aground. *Tiger* was approaching an enemy coast in conditions of extremely bad visibility. In these circumstances, it would appear to have been a grave dereliction of duty for the captain not to have been in direct personal charge of the deck and, indeed, it would seem from the evidence quoted in this chapter that his presence might well have averted the catastrophe. But he was dead, and in the circumstances the court evidently saw no benefit, indeed, probably positive disadvantage to the service, in underlining the obvious.

As it was, by recording a reprimand for the master and freeing Lieutenant Royer from all responsibility on the grounds that he was acting under the immediate directions of his captain, the court, it can be argued, had implicitly criticised the dead Captain Giffard. The president of the court, William Fanshawe Martin, was the unreconstructed, if brilliant, old school Tory with whom Giffard, on half pay, sailed as a supernumerary in HMS *Trafalgar*, of which Martin was in command, at the trials in 1845. These trials, as we have already explained (page 169), had political undertones.[4] Tory officers were bent on the denigration of ships built under a Whig administration and Giffard, identified so completely with two Whig families, perhaps was subject to some suspicion on board *Trafalgar*. Had an officer of less extreme political commitment presided over the court martial, the verdict might perhaps have exonerated all concerned. As it was, the politics of the mid nineteenth century navy, from which he had on the whole benefited much in life, pursued Henry Giffard even beyond that lonely grave, surrounded by monuments of an alien culture and lost somewhere in the cosmopolitan city of Odessa.

Nevertheless, Giffard was generally treated by the contemporary media as having met an heroic death, and for once the media may well have been right. The probable solution to the mystery of his absence from the deck has already been hinted at in Able Seaman John Harfield's letter to George Giffard. An even stronger hint was given by the surgeon Domville in his brief evidence to the court, when he said

> I was surgeon on board the *Tiger*; Captain Giffard was not on the sick list
> at the time of the wreck; Captain Giffard had had an attack of ague two

4 For a detailed account of the background, see Lambert, *The Last Sailing Battlefleet*, London 1991, p 81.

days before the ship went on shore, but on the previous day he was in his usual health; on the night previous he was well.

In response to further questioning, Domville went on

He had an attack on the 10th before we left Sebastopol; he was well on the 11th, but he would most probably have had another attack on the 12th; his health was delicate.

What was this 'ague'? Henry Domville described the symptoms in his journal. He was writing of the long period when *Tiger* was lying in Constantinople.

The Squadron having enjoyed a fortnight of fine weather at this celebrated anchorage returned to the Bosphorus. The *Tiger* was for three following months stationed chiefly at the Golden Horn and during March and the latter end of the proceeding month having much cold and damp weather a great number of cases of Intermittent fever occured. But nearly all were men who had suffered from attacks in the previous autumn [when the vessel was lying in Besika Bay and many cases of fever were reported in the fleet] very few new cases presenting themselves. Of the effects of this troublesome disease I can speak feelingly having been a repeated sufferer, the attacks generally occuring at intervals of from ten days to three weeks and seldom lasting over the second or third paroxysm of a tertian form of the complaint, but coming on suddenly and at times when the patient feeling himself in all respects well recovered from the effects of the last attack would confidently declare himself free from his inveterate enemy; so often was this the case that latterly on hearing similar remarks I predicted with almost constant certainty that such a one would have another attack of ague in a day or two. The actual amount of physical suffering in this eccentric disease is small compared with its debilitating effects and the extreme depression of spirits that accompanied every attack.

The last sentence of Henry Domville's account is particularly relevant in the light of Captain Giffard's symptoms while he was a prisoner of war before his death. What Henry Domville described appear to be the symptoms of *Plasmodium vivax* (benign tertian) malaria, widespread in some temperate regions in the nineteenth century, including parts of the Aegean and on the coasts of Italy. Giffard had originally been infected as far back in his service as Navarino, when he contracted 'bad marsh fever' and was invalided home, his life despaired of (see Chapter 5). The effect over a long period would have been to bring on a general decline of health and a lessening, as a result of anaemia, in the body's ability to cope with new infections. Such a condition would account for his twice repeated wish for a home posting, even at a time when a war was welcomed by many of his contemporaries as an opportunity to gain distinction and further their careers. If, as Henry Domville predicted, he did indeed experience a further attack on the early morning of 12 May, the degree of physical and mental incapacity which would follow could well explain his absence from the deck, although the degree of physical incapacity (it is clear from his orders reported at the court martial that he was not suffering from mental confusion) must have been considerable to keep him below in the circumstances. His physical exhaustion and mental depression, coupled with the difficulty in breathing in the fog reported by John Harfield, which was probably due to his anaemia and would have been marked, and which perhaps suggests that he may have developed an asthmatic condition, could have led him to place too much confidence in Francis Edington who had, after all, been master with him since the commission of *Penelope* in 1846.

But there may be more to it than this. From Lieutenant Royer's account of his journey through Russia we know that he too was a victim of malaria. Such were the frequency and violence of his attacks that it would seem likely that his judgement may also have been impaired. The prevalence of the infection on board *Tiger* may account in some measure for the apparent failings of her officers. Moreover, since infection was widespread in the ships, malaria could have played its part in such affairs as the chaotic movement of the fleet through the Dardanelles and the Bosphorus in October 1853.

Whatever the complex of factors which led to the loss of the steam paddle frigate *Tiger*, as we saw in the last chapter the effect on Captain Giffard was traumatic and there seems little doubt that it was a contributory factor to his physical decline and death. The conditioning of the seaman has always been such that the loss, or even the grounding of a vessel without disastrous consequences, often has a profound effect on those responsible for her safety, and especially upon her captain, if a naval vessel, or her master, if a merchant ship. In the latter case, the effect may be greater, even, on the master than on the owner. Captain Karl Kåhre, president of the Åland Cape Horners, a master mariner of vast and varied experience, recently reminded us that the trauma has never been described better than by Joseph Conrad in his novel *The Heart of Darkness*.

> After all, for a seaman, to scrape the bottom of the thing that is supposed to float all the time under his care is the unpardonable sin. No one may know of it, but you never forget the thump – eh?. A blow on the very heart. You remember it, you dream of it, you wake up in the night and think of it – years after – and go hot and cold all over.

Research and field work, 1975–1990.
Writing, January 1991–January 1992 at Boetheric.

Sources and Bibliography

Primary Sources
BRITISH LIBRARY:
Babbage Mss, Add 37
Byam Martin Mss, Add 35; 41
Napier Mss, Add 40
HAMPSHIRE COUNTY ARCHIVES:
The Winchester papers
MUSÉE DE LA MARINE, Paris:
Journale de St. Petersbourg 4, m Série, No 435
NATIONAL MARITIME MUSEUM: *Official Correspondence, Logs, Private Letters and Memoirs:*
BGY/9/4; HWG letter to his father
ELL 30/12/4/20 ff 91–2. The Ellenborough papers
HTN/52a, Keppel, letters from the Baltic
JOD/30; /38; HWG
Log/N/A/21; 23; N/H/3; N/W/7; HWG
San/T/101 (Ms 60/008) The Hon Victor Montagu, letters home
PUBLIC RECORD OFFICE: *Official Correspondence and Records, Admiralty Correspondence, Minutes, Logs, etc:*
BT 107/268
ADM 1/ Secretary's In letters
ADM 1/5671, HMS *Tiger* court martial
ADM 12/ Digest
ADM 38/5136 0992, HMS *Tiger* muster book
ADM 53/ Logs
ADM 53/7874; HWG log
ADM 54/
ADM 83/
ADM 87/ Surveyor's Dept
ADM 92/ Surveyor's Submission Book

ADM 93/ Steam Dept
ADM 95/
ADM 101/
ADM 106/Navy Board Correspondence
ADM 106/1799/Woolwich
ADM 180/
ADM 2956–2957, Captain HWG logs
ADM AO 1874 564
ADM AO 7782
ADM AO 8168 449
ADM PAR 20, Nos 66, 117
ADM PAR 21, 203
ADM PAR 26, ff 1–10. (Sir Wm Parker correspondence)
ADM PAR 97, 210, Private
Log N/H/3 Lt HWG
Melbourne Ms 859 9–13
Parliamentary papers, 1859, vol XV
SCIENCE MUSEUM:
The Goodrich papers, 1618, Field to Byam Martin
SCOTTISH RECORD OFFICE:
GD 1/135
WILLS MEMORIAL LIBRARY, University of Bristol:
Report on Screw Propulsion by I K Brunel
UNPUBLISHED MSS:
In private hands: *the Laird correspondence*
In the authors' possession: Mary Giffard, *What I can remember about the Ancestors*
In possession of His Grace the Duke of Wellington: *The Wellington papers*

Alphabetical List of the Main Articles and Books Consulted
AHLSTRÖM, Christian, 'The port of Odessa and Finland's Shipowners'
Nautica Fennica, 2 (Helsinki 1979)
American Historical Review, The
Artisan, The, 1843
Athenaeum, 1808
BAGWELL, Philip, 'The Post Office Steam Packets and the Development of Shipping on the Irish Sea, 1821–36', in *Maritime History* (Newton Abbot 1971)
Bath Independent, The (Maine 1929)
BAXTER, J P, *The Introduction of the Ironclad Warship* (Harvard 1933)
BECKETT, J V, *The Aristocracy of England 1660–1914* (Oxford 1986)
BERNARD, W D, *Narrative of the Voyage and Services of the Nemesis from 1842–3* (London 1844)
BIDDLECOMBE, George, *The Art of Rigging* (London 1848)
BLAKE, Clagette, *Charles Elliot, RN., 1801–1875* (London 1960)
BODY, Geoffrey, *British Paddle Steamers* (Newton Abbot 1971)

BONHAM-CARTER, Victor, *In a Liberal Tradition: A Social Biography, 1700–1958* (London 1960)
BONNER-SMITH, D and DEWAR, A C, eds, *Russian War, 1854, Baltic and Black Sea*, Vol
     LXXXIII (London 1943)
BOURCHIER, Jane, *Memoirs of The Life of Admiral Sir Edward Codrington* (London 1873)
BOURNE, J, *Treatise on the Screw Propeller* (London 1852)
BOURNE, J M, *Patronage and Society in Nineteenth Century England* (London 1986)
BRADLEE, Francis, *Some Account of Steam Navigation in New England*, Essex Institute Historical
     Coll, (Salem, Mass, 1919)
BRIGGS, Sir John, *Naval Administration, 1827–1892* (London 1893)
British Journal of Sociology, 1978
BROCK, Admiral P W and GREENHILL, Basil, *Steam and Sail* (Newton Abbot 1973)
BROWN, D K, *Before the Ironclad* (London 1990)
BRYSON, *Report on the Climate and Principal Diseases of the African Station, 1847*
BUCHANAN, R A and DOUGHTY, M W, 'The Choice of Steam Engine Manufacturers by the
     British Admiralty, 1822–1852', *The Mariner's Mirror*, Vol 64, No 4
BURN, W L, *The Age of Equipoise* (London 1964)
BYRN, Jnr, John D, *Crime and Punishment in the Royal Navy* (Brookfield, VT 1989)
BYRNE, *On the Best Means of Propelling Ships at Sea* (London and New York 1841)
CEDERLUND, Carl Olof, *Rapport Over Den Marinarkeologiska Undersokningen av Hjulangfartyget
     E*, Nordevall, *1985–1988* (Stockholm 1989)
CLOWES, Sir William Laird, *The Royal Navy – A History* (London 1901)
COLBURN's *United Services Magazine* (London 1854, 1855)
COLLEDGE, J J, *Ships of the Royal Navy* (London 1987)
COLUMB, V Adm P H, *Memoirs of Admiral the Rt. Hon. Sir Astley Cooper Key* (London 1898)
COOPER KEY, Adm Sir Astley, *A Narrative of the Recovery of HMS Gorgon* (London 1847)
CORLETT, Dr E C B, *The Iron Ship* (London 1990)
CRANKSHAW, Edward, *The Fall of the House of Hapsburg* (London 1987)
CREUZE, Augustin F B, article in *United Services Journal*, 1840
CURTISS, John Shelton, *Russia's Crimean War* (Durham, NC 1979; *The Russian Army Under
     Nicholas I, 1825–1855* (Durham, NC 1965)
CUSTINE, The Marquis de; trans anon, *The Empire of the Czar* (New York 1989)
DANA, Jnr, Richard Henry, *The Seaman's Manual* (London 1855)
DANDEKER, Christopher, 'Patronage and Bureaucratic Control – The Case of the Naval Officer in
     British Society, 1780–1850', *British Journal of Sociology*, 1978
DANIEL, Owen Fisher, *Some Reminiscences of a Midshipman in the Fifties* (no place stated, 1906)
DAVIDOFF, L and HALL, Catherine, *Family Fortunes: Men and Women of the English Middle Class
     1780–1880* (no place stated, 1987)
DEVEREUX, W Cope, *A Cruise in the* Gorgon (London 1869)
DEWEY, Clive, *The Passing of Barchester* (London 1991)
Dictionary of American Naval Fighting Ships (Washington 1976)
Dictionary of National Biography
DIN-TSUN CHANG, 'The Evolution of Chinese Thought on Maritime Foreign Trade from the
     sixteenth to the eighteenth Century', *International Journal of Maritime History* (St Johns, Nfld
     1989)
DODD, George, *An Historical and Explanatory Dissertation on Steam Engines and Steam Packets*
     (London 1818)
EDWARDES, Michael, *Playing the Great Game* (London 1975)
FANNING, A E, *Steady As She Goes* (London 1986)
FINCHAM, John, *History of Naval Architecture* (London 1851)
FISHER, S, ed, *Innovation in Shipping and Trade* (Exeter 1989)
FRASER, George Hamilton, *Flash for Freedom* (London 1971); *Flashman at the Charge* (London 1973)
FREMANTLE, Anne, ed, *The Wynne Diaries* (London 1952)
GELLNER, Ernest, *Nations and Nationalism* (Oxford 1983)
GILDEA, R, *Barricades and Borders, Europe 1800–1914* (Oxford 1987)
GLADSTONE, Rt Hon W E, *Two Letters to the Earl of Aberdeen on the State Prosecutions of the
     Neapolitan Government* (London 1851)
GOGOL, Nikolai, trans MAGARSHACT, David, *Dead Souls* (London 1961)
GONCHAROV, Ivan; ed and trans WILSON, N W, *The Voyage of the Frigate Pallada* (London 1965)
GORDON, Lt W, RN, *The Economy of the Marine Steam Engine* (London 1845)
GRAHAM, Prof Gerald S, *The China Station* (Oxford 1978)
GRANT and TEMPERLEY, ed and rev PENSON, Lilian, *Europe in the Nineteenth and Twentieth
     Centuries* (London 1953)
GREENHILL, Basil, 'The *Great Northern*', in FISHER, S, ed, *Innovation in Shipping and Trade*
     (Exeter 1989)
GREENHILL, Basil, and CORLETT, E C B, 'The Iron Screw Steamship *Bangor II*', *International
     Journal of Maritime History*, 1990

GREENHILL, Basil and GIFFARD, Ann, *The British Assault on Finland, 1854–55* (London 1988); *Women Under Sail* (London 1971)

GREENHILL, Basil, and HACKMAN, John, *Herzogin Cecilie* (London 1990)

GRIFFITHS, Denis, *Brunel's Great Western* (Wellingborough 1985)

GUEST, G A, ed, *Record of the Services of Admiral George Evans* (London 1876)

HALL, Capt Basil, RN, *An Account of the Ferry Across the Tay at Dundee* (Dundee 1825)

HALSTEAD, E P, *The Screw-Fleet of the Navy* (London 1850)

HAXTHAUSEN, Baron von, *The Russian Empire* (London 1856)

HEATH, Admiral Sir L G, *Letters from the Black Sea* (London 1897)

HEYLE, Erik, *Early American Steamers* (Buffalo, NY 1953)

HIBBERT, Christopher, *The Dragon Wakes* (London 1984); *Garibaldi and His Enemies* (London 1987)

HOSKEN, Admiral James, *Autobiographical Sketch of the Public Career of* (Penzance 1889); *The Logs of the First Voyage, made with the unceasing aid of Steam, between England and America, by The Great Western of Bristol* (Bristol 1838)

HYDE, Prof Francis E, *Cunard and the North Atlantic, 1840–1873* (London 1975)

Illustrated London News, The, 1854

International Journal of Maritime History (St Johns, Nfld 1989, 1990)

JACKSON, Gordon, 'Operational Problem of the Transfer to Steam: Dundee, Perth & London Shipping Company, c. 1820–1846' in Smout, T C, ed, *Scotland and the Sea* (Edinburgh 1992)

JOHNSON, William, *Imperial Cyclopedia of Machinery* (London 1853)

JONES, A G E, *Ships Employed in the South Sea Trade, 1775–1861* (Canberra 1986)

JORDAN, C H, Some Historical Records and Reminiscences Relating to the British Navy and Mercantile Ships, (London 1925)

Journale de St. Petersbourg , 1854

KENNEDY, John, *The History of Steam Navigation* (Liverpool 1903)

KEPPEL, Admiral of the Fleet, the Hon Sir Henry, *A Sailor's Life under Four Sovereigns*, 3 vols (London 1899)

KEVILL-DAVIES, Sally, *Yesterday's Children – The Antiques and History of Childcare* (London 1991)

KOHL, J G, *Russia and the Russians* (London 1842)

LAING, E A M, 'The Introduction of Paddle Frigates into the Royal Navy', *The Mariner's Mirror*, Vol 66, No 4

LAMBERT, A D, 'Anglo-French Rivalry: 1854–1856', *Service Historique de la Marine* (Vincennes 1990); 'Preparing for the Russian War: British Strategic Planning, March 1853–1854', *War and Society*, Vol 7, No 2, Sept 1989; *The Crimean War, British Grand Strategy Against Russia, 1853–56* (Manchester 1990); *The Last Sailing Battlefleet* (London 1991); 'The Royal Navy and the Introduction of the Screw Propeller: 1837–47' in Fisher, S, ed, *Innovation in Shipping and Trade* (Exeter 1989)

LARDNER, Dionysius, *Steam Communication with India* (Calcutta 1837)

LEE, *Parliament and the Appointment of Magistrates* (London 1959)

LEWIS, Michael, *A Social History of the Navy, 1793–1815* (London 1960); *The Navy in Transition, 1814–64* (London 1965); 'The Royal Navy and the Slavers' (Review) in *The Mariner's Mirror*, 1969 Vol 55, No 3.

LLOYD, Christopher, *The Navy and The Slave Trade* (London 1949)

Lloyd's List, 1826

Lloyd's Register, 1840

London Mechanics' Magazine, The

LOW, C R, *History of the Indian Navy, 1613–1863* (London 1877)

MABER, John M, *North Star to Southern Cross* (Prescot 1967)

MacDONALD, Fraser, *Our Ocean Railways* (London 1893)

MacGREGOR, David, *Merchant Sailing Ships 1815–1850* (London 1984)

McMURRAY, Campbell, *Old Order, New Thing*, (London 1972)

MARCH, Septimus, *Memorials of Charles March* (London 1867)

Mariner's Mirror, The

Maritime History (Newton Abbot 1971)

MARTIN, S B and McCORD, N, 'The Steamship *Bedington*, 1841–1854' in *Maritime History* (Exeter 1971)

MAUDSLAY SOCIETY, *Henry Maudslay, Sons & Field Ltd.* (1949)

MONTAGU, Rear Admiral, the Hon Victor A, *A Middy's Recollections 1853–60* (London 1898)

MORRISON, John H, *History of American Steam Navigation* (New York 1903)

MOULD, Daphne Pochin, *Captain Roberts of the Sirius* (Cork 1988)

MURRAY, Robert, *Rudimentary Treatise on Marine Engines* (London 1852)

NARES, Vice Admiral Sir George S, *Narrative of a Voyage to the Polar Sea* (London 1878)

Nautica Fennica, 1979

Nautical Magazine, The (London 1842, 1843)

NOLAN, E H, *The Illustrated History of the War against Russia*, 2 vols (London 1857)

O'BYRNE, Robert, *Naval Annual* (London 1855)
O'BYRNE, William, *A Naval Biographical Dictionary* (London 1849)
OMAN, Carola, *An Oxford Childhood* (London 1976)
OPIE, Iona and Peter (eds), *The Oxford Dictionary of Nursery Rhymes* (Oxford 1955).
OSBON, G A, 'Paddle Wheel Fighting Ships of the Royal Navy' in *The Mariner's Mirror*, Vol 68, No 4
OTWAY, Cdr Robert, *An Elementary Treatise on Steam* (London 1834)
PALMER, Sarah, 'Experience, Experiment and Economics: Factors in the Construction of Early
    Steamships' in Matthews, K and Panting, G,eds, *Ships and Shipbuilding in the North Atlantic
    Region* (St Johns, Nfld 1978)
PARRY, Ann, *Parry of the Arctic* (London 1963)
PEAKE, James, *Rudiments of Naval Architecture* (London 1851)
PENN, Geoffrey, *Up Funnel, Down Screw!* (London 1955)
PINCHBECK, I, and HEWITT, M, *Children in English Society*, vol 2 (London 1973)
PITCHER, Harvey, *When Miss Emmie was in Russia* (London 1977)
POND, E Leroy, *Junius Smith* (New York 1927)
Portsmouth Times and Naval Gazette, 1855
Proceedings of the Institute of Mechanical Engineers (London 1930)
QUARM, R, and WILCOX, S, ed, *Masters of the Sea* (Oxford, Greenwich, Newhaven 1987)
RADCLIFFE and CROSS, *The English Legal System* (London 1954)
RASOR, Eugene, *Reform in the Royal Navy* (Connecticut 1976)
RAWLINSON, John L, *China's Struggle for Naval Development, 1839–95* (Harvard 1967)
RIDLEY, Jasper, *Lord Palmerston,* (London 1970)
RIGBY, Elizabeth (Lady Eastlake), *Letters from the Shores of the Baltic*, 2 vols (London 1842)
RITCHIE, Rear Admiral G S, *The Admiralty Chart* (London, Sydney, Toronto 1967)
ROBERTS, Stephen S, 'The French Trans-Atlantic Steam Packet Programme of 1840' in *The
    Mariner's Mirror*, Vol 73, No 3, 1987
ROBERTSON, Fredrick Leslie, *The Evolution of Naval Armament* (London 1968)
ROBINSON, Cdr R S, *The Nautical Steam Engine Explained . . . for the Use of Officers of the Navy,
    etc.* (London 1839)
RODGER, N A M, 'Officers, Gentlemen and Their Education, 1793–1860,' paper in *Les Empires en
    guerre et paix 1793–1860* (Vincennes 1990); *The Wooden World: An Anatomy of the Georgian
    Navy* (London 1986)
ROYER, Alfred, *The English Prisoners in Russia* (London 1854)
RUSSELL, W H, *The Atlantic Telegraph* (London, undated)
SAGER, Eric W, *Seafaring Labour, The Merchant Marine of Atlantic Canada, 1820–1914* (Montreal 1989)
SCHMITT, B E, 'The Diplomatic Preliminaries to the Crimean War' in *The American Historical
    Review*, Vol XXV, No 1, 1919
SCOTT, Charles Henry, *The Baltic, The Black Sea and the Crimea* (London 1854)
SEAWARD, Samuel, 'Memoir on the Practicability of Shortening the Duration of Voyages By the
    Adoption of Auxiliary Steam Power to Sailing Vessels' in *Transactions of the Institute of Civil
    Engineers* (London 1842)
SETON-WATSON, Hugh, *The Russian Empire, 1801–1917* (Oxford 1967)
Shipping Gazette, The, 1842
SKELTON, Eng V-Adm R W, *Progress in Marine Engineering*, Proceedings of the Institute of
    Mechanical Engineers, 1930.
SLAVEN, Prof Anthony, 'Scottish Shipbuilders and Marine Engineers' in SMOUT, T C ed, *Scotland
    and the Sea* (Edinburgh 1991)
SLOANE-STANLEY, C, *Reminiscences of a Midshipman's Life, 1850–59* (London 1893)
SLOCUM, Joshua, *Sailing Alone Around the World* (London, undated)
SMILES, Samuel, *Lives of the engineers Boulton and Watt* (London 1904)
SMITH, Eng Capt Edgar C, OBE, RN, *A Short History of Naval and Marine Engineering* (Cambridge 1937)
SMOUT, T C, ed, *Scotland and the Sea* (Edinburgh 1992)
SOULSBY, H G, *The Right of Search and the Slave Trade in Anglo-American Relations* (Johns
    Hopkins University, 1933)
SPRATT, H Philip, *The Birth of The Steamboat* (London 1958)
STEPHENSON, Sir Frederick C A, GCB, *At Home and on the Battlefield* (London 1915)
SULIVAN, Henry Norton, ed, *Life and Letters of Admiral Sir B.J. Sulivan KCB, 1810–90* (London 1896)
SURTEES, R L, *Mr. Sponge's Sporting Tour* (London 1852)
SUTTON, Jean, *Lords of the East* (London 1981)
TEMPERLEY, H M V, *England and the Near East, The Crimea* (London 1936)
THOMPSON, F L M, *English Landed Society in the Nineteenth Century* (London 1963)
THOMPSON, Hilary, *A Portscatho Mariner, Edward Peters* (Roseland, Cornwall 1990)
Times, The
TIMEWELL, H C, 'Paddle Frigates of the Royal Navy' in *The Mariner's Mirror*, Vol 67, No 1
Transactions of the Institute of Civil Engineers (London 1842)

Transactions of the Royal Historical Society (London 1981)
United Services Magazine (1854, 1855)
United Services Journal (1840)
VINCENT, Prof John, 'The Parliamentary Dimension of the Crimean War' in *Transactions of the Royal Historical Society* (London 1981)
WALKER, James, *The First Trans-Atlantic Steamer* (London 1898)
WALVIN, James, *A Child's World: A Social History of British Childhood 1880–1914* (London 1982)
War and Society, Vol 7
WARD, W E F, *The Royal Navy and the Slavers* (London 1969)
WHITE, *Yankee from Sweden* (New York 1960)
WIENER, M J, *English Culture and the Decline of the Industrial Spirit 1850–1980* (Cambridge 1981)
WILLIAMS, H Noel, *The Life and Letters of Admiral Sir Charles Napier KCB* (London 1917)
WILSON, Robert, *The Screw Propeller* (Glasgow 1860)
WIMSHURST, 'The *Novelty* Steamship' in *The Nautical Magazine* (1843)
WOODHOUSE, C M, *The Battle of Navarino* (London 1965)

Index